THE UNIVERSITY OF
WINCHESTER

Martial Rose Library
Tel: 01962 827306

To be returned on or before the day marked above, subject to recall.

GEORGE GROSSMITH.

BORN 1847.

HIS inimitably funny actor and entertainer was the son of a humorous lecturer, and, after being educated at the North London Collegiate School, commenced life as a reporter at Bow Street, at which occupation he continued till he was thirty, becoming well known as an amateur actor and comic singer of great promise. In 1877 he made his *début* on the London stage as *John Wellington Wells* in " The Sorcerer," and afterwards played in all the Gilbert-Sullivan operas until 1889. Since that time he has chiefly restricted himself to entertain-

ments, writing many of the bright sketches in which he appears. His latest production is the music of " Haste to the Wedding " at the Criterion.

GEORGE GROSSMITH

Biography of a Savoyard

by

TONY JOSEPH

Published by
Bunthorne Books

© Tony Joseph, 1982

Reprinted 2000 (by Bunthorne Books, Bristol)

ISBN: 0 9507992 0 3

Published by
Tony Joseph
55 Brynland Avenue
BRISTOL
BS7 9DX

Printed by:
J. W. Arrowsmith Ltd
Winterstoke Road
BRISTOL
BS3 2NT

Contents

Illustrations

Acknowledgments

My thanks go first to members of the Grossmith family for their encouragement and help: to J. C. G. George, *Garioch Pursuivant*, Grossmith's great-grandson, with whom I discussed the writing of this book originally, who has since guided me on any number of points, and to whom I also owe four of the illustrations (nos 4a, 4b, 5a and 11b); to George Grossmith IV, Grossmith's grandson, who has a fund of background stories and anecdotes; to the late Mrs Phyllis Bevan, Grossmith's granddaughter-in-law, for allowing me to make use of the extensive collection of letters sent to Grossmith by various contemporaries and other relevant material then in her possession; and to her son Dr James Bevan, who holds this material now, and her daughter Mrs Deborah Jeffs, who have likewise given me permission to use it. These "Grossmith Letters" (to give them a convenient name) have been among my most valuable sources.

Thanks, too, to the following for permission to quote other unpublished and copyright material: to the Archives of *The Times* for the letters from *The Times* Managers' Letter Books quoted on pages 21 and 85; to the Lord Ponsonby of Shulbrede for the letter to Grossmith from Sir Henry Ponsonby on page 135; to Geoffrey Ashton, librarian of the Garrick Club, for the "Sudbury" letter on page 138; to Mary Anne Bonney, librarian of *Punch*, for the use of facts and figures contained in the *Punch* contributors' ledgers; and to J. M. Dent & Sons Ltd for permission to quote the passage from *Gilbert & Sullivan* by A. H. Godwin on page 90.

Grateful thanks are extended to the Royal General Theatrical Fund Association, 11, Garrick Street, London, WC2E 9RA, as owner of the subsisting copyright in Sir William S. Gilbert's unpublished writings, for permission to quote from letters written by Sir William Gilbert.

The extract from Queen Victoria's Journal (page 136) is quoted by the gracious permission of Her Majesty the Queen.

The two *Sorcerer* illustrations (nos 2 and 3) are reproduced by permission of Raymond Mander and Joe Mitchenson of the Mander and Mitchenson Theatre Collection; three of the other illustrations (nos 11a, 13a and 14) are reproduced by permission of the British Library.

I am grateful also to the Inter-Library Loans Department of Bristol University Library for all the material they obtained for me, and the countless journeys to libraries elsewhere they saved me in consequence; to George Rowell, of the University's Drama Department, for many helpful suggestions; and to my wife, whose support and encouragement throughout the whole period of the book's writing and production have been invaluable, and who could hardly be blamed if she wondered at times if I'd ever talk about anything else.

An author who publishes his own book has to deal with a host of matters and take a hundred and one decisions that would be taken *for* him if the book was being brought out by a regular publisher. But in this respect I could not have been luckier. To Victoria Arrowsmith-Brown, Gordon Young, Barry Priddle and all the staff at Arrowsmith's go my lasting thanks for easing me through those decisions, and for the immense help and cooperation they gave me from the moment I offered them the book to produce.

INTRODUCTION

THE FIRST NIGHT OF THE SORCERER

The First Night of The Sorcerer

It is Saturday, November 17th, 1877; the time early evening, the place the Opera Comique in Wych Street, an unsavoury thoroughfare off London's Strand. Built just seven years earlier, the "Op. Com." is thus virtually a new theatre. But it has also, even in that short time, acquired the reputation of being an unlucky one. Nothing staged there previously has made any lasting impact. Farces, comedies, burlesques, light musical productions, French *opéra bouffe* – each once or more than once has had its unsuccessful turn.

All that, though, is now in the past. For tonight everything promises to be different. Tonight the atmosphere has about it an air of considerable and definite expectation. The audience, surging through the various entrances – the chief of these a remarkable "tunnel" or covered passage leading from the Strand under part of Holywell Street at the side – into the theatre foyer, is talking animatedly of the evening's entertainment to come.

The main work that awaits them is billed as "An Entirely New and Original Modern Comic Opera"; its title *The Sorcerer*; libretto by W. S. Gilbert, music by Arthur Sullivan. W. S. Gilbert! Arthur Sullivan! Anybody who knows anything about the arts at this time will be familiar with their names: Gilbert, London's most prolific playwright, Sullivan the shining star of British music; may well have seen their previous joint work, the one-act *Trial by Jury* that had taken the theatrical world by storm back in 1875. Small wonder, then, that a full-length work by these same gifted collaborators should arouse such anticipation, should have led to a huge demand for tickets for that new work's first night.

Cloakroom attendants take charge of coats, wraps, umbrellas. Programme sellers distribute programmes, opera glasses, copies of the libretto. Inside the theatre the unsavoury surroundings are forgotten. The auditorium is ornate, rich in design, its dominant colours white and gold. The audience settles into its seats, bewhiskered, stiff-collared men, elaborately coiffured, elegantly dressed ladies. In front of them the orchestra is assembling; tuning instruments, checking music sheets. Excitement mounts with every second.

Concealed as yet behind the scenes, the actors feel that excitement too. They cope, each in his or her own way, with first night nerves. They prepare for the show, though, in conditions of marked discomfort. The dressing-rooms are mostly some way from the stage, up a long and steep flight of stone steps in houses along Holywell Street. They are small, cramped, essentially makeshift. They are also few in number. Even the principals are crammed in three or four together.

Eight o'clock. Time for the performance to begin. Here and there seats still unoccupied, for it does so not with the main work but, rather, the customary curtain-raiser. The curtain-raiser on this occasion is a piece called *Dora's Dream*; libretto by Arthur Cecil, music by Alfred Cellier. Into the orchestra pit to the evening's first round of applause steps the moustached, tidy-haired figure of Cellier to conduct it himself. The gas house lights dim. He raises his baton and the first notes ring out. Up goes the curtain. *Dora's Dream* has just two characters, a pair of lovers. For the two actors concerned, soprano Giulia Warwick and baritone Richard Temple, the ordeal of waiting for their call is quickly over. They go through the half-hour piece with pleasant and easy confidence. At the end the curtain comes down for the first of the evening's two intervals.

The orchestra reassembles. The empty seats – those of the ultra-fashionable whose pleasure it is to dine late and thus arrive late – fill up. But for ten minutes, twelve minutes, nothing happens. The unwonted, unexplained holdup, though, only increases anticipation. The time approaches nine o'clock. And now at last the great moment has come. For there, taking that place in the pit that Cellier has occupied before, is the man who is the darling of musical London, Arthur Sullivan. Sullivan is short, dark, monocled. He beams round, acknowledging his reception, radiating bonhomie. The house lights are dimmed again. He turns to conduct the overture. *The Sorcerer* is under way.

It opens, however, on a somewhat odd note. This is – unquestionably – the first performance of a brand new opera, but the "overture" Sullivan conducts proves to be a movement from music to Shakespeare's *Henry VIII* which he has written just a few months earlier. It is light, tuneful and has a leisured, courtly grace, though its qualities and suitability to the occasion – or otherwise – hardly register, for people talk right through it. The British public always talks through overtures. Sullivan handles the orchestra in a controlled, unflamboyant manner.

The "overture" completed, the resulting applause dying down, Sullivan raises his baton again. A few bars, and up once more goes the curtain to reveal the garden of an old-world country mansion on a bright summer's day, and grouped around the stage a chorus of peasantry, roughly forty of them, the men amusingly dressed in smocks, chimney-pot hats, corduroy trousers and hobnailed boots. And through almost immediate laughter the yokels break into the strains of a lively number that inaugurates the opera proper:

> "Ring forth, ye bells,
>   With clarion sound –
> Forget your knells,
>   For joys abound.
> Forget your notes
>   Of mournful lay,
> And from your throats
>   Pour joy today."

They sing lustily and with well-drilled precision. They point their words with clarity.

> "For today young Alexis – young Alexis Pointdextre
> Is betrothed to Aline – to Aline Sangazure,
> And that pride of his sex is – of his sex is to be next her,
> At the feast on the green – on the green, oh, be sure!"

Off stage, the majority maybe still in their dressing-rooms, the principals wait, keyed up. The first two of them are on now: chubby Harriet Everard, playing Mrs Partlet, a pew-opener; Giulia Warwick making her second appearance of the evening as her daughter, Constance. And gradually thereafter, all the others make their first appearances in turn. Stolid Rutland Barrington, playing Dr Daly, the vicar. Neat, slim Richard Temple again, this time portraying an elderly baronet, Sir Marmaduke Pointdextre. Temple is in fine voice, but Charles Bentham, the tenor who comes on with him as his grenadier guardsman son Alexis, is suffering, as has indeed been announced before the opera starts, from a swollen face and sore throat. Following them, vivacious Alice May as Alexis's fiancée, Aline. Her song, a lilting aria in waltz time, is received rapturously. Smiling up from the pit, Sullivan grants her the evening's first encore. Next, the commanding figure of Mrs Howard Paul, principal contralto, in the character of her (Aline's) mother, Lady Sangazure. A

5

stately duet between Mrs Paul and Temple brings encore number two, even though Mrs Paul is another who seems to be struggling with her voice. The encore concluded, on comes Fred Clifton as an elderly Notary.

The Notary presides over a ceremony sealing the betrothal of Alexis and Aline; whereupon the two young lovers are left alone. And Alexis, it now turns out, has some far-reaching ideas. He believes, he says, that true love is the source of every earthly joy. And to give this belief effect he proposes to take a desperate step. Have you, he asks Aline, ever heard of the firm of J. W. Wells and Co., the old-established family sorcerers in St Mary Axe?

The plot is taking shape. There is just one more character to appear, the Sorcerer himself, plainly the figure who will act as the opera's catalyst. In the wings the actor who is playing that role is waiting, more tense, more fidgety, more excited perhaps than anyone. For not only has he had quite the longest wait for his call, but this is also his first appearance on the professional stage – a fact actually stated in the programme. His name is George Grossmith.

The build-up to his entrance is almost complete. Alexis summons a Page.

"Is Mr Wells there?"
"He's in the tent, sir – refreshing."
"Ask him to be so good as to step this way."

Forty seconds, maybe, to go. Three more short speeches: Aline – Alexis – Aline – and then the speech of Alexis that is his cue. Thirty seconds; twenty; ten; five; four; three; two; one . . .

Zero. And now he is on. The audience takes him in. For one of his supposed calling he looks a singularly incongruous individual. Short and slight in build, eager yet deferential in stance, an apparently conventional contemporary tradesman, unremarkably dressed in frock coat, check trousers and tall top hat. He has to speak immediately.

"Good day, sir."

Alexis responds.

"Good day. I believe you are a sorcerer."

Still diffident, deferential, but perky, alert and with an unmistakable hint of cockney in his voice, Grossmith goes on, trotting out in true tradesman style a description of his wares.

"Yes, sir, we practise necromancy in all its branches. We've a choice assortment of wishing-caps, divining-rods, amulets, charms and counter-charms. We can cast you a nativity at a low figure, and we have a horoscope at three-and-six that we can guarantee. Our Abudah chests, each containing a patent hag who comes out and prophesies disasters, with spring complete, are strongly recommended . . ."

6

Fig. 2. Grossmith as John Wellington Wells.

7

And so on for six sentences more. It is a long speech for anyone to be faced with at the start of a stage career. And no sooner has he reached the end of it than Sullivan has launched the orchestra into the introduction to a fast patter song. With scarcely time to draw breath, Grossmith has embarked on the opening verses, reeling them off at a truly cracking pace.

> "Oh! my name is John Wellington Wells,
> I'm a dealer in magic and spells,
>> In blessings and curses,
>> And ever-filled purses,
> In prophecies, witches and knells.
>
> "If you want a proud foe to 'make tracks' –
> If you'd melt a rich uncle in wax –
>> You've but to look in
>> On our resident djinn,
> Number seventy, Simmery Axe."

The audience, it is clear, is intensely amused. The singer's voice, a very light baritone, is by serious operatic standards negligible. But his diction is crisp, clear and unforced, every word reaching to every part of the house.

> "We've a first-class assortment of magic;
>> And for raising a posthumous shade
> With effects that are comic or tragic,
>> There's no cheaper house in the trade.
> Love-philtre – we've quantities *of* it;
>> And for knowledge if anyone burns,
> We keep an extremely small prophet – a prophet
>> Who brings us unbounded returns"

– and so on through a continuing change of rhymes and rhythms until, at the end, the applause breaks out in a storm. Beaming still more, Arthur Sullivan raises his baton to signal yet another encore. Grossmith has to sing the whole song again, right through from the beginning.

There is no doubt. The singer has made a hit. He goes on with confidence increasing every minute. Some dialogue with Alexis and Aline, and now the stage grows dark and the music takes on a pseudo-eerie air for an incantation scene in which Grossmith, the Sorcerer, is to bring Alexis's dreams to fulfilment by introducing a love-potion into – of all things – a teapot that will be used to dispense the tea all the other characters will drink at a coming party. The fiendish and comic spells cast, daylight returns, and Grossmith, stooping low and brandishing the fizzing teapot before him, shuffles right round the stage with it as though it is the hissing funnel of a railway engine. The house roars and

8

Fig. 3. *The Sorcerer*: Incantation Scene. Drawn by Harry Furniss.

rocks with laughter. Bentham and Alice May are hard pressed to avoid laughter too. For this "locomotive" gag has been totally unrehearsed, a surprise Grossmith has kept until this moment entirely to himself.

Next, forming the finale to Act I, comes that tea party. And then the interval. Enthusiastic chatter breaks out all over the auditorium. The atmosphere, thanks to the gas lighting, has by now become hot, stuffy and somewhat unpleasant-smelling. But as proof of how well *The Sorcerer* is going, hardly anyone notices. Excitement mounts again as Sullivan returns to conduct Act II. This time the setting is the village market place. And immediately it becomes clear the Sorcerer's love-potion has worked. But it has done so with results that are, to say the least, disturbing. Constance, for example, has attached herself to the old Notary. Sir Marmaduke has taken up with the pew opener, Mrs Partlet. What other calamities are there in store? On again comes Grossmith, the little man, the Sorcerer. And Mr Wells is suffering from unwelcome remorse over the way things are turning out:

> "Oh, I have wrought much evil with my spells!
>   And ill I can't undo!
> This is too bad of you, J. W. Wells –
>   What wrong have they done you?"

Depressed, he sits at the foot of the market cross. But as he does so someone else approaches: a woman, elderly, downcast and – still unattached. It is Mrs Howard Paul, Lady Sangazure. And Mrs Paul, below par though she may be voicewise, is in fine fettle as an actress. All at once she notices him. Instantly her spirits rise. She bursts into eager recitative:

> "What is this fairy form I see before me?"

He leaps up, dismayed. He has not himself drunk the philtre. But he is not, it seems, immune from the effects of it on other people.

> "Oh, horrible!" – he sings in return – "she's going to adore me!"

And then he starts to wriggle, both verbally and physically, to say, to do anything he can to shake her off. But she, nothing daunted, will have him irrespective, no matter what his feelings, no matter how unsuited to each other they may be. At length he makes a dramatic pronouncement. He may not love her, because – pause – he is engaged! It is untrue; but she believes him all too readily. Voice rising in anguish, she utters a wild warning. It will be all his fault, she declares, if she goes straight to her family vault to bury her lifelong woe.

10

She rushes off as though to do just that. Resigned and even more guilt-ridden than before, he goes off after her, prepared to make reparation for all he has done by accepting her. But there is still one more upset to come. Aline, having herself taken the philtre at Alexis's insistence, immediately falls, powerless to resist the pull, into the arms of Dr Daly, the vicar. Alexis is furious. Yet how can the mischief be undone? Grossmith returns, miserably, in the wake of Lady Sangazure. There is one means, he suddenly remembers, by which the spell may be removed. Either Alexis or himself must yield up his life to a spirit fiend, Ahrimanes. He leaves the choice to the company as a whole.

The company make their decision: the sacrifice must be his. And with a fleeting twist of pathos he accepts his fate:

"Be happy all – leave me to my despair –
I go – it matters not with whom – or where!"

A gong sounds. And as the rest of the characters take up their positions for a brief finale, red fire envelops him, and he sinks slowly and with a comically mournful expression through a trap door in the centre of the stage, winding up his watch, buttoning his gloves and calmly brushing his hat as he goes. The final chords of the music echo round. The opera is at an end.

The applause is immense. The actors, in response, make their bows. Then, more or less simultaneously, there are calls and shouts: "Authors! Authors!" Sullivan leaves the orchestra pit. Moments later he and Gilbert appear together on the stage, he himself smiling delightedly, completely at his ease, Gilbert, on view for the first time, towering beside him, stiff, erect, awkwardly self-conscious, bowing their thanks in turn.

The curtain comes down for the last time. Slowly the audience begins to rise, to head for the doors. Coats, wraps and other property are reclaimed. Outside in the Strand the linkmen call the carriages. The bewhiskered men, the elegantly dressed ladies surge back along the "tunnel", still smiling, still chuckling. There is no question as to *their* enjoyment of the evening's performance.

On the Sunday, and over the days and weeks that follow, it is the turn of the press to have its say. And here too the general reaction is glowing. All the cast without exception come in for praise; and almost none more than the central figure, the newcomer, George Grossmith – even though, in the case of the *Musical Times*, this praise is somewhat two-edged; "Mr G. Grossmith," remarking that journal's critic, "singing as well as he could do, considering that nature had not gifted him with a voice." But from others the accolades flow freely; whether in the straightforward phraseology of the *Saturday Review* – "Mr Grossmith's

11

acting of the part . . . has true original force" – or the contorted humour of *Punch*: "Mr George Grossmith as Wellington Wells is the Sorcerestest Sorcerer that ever I did see or hear." Best of all perhaps is the assessment of the *Tatler*: "Mr Grossmith is an acquisition of great importance, and is a genuine comedian, as well as an effective singer. Would there were more like him on the stage!"

Clearly a new figure of talent has arrived on the London theatrical scene. Henceforth the name "Grossmith" will become familiar to all the capital's play and operagoers. Yet it is by no means the first time that name has been on the lips of entertainment-seekers. For Grossmith hails from a talented family, successive members of which have made their names not only on the stage but, with no less panache, in a variety of other forms of entertainment too.

PART ONE
EARLY LIFE, 1847–1877

CHAPTER ONE

Family Background and Boyhood

The story may conveniently begin around the turn of the nineteenth century with the Gilbert and Sullivan actor's paternal grandfather, a Grossmith whose christian name was William. William Grossmith was a man of many parts. Corpulent and amiable, he has been likened to that well-known plump man of fiction, Dickens's Mr Pickwick. Born possibly at Oxford about 1793, he was to be found early in life living in Reading, then a typical English market town, where he established a business making and selling looking glasses and picture frames. The business flourished and expanded. In due course he branched out into a quite different field: perfume, soap, shaving soap and toothpowder manufacture, topping his achievements here with "a superior article of great utility" which he called the "Reading Wash Cake". He also branched out geographically, opening premises in London (135, the Strand) in the early 1840s. In addition – and this is the side that links him most obviously with his famous grandson – he took more than a passing interest in the stage, to the extent of reputedly becoming at some point manager of the small but attractive Reading town theatre. And to complete the catalogue – and tightening that link, as it were, still further – he was to compose and have published a number of dance tunes and other light musical pieces.

Meanwhile he had got married. Lucy Grossmith, née Briant, was a native of Whitchurch in Oxfordshire; and Lucy Grossmith, whatever her feelings may have been as regards looking glasses and perfume, had very decided views on her husband's other main interest. To her, the theatre was anathema. She was, or so it was said, "sternly opposed" to

15

both playgoing and the acting profession. It was a viewpoint which, so far as her own household was concerned, carried within it the seeds of endless possible tension. For the interest William Grossmith himself took in the theatre was transmitted even more strongly to the next generation. Over the years the couple produced four sons;[1] and of that quartet no fewer than three were to become public entertainers of one sort or another, two of them, moreover, at an age so early as to be close on preposterous.

The torch was lit straight away by the eldest, William Robert Grossmith, born in 1818.[2] William Robert was a child prodigy. Right from the word go he began to display unusual intelligence and awareness, together with a remarkable memory. A visit to the Reading theatre at the age of five, and the urge to perform on his own account caught hold of him completely. His father took him up to London, where the managers of both Covent Garden and the Coburg theatres pronounced themselves amazed by the youngster's talents and, as a result, within days (the date was April 1824) he had made his stage debut at the latter establishment,[3] singing two character comic songs to rapturous applause on three or four separate evenings.

Back home, however, there was mother. Lucy Grossmith was not having any of that. On her entreaty his father agreed that all further theatricals for the youngster were out. But William Robert had other ideas. Quiet but determined, he succeeded after several attempts in persuading his father to buy him a copy of Shakespeare's *Richard III*. A month later he knew the whole play by heart. His father, astonished, realised his predilection for acting was not to be checked, and the upshot was a renewed Coburg appearance on July 5th that same year when he duly gave scenes from the play as part of a quadruple bill. It was an occasion that could hardly have gone better. The house was "crowded to excess" with an audience both fashionable and enthusiastic. The critics were there, and the critics were more than impressed. Fame was his from that night on. So too was a sobriquet. The boy was "The Young Roscius of the Age".[4]

And so the "Young" or "Infant" Roscius he became and so for many years he remained, the term "Roscius" deriving from an ancient Roman

---

[1] Plus, apparently, two or even three daughters; though all further knowledge regarding this feminine contingent is lacking.

[2] Or possibly 1819; or 1817; or even 1816. The evidence is hopelessly contradictory.

[3] Now the Old Vic.

[4] He was not, even so, the only one. Twenty years earlier another (in this case teenage) "Young Roscius", a certain Master Betty, had been the object of still greater public attention and adulation.

actor, Quintus Roscius Gallus. A portrait published the following year shows him looking suitably boyish, with curly hair parted down the middle and an alert, hopeful expression on his face. His triumph at the Coburg was followed by a week each at the Surrey Theatre and Sadler's Wells. Once more the public reaction was all he could have asked for.

Again, though, his mother begged or insisted that all this must stop. And again his father, torn between the two of them, bowed to her wishes. But again, after a short interval, the youngster won the battle. On Wednesday and Thursday, November 10th and 11th – and by this time with Lucy Grossmith's active, if reluctant, consent – he made his first public appearance in the provinces. The location was the town hall at Reading itself. A full column announcement in the *Reading Mercury* blazoned the versatility of the youthful phenomenon who would then be presenting himself. Since the summer he had widened his repertoire to a degree quite remarkable. His Reading entertainment would begin with a specially written prologue, to be followed first by his "introduction to the audience" and then by *Adventures in the Reading Coach*, in which he was to take off such characters as an irritable lady, John Bull, a Frenchman, an affected lady, the coachman, a lisping lady, a Scotsman and a drunk; moving on to a

"description of the company at an hotel in London; London cries; ballad singers; his interview with the manager of a London theatre; description of a green-room; imitations of many candidates for the stage; his own success with the said manager, etc. etc. In the course of which he will introduce a variety of new and admired comic songs . . ."

And that was only part one! Part two would comprise scenes from *Richard III*, *Macbeth* and John Home's *Douglas*, "which scenes will be varied each night," plus a piece played on "the musical glasses" one night and an additional song with violin accompaniment (by himself) the other, the whole performance to take place on a specially constructed stage. And to allay any suspicion that he might be exploiting the talents of so young a child for his own ends, his father added to all this the ingenuous footnote:

"Mr Grossmith, fearful lest the exertions of Master G. should be thought too much for him, begs leave to assure the public that Master G. does not feel the slightest inconvenience or even fatigue from his performance, and that he often goes through the whole twice and three times a day for his own amusement."

He need not have worried. The youngster's London triumphs had aroused too much interest to set anyone raising awkward questions on that score. More than three hundred people turned up the first night, another substantial gathering the second, and lapped up everything he offered them. His solo performance on each occasion lasted all but three hours. A third Reading performance was announced for, and given, the following Tuesday. And thereafter he, his father – who in effect acted as his manager[5] – and his portable stage went on tour: Newbury, Henley, Marlow, Maidenhead, Windsor, Egham, Chertsey, Kingston, Woking-ham – all received him with acclaim. Only at Windsor, where the weather was abominable and it was·anyway the week before Christmas, did he fail to attract large audiences.

The success of this tour removed the last doubts about his capabilities entertained by his father. It had an even more striking effect upon his mother who, conceding that the busker's life had neither impaired his health nor (which would have been far worse) corrupted him morally, now consented "heartily" to his making a tour over a still wider area of the country. This second tour, on which he embarked within a day or two of his return from the first, took him west into Gloucestershire and north from there into Staffordshire, Worcestershire, Shropshire and Warwickshire. A third tour later that same year (1825) encompassed, principally, Cheshire and Lancashire; a fourth, in 1826, saw him back in the south. But it scarcely mattered where he went, the result was the same: the press continued to rave, the crowds to flock in. So well known and popular indeed did he become that as early as 1825 there was published in Reading an anonymous booklet detailing in full his career to that date, which ran (with some later updating) through five editions or more in much the same number of years. He was the subject of at least two laudatory poems; his success too produced a number of imi-tators. These imitators, as might be expected, each came and went – all, that is, except one, and he was less an imitator than a brilliant performer in his own right. That exception was his youngest brother, Benjamin.

If anything, Benjamin's rise to fame was even more meteoric than his own. Born in 1826 (or possibly '27 – again the evidence is confusing) Benjamin had launched himself into public notice by the end of 1831, combining with William Robert for regular performances and tours and immediately displaying, in the words of the *Reading Mercury*, "the most various and extraordinary precocity of talent". He was, declared the same paper, a "wonderful little fellow"; and well before the decade was out it was *his* name that was topping their advertising billing. "Master B. Grossmith, now ten years old, will produce his entirely new, moral and instructive entertainment for 1838," began one such announcement.

[5] He announced meanwhile that he had engaged a Mr Cross, a "classical professor", to complete the youngster's education and to "manage the stage". But nothing further seems to have come of this.

"His brother will also appear." The occasion of this was what had become known as their "Reading Biennial Gala"; and the "entertainment" itself was a fair example of their general style of programme.

First came *A Comic Introductory Dialogue Address*; second *My Cousin Tom; or, Chambers in Lincoln's Inn*, a "mono-dramatic divertisement" offered by Benjamin in which he "sustained the entire cast of characters, changing both dress and appearance with extraordinary rapidity." Part three featured the two of them in another piece involving various character changes: *Poets, Proctors and Doctors; or, a Laugh at Life*. While part four, yet another such piece, went under the title *Eyes Right; or, the Short-Sighted Gentleman*. This last piece they called a "farcette"; as was normally the case with both of them, the comedy side clearly predominated.

For this one-night "Gala" performance the town hall was crammed with more than eleven hundred people; and similar evidence of popularity continued to greet them not only in Reading but in a hundred other cities and towns throughout the British Isles. They could, it seemed, have gone on indefinitely. But this was not to be. Suddenly at the beginning of 1843, and while still at the height of their fame, they announced their retirement. Their final appearance was billed for Reading that February. When the evening arrived they played to their usual packed house. It was an emotional occasion. At the end Benjamin made a short farewell speech, thanking the audience for their constant and loyal support in the past no less than for their cheering reception that night. The effort, reported the *Mercury*, "much affected" him. It was hardly surprising. He was still no more than a teenager.

The reasons for this early retirement may not be too difficult to guess. Constant touring, with themselves the sole performers wherever they appeared, must have been an immense strain. Maybe they had begun to feel burnt out. Maybe too, fame won so early in life had begun to pall. Or was it even that something of their mother's initial hostility had worked into them over the years and in spite of themselves? At all events, their future careers could scarcely have been further removed from what they had been doing before. Already, it seems, William Robert had taken up an apprenticeship with a London businessman. The firm in question, situated in Fleet Street, was eminently respectable – if somewhat out of the ordinary: it manufactured artificial limbs. That year, 1843, the current owner died; and thereupon the erstwhile "Young Roscius", now in his mid-twenties, took the business over and eventually married the latter's widow.

He threw himself into limb-making with the same single-mindedness he had previously devoted to entertaining. He even, in 1857, published

19

a short book on the subject, describing therein the various improvements he had brought about in this field and giving charts, with annotations, of more than two hundred cases in which the products of his firm had been satisfactorily applied. It was a line of business in no sense to be entered upon lightheartedly. To quote, for instance, from the section headed "Artificial Legs":

> "Simple as the manufacture of a leg on the English principle may seem to be from its appearance, by those who are accustomed to see the beautiful specimens of art displayed in our saloons and drawing-rooms, it is not by any means an easy task to accomplish."

Enough said.

If William Robert on his retirement from entertaining settled for a berth in the world of manufacture and trade, Benjamin had leanings of an altogether different nature. Not for him anything so down to earth, so tangible, so unwittingly comic, as artificial legs;[6] for him life henceforth was to be devoted to religion. But the tragi-comic caught up with him in the end too. For he sailed out to Africa as a missionary, never to return; and the story went that he had been eaten by a lion. It may have been true; equally it may have been pure fabrication – no lion ever came forward with evidence one way or the other. But true or not it was a story that has since become fixed firmly and irrevocably in Grossmith family legend.

So ended the tale of the two child prodigies. But what meanwhile of the other two brothers, who had somehow got left out of the juvenile act? In the case of the third, Charles, nothing definite is known. He may have gone into the Army; he may even at a later date have succeeded his father in the soap and toothpowder business. There is also a possibility that at some stage in his life he landed himself in trouble with the law. But where the second brother was concerned, things were different again. That second brother was christened George. He was to be the first of four generations of George Grossmiths, and father of the subject of this book. And fame was shortly to come to him in turn.

II

George Grossmith I – "George the First" as he was eventually to become known in family (and even some non-family) circles; "George senior" as he will be referred to where necessary in the pages that

---

[6] Or, at any rate, not for long. He may conceivably have filled in a year or so working with his father in the Strand.

follow – was born on August 20th, 1820, two years or thereabouts, that is, after William Robert, six or seven years before Benjamin. But while these two were touring the country and bathing themselves in the limelight, George stayed quietly at home and at length took up journalism. First he got a job on the *Reading Mercury*. But after a few years the wider world called him too, for in 1844 or '45 he moved to London to rooms in the Temple and a new job as a reporter for no less a paper than *The Times*.

In this capacity he was assigned in due course to cover Bow Street Police Court, reports from which featured regularly on the paper's law pages. It was a niche into which he settled with assurance and ease. His journalistic standing and relationship with the paper may be gauged from the following letter which he received a number of years later from the then *Times* manager, Mowbray Morris.

> "Mr Grossmith.
> Dear Sir,
>   The enquiry which I told you would be made of the Bow Street magistrates, to discover their opinion of the reports of the proceedings in their court which appear in *The Times*, has been satisfactorily answered . . . also to my question, whether the reports you supply to us are exclusive, is also satisfactory."[7]

In addition, the suggestion of a possible alteration in Grossmith's terms of employment had been mooted – apparently by the latter himself.

> "There appears, therefore" (Morris went on) "no sufficient reason for a sudden termination of your engagement, and I am unwilling to take advantage of your offer to resign your salary in lieu of the customary payment by the line. The fairer way will be to continue the present arrangement for twelve months, and to take an account of your performance during that interval. If your salary should be found very greatly in excess of the remuneration that would be given under the linear system of payments, it may perhaps be thought necessary to adopt this method thenceforward."

All very amicable. And so George Grossmith's journalistic career proceeded on its relaxed and untroubled way. But by this time – indeed since the day he had first arrived in London – journalism had become for him no more than a second string. His real interests lay elsewhere. Early in his twenties, while still living at home, he had become first acting and then full honorary secretary of a mechanics' institution founded at Reading in 1840. The institution provided a variety of facilities: among them elementary classes, essay and discussion meetings and, above all, lectures. After a somewhat unconvincing start it blossomed

---

[7] It would seem from this and from incidental evidence from other sources that Grossmith was also covering the court for most other papers by this time. One such source, in fact, refers to him significantly as the "chief" reporter there.

and flourished impressively. The prevailing enthusiasm stimulated Grossmith into expanding his activities still further. He began to give "recitations" – that is, readings from popular literary works of the day. Soon he found his name as a reciter becoming known. In due course, when he moved to London, he severed his connection with the institution. But by now he was established. The next step followed more or less logically. Acting on the advice of Thomas Noon Talfourd, a prominent Reading figure – not to mention the institution's second president – he decided to take up lecturing and reading professionally.

It was a decision he never regretted. And on Tuesday, December 21st, 1847, some four months after his twenty-seventh birthday, he gave his first professional lecture. Like his elder brother beginning his provincial career twenty-three years previously, he cast off plumb in home territory: as guest of the Reading institution itself. His name on the boards brought keen anticipation in the days beforehand, and on the night itself an immense audience turned up, completely filling the large hall in which the institution lectures were customarily held. The coming festive season had given him the inspiration for his choice of subject: "Wit and Humour – their use and abuse".

"All who attended the lecture," reported the *Reading Mercury*, "went filled with mirthful anticipation, and all seemed heartily to participate in the holiday spirit of the occasion. . . . The address embraced an allusion to the history of wit and witty authors; some remarks upon its peculiarities, under the headings of genuine wit, humour, punning and satire; and on their powerful agency in correcting follies and abuses; with a criticism of the leading comic writers of the day"; the points being illustrated by a stream of anecdotes, examples of repartee and "puns and jokes innumerable". It was all, the paper continued, "exactly what it professed to be – an evening's entertainment of a most amusing character. But Mr Grossmith's voice must be heard, and his gestures seen, to properly estimate his comic powers. A wit himself, a practised and accomplished reciter, an exquisite mimic, with an admirable perception of the grotesque and the ludicrous, he could not, and did not, fail to please and to amuse all present; and abundant applause with, better still, peal after peal of merry laughter, testified to the success of his efforts."

The description was one that could have been applied with equal accuracy to any of his lectures at any time. Those "comic powers" he retained for the rest of his life. And having appreciated from the outset that humour was his métier, it was no less clear that in lecturing he had found for that humour the ideal medium. Short in height (only just over five foot), plump, increasingly inclined to *embonpoint*, he thus bore a distinct resemblance to his father and, as with his father, he has been likened visually to Mr Pickwick. "He looked a humorist, that old fellow," as one later writer put it; and with a powerful, resonant delivery, the voice as clear as a bell, and without music, costume or notes, he could keep any audience creased with amusement for a full couple of hours nonstop.

Most lecturers, whether professional or otherwise, have a subject they make their particular speciality. For George Grossmith that speciality was Dickens. From the first he devoted himself to interpreting and expounding the works of the renowned novelist; and as a reader of Dickens he was considered in some quarters superior to that indefatigable author-reader himself. Among other writers who featured prominently in his repertoire were George Eliot, Thomas Hood and the American humorists Artemus Ward and Mark Twain. He also became noted for his skilled, though invariably good-natured mimicry of other – more earnest – types of lecturer.

Soon he had as many engagements as he wanted. And soon too he had become a welcome and familiar figure at literary and other institutes all over the country. His following increased almost daily; "we were never so pleased," recorded one of his admirers, "as when it was passed about that [he] was coming to lecture, or rather to amuse, in the town hall." As the years went by, reading and lecturing came to occupy more and more of his time, his commitments taking him on occasion right away from town for whole weeks at a stretch; and when this happened he would entrust his work at Bow Street to a deputy (*The Times*, it can only be assumed, fully accepting the arrangement). It was a life rich in experiences, and provided him with an ever-growing fund of anecdotes that he never failed to relish telling.

There was one story, for instance, that concerned a brazen attempt to cut the amount of his fee. The place was "some out-of-the-way spot in Scotland". His hosts on that occasion proved to be a group of elderly gentlemen. This august deputation met him at the station on arrival, conducted him from there to his hotel, from the hotel to the lecture-hall and the lecture-hall back to the hotel, and turned up yet again next morning to see him back to the station. And there on the platform the leader said:

"You'll be sorry to hear, Mr Grossmith, that we find, on making up the accounts, we are exactly £1–14–6 out of pocket by your lecture. We thought you would not like to leave the town with that upon your mind; and so we give you the opportunity of returning the deficit and enabling you, with a clear conscience, to say we have not lost by your visit."

23

Mr Grossmith was fully equal to that one. The punch line of the story as he loved to relate it lay in his reply. "I told the deputation it was most kind of them to afford me the opportunity, and I certainly would carefully consider the matter. I kept my word; for although that occurred many years ago, I have been carefully considering it ever since."

Then there was the time he was invited down to one of those little country towns "where they don't often have lectures but where, oddly enough, whenever they have *one*, they are pretty certain to have *two* the same night." And while he himself was holding forth on the *Sketches by Boz* in one room, another man in a different room was doing likewise with *The Pilgrim's Progress*. In the front row of Grossmith's audience sat a lady, "elderly, very respectable, but not very intelligent", who had turned up for the latter but come into his own lecture by mistake; and who, "putting on the most solemn countenance it was ever my misfortune to behold, became a listener to my discourse on the writings of Boz" without, for a good twenty minutes, realising the error she had made. But trouble was in the offing; for

> "when I at length referred to my author's description of a country fair, and the servant girls out for the day, 'not allowed to have any followers at home, but now resolved to have 'em all at once,' the dear old soul gave a shriek of horror and said, quite audibly, 'Oh, how shocking!' This exclamation was repeated when I described 'the fat old lady with the Jack-in-the-box, and three shies a penny'; and at last I became somewhat unnerved. I tried not to look at the old lady; but there is nothing in creation more difficult than the effort *not* to look at a thing you don't want to see."

And then, a few minutes later, he embarked upon Dickens's description of a thimble-rig. "'Here's a little game to make you wake up and laugh six months after you're dead, buried and forgotten, and turn the hair of your head grey with delight. Here's three little thimbles and one little pea. Now then, with a one, two, three, and . . .'" And that finished it.

> "The old lady, mistaking me for the creature I was describing, and believing that I was offering to bet with the company, uttered another scream of horror and left the room. 'Poor lady,' said I to the quiet old chairman. 'Of course, she's mad. But why did the committee let her in?' 'No, sir,' said the chairman, 'that lady is not mad; *she is my wife!*' I apologised; but, to my comfort, the chairman was not so much offended as I supposed. For, addressing me again, he said: 'Never mind; you'd better get on with your lecture. *She's more trouble to me than she is to you.*'"

This second story, as Grossmith recounted it, was almost certainly fictionalised and may even have been made up altogether. For the main theme of the article of which it formed a part was fiction beyond doubt, a hilarious account of how he had received a lecturing invitation from a man who described himself as "President of the Early-Rising Association"; how the latter turned out to have a wooden leg; and how, when staying at his house the night after the lecture, he (Grossmith) had been woken three times before six o'clock the following morning by the deathless clump of that wooden leg on the stairs.

The work in which this *Visit to the President of the Early-Rising Association* appeared was the second of two volumes of prose and poems brought out in the 1860s by members of the London Savage Club. The Savage Club was then of fairly recent foundation; and Grossmith, on being elected, had become one of its most prominent and popular habitués. For his humour was not confined to the lecture platform but bubbled over into all his private and personal relationships. "Returning from the dentist's once, we found him in the bus and he chucked me under the chin," recalled one little girl. "He had, I think, a geniality that none of his descendants have inherited; somehow I cannot imagine any of them chucking me under the chin except as stage business." Which is a debatable point – that is, so far as the rest of them were concerned. But it provides a neat, convincing cameo of George senior's own personality. His popularity too was reflected in an ever-active social life elsewhere. Invitations to dinners and parties were lavished upon him endlessly; hospitality was his wherever he went. And he himself was lavish with hospitality in return. To his home over the years came a regular stream of visitors whose names when listed read like part of a mid-Victorian literary, artistic, theatrical and humorists' "who's who".

But this is to take the story too far ahead. For home to George Grossmith also meant family. Back in the 1840s he had got married. His bride's name was Louisa Emmeline Weedon. The two of them possibly set up their first home in Grossmith's rooms in the Temple. But whether in the Temple or elsewhere, there was born to them in the course of time a son, George Grossmith II, whose fame as an entertainer, writer and, above all, Gilbert and Sullivan actor was to rival and outlast the fame of all his elders put together.

III

George Grossmith II was born on Thursday, December 9th, 1847 – or, at least, that has always been the accepted date. With regard to the year and the month there is indeed no dispute. The only doubt concerns the day, and it arises because of a remark apparently made by his father years later at his coming-of-age. "I went down to Reading," George junior quotes him as saying on that occasion, "to make my first appearance in *public* at *my* native place; and, on my return, found my eldest son had made his first appearance in *private* at *his* native place."

That first public appearance was the lecture on wit and humour that took place – as already mentioned – nearly two weeks later, on December 21st. But whether this confusion of dates was due to faulty memory on George senior's part, or whether Grossmith himself got the whole thing wrong, it is now impossible to say. Whichever way, it is a small matter, a minor curiosity and no more. It made a neat raconteur's point; and that, for both father and son, was what really counted in any such situation.

George junior's first significant memory of his own was of being taken, shortly before his fifth birthday, to a house in the Strand to watch the funeral procession of the Duke of Wellington. But inevitably, many if not most of his other earliest recollections were connected with school. Starting school at the age of five (the school in question being somewhere near Bloomsbury, where his parents were now living) he immediately fell in love with one of the little girls among his classmates. Love knew no scruples. It was only natural, he claims, that he should wish to make his "fiancée" a suitable gift as a token of their engagement; so "I presented her with a set of large gold shirt-studs, which I annexed from my father's dressing-table." This innocent purloining, however, produced a sequel he had not anticipated. The little girl's mother promptly went round and returned the studs to his father. And his father, equally promptly, explained to him "in a sweet, simple and comprehensive manner" the whys and wherefores of such matters and extracted from him a promise never to help himself to other people's property again.

That, though, was not quite the end of the affair. To sustain him in keeping his promise George senior handed him a sovereign – but with an injunction not to spend it. It was an injunction that naturally mystified him. And then, on examining the coin a few days later, he began to get suspicious. On one side of it was some lettering which he was too young to decipher, and on the other, instead of the head of the Queen, there was simply the impression of a hat. "I was much worried and concerned about that hat," he records. "I perfectly remember going to my parents and saying, 'I would rather have a sovereign without a hat on.'" This remark sent them both into roars of laughter. For that "sovereign", as they then or later told him – or he discovered for himself – was merely a brass disc advertising the "Gibus Opera Hat".

At seven or eight he was sent – as a boarder – to a preparatory school, Massingham House on Haverstock Hill in the then semi-rural district of Hampstead. Massingham House was run by three sisters named Hay, and in different ways these prim but understanding maiden ladies encouraged the boy in developing his various latent talents. One of them helped him with the piano, which he had begun learning around the age of five. Another gave him elocution lessons and provided him with pieces of poetry to recite. In turn, using his own initiative, he started devising and acting in a number of what he called shadow pantomimes, and it was at Massingham House too that he first showed an inclination to play the fool. One day when his mother called at the school, she enquired of the "poetry" sister how he was progressing. The answer came, in effect, in two parts. He was, she was informed, getting on very well with his music; but – and this was said with a sort of straight-faced amusement – "I am afraid he will one day be a clown." It was a splendidly accurate prophecy.

Then in 1857 the family themselves moved to Haverstock Hill, just a few doors away from the school, and George changed from a boarder to a day-scholar. Meanwhile, though, the family had grown. Back in 1854, on June 9th that year, a second son had been born. His parents christened that second son Walter Weedon, the "Weedon" clearly deriving from his mother; and they might just as well not have bothered with the Walter at all, for Weedon was the name by which he became known almost universally from the start. Furthermore, between the two boys there had also, it seems, been a daughter, Emily. But she has virtually no part to play in the story, for like so many Victorian children she died young. Weedon in his reminiscences gives her a single passing mention.[8] George in *his* makes no mention of her at all.

The fact of her death, though, whatever its cause, left no permanent scars on what was almost invariably a laughing, happy household. The chief fount of laughter, give or take the occasional off moment, was undoubtedly George senior – that is, when he was at home and not away on a lecture tour somewhere the other end of the country. To the two boys he was, in the familiar endearment of the period, "The Guv'nor", at once their mentor, their model and their companion.

It was to his father, for example, that little Weedon at the age of six or seven essayed his first conscious witticism. He had been looking through the pictures in a travel book and had accidentally torn one of the leaves. "The Guv'nor" was naturally annoyed at finding one of his favourite books thus damaged. Eyeing his younger son with suspicion, he demanded to know who was responsible. Cornered yet unabashed,

---

[8] In a reference to his own arrival. "My parents, who were not too prosperous . . . already owned two luxuries in the shape of a boy and a girl." Burial records suggest she died in 1859.

Fig. 4a. Grossmith (right) and Weedon as boys with their parents.

Fig. 4b. William Robert Grossmith, the "Young Roscius".

28

Weedon glanced at the cover of the book for inspiration. Improbably, inspiration came. "Father," he announced, "it says on the cover who did it. Look! *Tour by a German Prince.*"

Then there were holidays – most memorably at Llandudno and, one year, Edinburgh; there were occasions when he took them to a London theatre. But, more than that, his interest in everything that concerned his sons included a readiness to join in their activities as one of themselves, and this delight in participation was never better exemplified than when they all three acquired bicycles. In the winter, with no flowers around they could damage, they used their back garden path as a cycling practice circuit. The two youngsters, lithe and adaptable, obtained endless amusement from the valiant efforts made by their tubby, unathletic father to cope with his heavy machine. Even from indoors, recalled George, they could hear him distinctly:

> "loud as he approached the house, the noise becoming less as he reached the bottom of the garden. Sometimes the noise would suddenly cease. Ha! We in the house knew instinctively what had happened, and [would] rush to the windows to look out. Yes; there he was, in the thick of the gooseberry bushes. Not on the bicycle – oh dear, no! Under it, most decidedly under it. Sometimes on these occasions we would push up the windows and, in conjunction with our dear mother, greet him with a loud guffaw. Sometimes we would preserve a strict silence and listen. We [would] hear him wheel the vehicle back, place it against the lattice-work of the verandah, open the door and, as usual, call for me.
>
> 'George – George!'
>
> 'Here I am. What is it?'
>
> 'Oh, I say, George, have you got a piece of sticking-plaster?'
>
> "He always appealed to me for this article, knowing" (George explained) "that I was in possession of a few quires of court plaster; for it was at this period I had commenced to shave."

George, then, was growing up. Growing up physically, though to no great height, a wiry, agile, zestful boy with a zestful, agile mind to match. In 1859 he transferred to the North London Collegiate School in Camden Town. Life seemed now to revolve in typical youthful-adolescent fashion round a succession of crazes. Cycling was one such. Another – earlier – had been pugilism. A third was photography, and a fourth that odd schoolboy predilection for gunpowder and explosives. This predilection had been encouraged, improbably enough, by the third and eldest of the Hay sisters, who had allowed him on occasion to fire off a brass cannon she kept – even more improbably – in her kitchen. That might have been as far as George would have gone if left to himself. But then, at some point, Weedon came into the act to spur him on with an idea of his own.

Weedon was one of those boys who are forever playing the daredevil. On this occasion he got the urge to try his hand at making gas. George who really (claimed his younger brother) ought to have known better, but quite patently did not, was all for the suggestion. Adjoining their house was a coach house which had previously been converted into a breakfast-room, and it was in this breakfast-room that the two of them set to work one day boiling up a pint or so of turpentine or benzoline in a large workman's oilcan that had been left behind after the conversion. A few minutes of excitement, and then – disaster! Hissing and roaring, the gas began to shoot out of the narrow neck of the can, and all at once it ignited. There was a tremendous explosion, a huge flame shot across the room, and both boys were literally blown through the doorway. Clouds of thick, evil-smelling smoke curled round the ceiling, bringing down solid lumps of plaster. And suddenly there was their father, brought hotfoot to the scene by the noise of the explosion. It was one of those rare moments when his equanimity was shattered. Speechless at first, all he could finally say was: "Blow your heads off as much as you like, but don't blow up my house!"

Cycling, boxing, experimenting with gas, the processing sides of photography were all phases and crazes that passed. But it was in these same early years that the two boys made their first ventures into another realm of activity that, starting simply as youthful amusement, became in due course for each of them his full-time career. These ventures took several forms; but the essence of them all can be summed up in a single phrase: acting and performing. For George performing from the start revolved primarily round the piano. There had been times when that piano, with all the dedication, the practising its playing entailed, had been the cause of misery, of damp eyes and raps on the knuckles, when he had almost given it up. It was his mother who urged him to stick to it, claiming – with a clairvoyance here of her own – that his piano would turn out eventually to be his best friend. And so he stuck to it, with ever increasing skill and enjoyment, and with the result that, by the time he was twelve, whether playing from music or by ear, he had the instrument thoroughly mastered. More, it became for him, as a later admirer was to write, "almost an instinctive form of expression".

He might, with this skill, have played music of any type. But his real forte, as he discovered well before he reached his teens, was comedy and, in particular, the comic song. These songs he would sing himself, picking out his own accompaniments as he went along; and, in consequence of his prowess in this respect, he began to find himself increasingly in demand among his young contemporaries at parties. There was one such party when, asked to sing by some of the adults who were

30

gathering towards the end to take the children home, he launched into a song the tune of which was currently all the rage with everything from bands to barrel-organs and the lyric of which he had picked up from a penny song book; and the reaction stunned him. For that lyric, as he had not previously realised, was somewhat risqué. "I never heard so much laughter in a room before. There was a general request for the song to be encored. But this was just a little too much for the feelings of my fond and hitherto proud mother, who made a dash at me, and shut me and the piano up at the same moment."

But his performing was by no means confined to parties for children and adolescents. As his reputation increased, so he became allowed, while still a boy, to go to adult parties too – and to stay up late into the bargain. In addition during these years there were opportunities for entertainments and amateur theatricals in which he would play a leading role and in which Weedon joined with all the zeal of a younger brother eager to emulate the elder. One of their first notable histrionic triumphs was in a school production of the trial scene from *Pickwick*, with George cast as Sam Weller and Weedon as Justice Stareleigh.[9] Another came in April 1864[10] during a long, virtually all-night party at home when, having first got things going with music, conversation and dancing, they went on to present a twenty minute burlesque of *Hamlet* written for them by their father. In this George played the title-role, Weedon doubled as – of all combinations – Ophelia and the Gravedigger, while a number of their schoolfellows filled the other parts. The excruciating finale George later quoted in his reminiscences with unashamed relish. The characters are all lying on the floor, supposed to be dead.

> Hamlet (*sitting up*): What! Everybody dead? Why, that won't do;
>   For who's to speak the tag? I must –
> Horatio (*rising*):   Not you.
>   You've had your share of talking; so now stow it.
>   I'll speak the tag –
> King (*jumping up*):   Not if I know it.
>   They've kept me back until the very last.
>   Now, *I*'ll speak the tag. Friends –
> Queen (*getting up*):   *Not* so fast.
>   Your notion, King defunct, is most absurd;
>   The lady always utters the last word!

And so on for another four lines and a final brief burst of song to bring down the (imaginary) curtain.

---

[9] Still North London Collegiate, which Weedon also attended for a short time.

[10] April Fool's Day, as it happened. But let that pass.

Thanks no doubt to the vigour of their performance, the burlesque went off so well that, to their pride and delight, they were later asked at least twice to repeat it at parties elsewhere. Meanwhile, towards the end of that same year, 1864, young George began taking part in local "penny readings". Increasingly he was learning the art of performing to an audience, discovering in particular the pleasure of making an audience laugh. He seemed destined to follow in his father's footsteps, to fashion a career for himself if not admittedly as a lecturer, then certainly in some field of public entertaining.

His father's footsteps were indeed to act as his guide. But those footsteps did not lead only to the lecture platform and the world of entertainment. They also led, more prosaically, to Bow Street Police Court.

CHAPTER TWO

Bow Street Reporter

Bow Street Police Court (or "Police Office" as it was no less frequently called) was a small, "squeezed", badly laid out building situated in the bow-shaped thoroughfare adjacent to Covent Garden from which it took its name. Erected in 1825 to replace an older court, it was featured thirteen years later by Dickens in *Oliver Twist*, and since then had changed all too little. The courtroom itself, as Dickens described it, had a certain impressiveness. At the upper end stood

> "a raised platform railed off from the rest, with a dock for the prisoners on the left hand against the wall, a box for the witnesses in the middle and a desk for the magistrates on the right; the awful locality last named being screened off by a partition which concealed the bench from the common gaze, and left the vulgar to imagine (if they could) the full majesty of justice."[1]

But it was an impressiveness dwarfed by an irredeemable squalor. For the room, ill-ventilated,

> "smelt close and unwholesome, the walls were dirt-discoloured and the ceiling blackened. There was an old smoky bust over the mantelshelf, and a dusty clock above the dock – the only thing present that seemed to go on as it ought; for depravity, or poverty, or an habitual acquaintance with both, had left a taint on all the animate matter hardly less unpleasant than the thick greasy scum on every inanimate object that frowned upon it."

This, then, was Bow Street, a "public scandal" (as another writer put it) a place of grease and grime and yet one of life and bustle too, for it

---

[1] That partition, to judge from the way Grossmith described the courtroom himself, seems by his time to have disappeared.

was the court where nearly all the major contemporary criminal cases had their preliminary hearings. And it was here to Bow Street that young George Grossmith came one day in 1865 on instructions from his father to act as stand-in press reporter for a short though unspecified length of time. The reason for this call was quite simple: George senior had to go off to Liverpool; his deputy, a man named John Kelly Courtenay, who normally filled the breach in such circumstances, was away ill. George junior, though no more than seventeen, indeed still a schoolboy, must fill that breach instead.

It was a challenge; and he rose to it with all the carefree confidence of youth. After all, he had learned shorthand a few years previously – his father having made sure of this by doing the teaching himself; so what was there to worry about? The case under consideration that first day turned out to be a major bank fraud, involving intricate and complicated figures. Much if not all of it was beyond him. But his confidence remained unshaken. Not only did he have the wit to ask if he might check the figures he had taken down against those taken down by the chief clerk, but he even had the magistrate repeating solely for his benefit the gist of his closing remarks. Then he sat down to write his report, which was to be syndicated to most of the evening and morning papers,[2] along with the special report required by *The Times*.

The reports were duly printed; and that, apparently, was that. But then a few days later he received a letter from his father congratulating him on a worthy effort. That few days' gap had been deliberate – to allow time for any complaints to reach him from the papers concerned. No complaints arrived, so congratulations were clearly justified; and young George, proud at having distinguished himself on his reporting debut, proceeded in the days that followed to report other, less demanding cases while keeping on the lookout for an opportunity to distinguish himself again. At last, or so he thought, that opportunity had arrived:

"A poor woman was charged with purloining a shirt which was hanging outside a cheap hosier's in Clare Market somewhere. It was a windy day, and the end of the shirt was apparently flapping round the corner of the shop; so the prisoner, unable to resist temptation, filched it after the manner of a clown in a pantomime. Inspired by the punning humour of Tom Hood, I parodied one of his poems for the heading of my police report. The heading was 'The Tale of a Shirt'."

But this, as he was soon made aware, had "a most undesired effect":

"The serious papers wrote to complain of the flippancy of the title; the refined papers of its vulgarity; while the vulgar papers inserted the title which they emphasised by printing the word 'tale' in italic."

---

[2] "All" of them, if his own account is to be believed. Or was this stretching a point?

Even worse was to follow:

> "This caused sarcastic paragraphs to appear in other papers directed against my father who, of course, was the responsible reporter and who, consequently, wrote me a second letter anent my talents for reporting which differed widely from the first."

It made a good story; and it was only unfortunate that, when he wrote the above account of the incident more than twenty years later, memory had played tricks on him in a particularly ironic respect. For, to put it bluntly, he got the wrong shirt. The case to which he attached the punning title had nothing to do with theft but concerned a shirt that happened at the relevant time to be on a man's back. His report as it appeared in the *Evening Standard* and the *Morning Herald* opened in fact thus:

> *Bow Street.* "A Tale of a Shirt".
> "Wm Macklin and Joseph Head, members of the Corps of Commissionaires, were charged with assaulting John Hanford, the serjeant.
>   Mr Cottman, solicitor to the corps, conducted the case.
>   Hanford stated that on Saturday the prisoners, who were the worse for liquor, came into his room, and Macklin complained that he had been sent to Woking, and had had to pay his own fare. He demanded the money from witness. Witness refused to pay it, upon which the prisoners set upon him and pulled him about until his shirt was literally torn from his body. They had been hitherto well-conducted men . . ."

And so on. All mundane to a degree, and a case wherein no one but an incurable optimist would have seen an opportunity to distinguish himself on *any* count. Moreover, it is amusing to note that at least two papers, the *Daily Telegraph* and *The Times* itself, chose not to publish the report at all; and that two others, the *Morning Post* and the *Morning Star*, while printing the body of it pretty well word for word as above, were careful to omit a title altogether. The incident passed; but it was undoubtedly fortunate for everybody, as Grossmith remarks, that Mr Courtenay got well again and returned to work. This left Grossmith himself free to return to school. But the following year – 1866 – when he finally completed his education, it was decided he should go back to Bow Street to learn the business of reporting from the beginning, with John Courtenay acting as his teacher and general watchdog. There was, even so, no intention that journalism should be his career for life, for it had also been decided that he should at the same time study for the Bar. Family finances being what they were, though, it was clear he needed a remunerative occupation during the inevitably long period before the briefs began to come in. Journalism would take care of that period admirably.

In the event, however, things worked out rather differently. For when it came to the point, all his intention of preparing himself for the Bar was abandoned virtually from the outset. Instead, for the next four years[3] – until late 1870 – he stuck exclusively to reporting, and he continued as a reporter, if more intermittently, for another seven years after that. As to why his legal career never got off the ground there were perhaps two reasons: the first, as will become clear from the next chapter, was simply lack of time; the second, more immediately relevant, related to Bow Street itself. The job of a reporter, he found, suited him very well. The work unquestionably had its fascination; the grimy, squalid side of the place seemed to pass him by. His period of association with the court, he recalled in later years, was among the happiest phases of his life.

Soon he had settled into a daily routine, although "routine" is a dubious way of describing it, for the workload involved was decidedly erratic. Sometimes, as when there were long legal speeches to take down, the day could be a hard, grinding slog. One such speech – not surprisingly (if mercifully) his record in this respect – lasted with only about a thirty minute break for something like seven hours. And not merely did the speech have to be legibly transcribed, but no fewer than twelve copies of it had to be produced. For most of his reporting he worked on "manifold", sheets of oiled tissue with black carbonised sheets in between them. The amount of pressure required to produce twelve clear copies, and using to do so not a pen or pencil but a stylus, not to mention the state of the hands and fingers after sweating at this for any length of time could well, he suggests, be imagined.

On other days, that is, when there was little or nothing of consequence to report, things were less wearing. But then, by contrast, time could drag. Without a room of his own to retire to, it was all too easy to find himself simply hanging about waiting for something to turn up, loitering maybe in the passages, going to sit in the usher's room, or wandering into the gaoler's room to stare at the police and the prisoners. Sometimes on these blank or semi-blank days he would spend three or four hours over lunch, only to find that an important case had been disposed of in his absence. It was a situation that might have flummoxed a lesser man. It bothered Grossmith not a whit. He could generally write up a case just as well when he was absent, he considered, as when he was present – by copying from the notes taken by the court clerk.

The court normally sat six days a week, which meant – at least in theory – that six days a week a report of some sort had to be written.

[3] "Three", according to his reminiscences. But then he never claimed to be a mathematician.

A certain number of these submissions were always so much wasted effort, the papers not having the space to include them; but over the years a fair proportion were used. To take at random a single year, 1869, *The Times*, which almost certainly gave the law courts the most extensive coverage of any newspaper, printed reports of well over a hundred Bow Street cases, several of them involving more than one hearing. At this date it is impossible in most instances to state conclusively which of these reports were by Grossmith himself, which by his father (who, despite being so seldom there, remained throughout the period the official court reporter) and which by John Courtenay or – after the latter's death that October – by later deputies; records of particular reporters' contributions, at any rate in the case of *The Times*, no longer existing. Nor does straight reportage of this nature lend itself to individuality of style. But every so often among those thousands of printed words there peeps out a phrase, a sentence – something with a strong hint about it of the ridiculous or bizarre – that instinctively suggests a Grossmith pen at work. Thus there appeared one day a report concerning a certain George Roberts, who was brought into court "on the charge of returning from transportation before the expiration of his sentence, which was for life". Or again, from the report of a case involving the sale of two obscene oil paintings: "The latter, though most filthy, were executed with great ability" (it sounds more like a modern justification). Or yet again the following – a whole paragraph this time:

> "A gentleman who had been overcharged, as he supposed, by a cabman, applied to Mr Flowers[4] for a summons. He stated that his little baby, only seven weeks old, had been charged as a 'person'. It was well known that two children under twelve were allowed to travel as one fare, and he always understood that a baby did not count at all. Mr Flowers said it had been decided by the Court of Queen's Bench that a baby was 'a person' and must be charged for as such; but it was a consolation to know that two babies could be conveyed at the price of one. The applicant thought the public ought to know this fact, for it was a decided change in the law. Mr Flowers thought that a good many of the public had found it out, and it was now pretty generally known."

A Grossmith pen here? Making a not too unhopeful guess, yes; for George junior, as will be seen from other things he was eventually to write, had something of a fixation with babies.[5]

But even if, with the early incident of that shirt and its "tale" to act as a warning, wit and individuality had to be kept carefully under control, this was more than compensated for by the never-ending variety of cases with which the court had to deal.

[4] The magistrate that day.
[5] As of course did the librettist of *The Sorcerer* et al., W. S. Gilbert ("Bab").

On May 22nd, 1869 a medical student named Cassen was had up for attempting to steal three door knockers. On November 20th that year a "well-dressed" man named George Wilson was charged with stealing a book from the library of the British Museum. There were cases of begging and cases of pocket picking. There were men had up for burglary and men had up for receiving stolen goods. There were others accused of obtaining money by false pretences. There were still others accused of embezzlement.

Then there were cases of arson, cases of assault, cases of manslaughter, cases of murder, squalid affairs many of them, bringing into the open the seamiest sides of London life. Drunkenness as a cause of trouble was something that inevitably featured on occasion, and the drunks in question might come from almost any class of society. One such inebriate was a solicitor, no less, apprehended for "annoying ladies by laying hold of their arms as they passed along the Strand"; he was fined thirty shillings. Another was a young man employed by an undertaker taken into custody when "having a dead body in his possession of which he could give no satisfactory account". He was discharged.

Again there were people from no less a variety of backgrounds brought in for infringing some local police regulation; or worse, contravening an Act of Parliament.

From *The Times*, January 4th, 1869:

"Mr Samuel May, the popular theatrical costumier, was summoned under the new Workshops Regulation Act for having employed certain needle-women after the prohibited hours on Saturday week. Mr May stated that it was owing to the very great demands upon him for dresses for Boxing Night which it was compulsory to finish by that time. He thought such a case should prove an exceptional one. [The magistrate] was of an opposite opinion and fined Mr May £1."

The theatre indeed cropped up in innumerable Bow Street cases, for the court stood in a prominent theatrical area, with such playhouses as Drury Lane and the Lyceum just, so to speak, round the corner. And thus if it was May the costumier before the bench on one day, on another it was William Watkins brought in for loitering at the entrance to the Adelphi and on yet another it was a Frenchman, John Joseph Soyer, had up for causing a disturbance by "shouting and gesticulating" (not to mention assaulting the prompter) in the same building.

Theatrical disturbances, though, were far from uncommon at this time. Another such incident that resulted in a Bow Street case occurred in 1871 when a solicitor named Leopold David Lewis was charged with creating similar upheaval at the Queen's Theatre during the performance of a play called *Joan of Arc*. Lewis, sitting in the pit, decided he was unable to hear sufficiently clearly what was going on. He began calling to the actors to "speak up". Other members of the audience demanded he be turned out. The upshot was pandemonium; the performance was stopped. The acting manager tried to remonstrate with him – to no avail; and thereupon, with the help of some of his underlings, he dragged the offender right out of the auditorium and finished by pushing him down the stairs that led to the street. A policeman was called and hustled him off to the station, and because of this the case was dismissed; the officer should have confined himself, said the magistrate, to removing him from the theatre. Grossmith's report of the affair appeared in *The Times* on April 19th.[6] But the matter did not end there, for Lewis now issued a summons against the theatre proprietor for assault; and when the case was heard at Westminster, Grossmith was called as a witness, in order that use might be made of his shorthand notes of the evidence taken at Bow Street.

It was almost certainly an occasion of some embarrassment for him, since Lewis, who was not merely a solicitor but also a writer,[7] happened to be an acquaintance of his. And this situation – knowing somebody involved in a case, and especially if that person was actually in the dock – was one that cropped up (or so he seems to imply) with some frequency. What, he would wonder, ought his attitude on these occasions to be? The fact that the dock at Bow Street joined the reporters' box hardly helped. Suppose he were to lean across and shake hands? In the event, he admitted, "I never did," although "I do not see why I should not have done so. However, I thought it best to follow the footsteps of the magistrates – they did not shake hands with their friends when charged." There was one case that highlighted in the sharpest fashion the embarrassment – or worse – a false step in this respect might have caused. He had been giving a nightly entertainment down at Margate, and one evening while there had been introduced to a young man. The latter, pleasant, personable and free with money, took him out to supper. A lunch or two followed and finally, when the time of his engagement in the resort came to an end, an invitation to a special farewell banquet.

---

[6] In addition, a quite separate account of the incident was written more than forty years later by a dramatist and journalist, G. R. Sims, who happened to have been in the pit at the Queen's that same evening; and it is from him that the details about the manager's intervention are taken. His account, though, needs to be treated with some reservation. If nothing else, he slipped up on the name of the play.

[7] He is known chiefly now for his adaptation of *The Bells*, one of the most famous plays associated with Henry Irving.

A friend advised him to steer clear of this and, as a result, he stayed away; to his undoubted relief when, a few days later, the young man turned up in court on a charge of robbing his employer.

Most of the cases thus far mentioned attracted no more than passing interest among the public at large. But there were others – those of a particularly sordid or sensational nature – that evoked interest and excitement for weeks, if not months, on end. Grossmith in his reminiscences names five of these that he covered either wholly or in large part during their Bow Street stages. There were two linked cases involving Irish Fenians, one of which resulted in the country's last public execution. There was the case of Dr Gottfried Hessel, accused in 1873 of cutting a woman's throat, an affair known as the Great Coram Street Murder. There was the arraignment of four police detectives and a solicitor for conspiracy in a business that achieved notoriety as the De Goncourt Turf Frauds.

And in sharp, near-pantomimic yet salacious contrast there was the so-called Female Impersonation Case, which first came up in April 1870. Two young men in their early twenties, Ernest Boulton and Frederick William Park, appeared on a charge of frequenting the Strand Theatre (a theatre again!) with intent to commit felony while dressed – this being the salacious aspect – in the guise of women. The whole affair was a reporter's dream. The two men actually made their initial court appearance in their female get-up. On the one hand there was Boulton sporting a cherry-coloured silk evening gown trimmed with white lace, wearing bracelets on his wrists and a wig with a plaited chignon on his head. On the other there was Park flaunting a dark green, low-necked satin dress tricked out with black lace, with a lace shawl round his shoulders, white kid gloves, and with his hair flaxen and in curls.

This dressing up had been going on, it appeared, for above two years, and at length had attracted the attention of the police. On the evening in question a detective, watching a house in Wakefield Street off Regent Square which the two of them frequently used as lodgings, had followed them from there to the theatre in a cab. On arrival he spotted them going into a private box, along with two other young men dressed normally. At some point during the evening, he claimed, one of the pair went into the ladies' cloakroom and "desired an attendant to pin up some lace that had fallen from his skirts". The attendant obliged, quite unsuspecting; a tribute to the skilfulness and efficacy of the disguise if nothing else. Another policeman, going to the theatre and watching them in their box, described how one of them kept smiling and nodding to gentlemen in the stalls. Such behaviour could only serve to reinforce already strong suspicion of their motives. And now, when they left the theatre, they and one of the other two with them were arrested.

But this was only the beginning. For when the police investigated the Wakefield Street house inside, they found a number of photographs showing the two of them dressed both as men and as women, together with some distinctly suggestive letters and a complete feminine wardrobe astonishing in its variety, including: dresses, skirts and petticoats of all colours and materials, cloaks, jackets, bodices, shawls, about a dozen pairs of ladies' kid boots and shoes, "seven chignons, two long combs, ten plaits, one grey beard [The magistrate: 'The grey beard can hardly be called part of a woman's costume.' The prosecutor: 'It may be part of a disguise'] curling irons, sunshades, six pairs of stays, one low crossover, two tulle falls, chemisettes, garters, drawers, five boxes of violet powder, one of bloom of roses (rouge), silk stockings, eight pairs of gloves, one bottle of chloroform, artificial flowers and a great quantity of wadding used apparently for padding."

It was a case which, as that interjection about the beard will have indicated, gave Grossmith a chance to allow his humorous wings rather more than their normal spread. But it was also one that involved him in any amount of work. The Bow Street hearing extended to no fewer than eight sessions, each of which had to be reported in full; the longest of these reports covering more than three columns of close *Times* print. Then too it was a case that caused an enormous stir, sending ripples of unease through all the many citadels of mid-Victorian respectability; for the longer it went on the more serious and disturbing seemed the evidence adduced. The whole affair, declared one contemporary chronicler, was "but the outer eruption significant of a deeper social disease within".[8]

Which is as may be. But the existence of social disease, however deep or wide its hold, was not something that troubled young George Grossmith. Still less was he concerned to analyse or dissect it. Happy in disposition, to use his own words, he so thoroughly enjoyed the bright side of life that its shadows sank into insignificance. To social reformers, to men with long faces, to those obsessed by the evils of society, Bow Street (and similar courts elsewhere) doubtless provided more than sufficient evidence of the world's depravity and moral decay. To him it seemed instead an endless fount of humour. So firmly indeed did this humour strike him that some years later, in 1884, he used his experiences as the basis for a jaunty series of ten skits on court life which he contributed that year to *Punch*.

[8] Ultimately the two men were acquitted; though the full legal proceedings against them lasted over a year.

These skits, or sketches, went under the overall title *Very Trying: a record of a few trials of patience*, and incorporated a variety of comic characters with a variety of comic names: a policeman called Inspector Van Läden in one, an aristocratic gentleman, Lord Peter Beauchamp Majoribanks Cholmondeley Waterloo Rhodes in another, Mr Nowal, a chief clerk, in a third. But the most affectionate targets of his wit were the Bow Street magistrates, their identities disguised in the thinnest of fashions. Number four in the series, for instance, concerned a magistrate named Mr Bowers. In real life "Mr Bowers" was Frederick Flowers, he who had had to deal with that complaint about the cabman and the baby and, incidentally, with Messrs Boulton and Park. As a magistrate, Frederick Flowers was anything but conventional. Short, with iron-grey hair and whiskers, he seemed less like an administrator of the law than everyone's benevolent uncle, a man who hated having to mete out punishment of any sort. On one occasion he refused to convict a small boy for throwing a snowball that cut an elderly gentleman in the cheek. "I daresay," he explained when the latter protested, that "when you were a boy you were in the habit of snowballing old gentlemen. At all events, I know *I* used to snowball people, and I am not going to fine any boy for doing what I used to do myself." This readiness to acknowledge his own failings and fallibility, together with a penchant for humour on duty that would not be stifled, were both reflected in Grossmith's sketch:

"John Pummle was charged before Mr Bowers, the presiding magistrate, with assaulting Charles Short.

The complainant (*who had a black eye*) deposed: On Tuesday, your Worship, I was standing on a seat in the Strand, waiting for the Lord Mayor's Procession to pass. About four rows in front of me was the back of a man who I thought was Alf Watson.

Mr Bowers: And who is Alf Watson?

Complainant: He is a packer at the Stores, you know.

Mr Bowers: Well, I didn't know, but I'm always pleased to receive information. I hope he'll stick to his packing-cases and keep out of assault cases. (*Laughter*)."

A few moments later:

"Complainant: Well, your Worship, I calls out, 'Hulloh, Alf Watson!' and I leaned over and touched him gently on the back of his head with my stick – just so.

(*The complainant lightly tapped with his stick the ledge of the witness box*)

Mr Bowers: A rather *striking* illustration.

Defendant: (*interrupting*). Not a bit like it, your Worship. He tapped me like this.

(*The defendant here struck with his stick a tremendous blow on the ledge of the prisoner's dock*)

Mr Bowers: I cannot help thinking that that is a violent assault upon the court. (*Loud laughter, in which the chief usher joined*)."

And finally:

"Complainant: The defendant turned round, and I said, 'It's a mistake – I thought you were Alf Watson.' The defendant, in reply, said, 'Oh, is it? Wait till the Show has passed, and I'll "Alf Watson" you in the eye.'

Mr Bowers: A new form of assault, evidently. And what passed then?

Complainant: The Lord Mayor's Show did. (*Laughter*). The defendant then came down on me like a ton of bricks, as my eye will prove.

Mr Bowers: Ocular evidence. (*To defendant*). Now is your time to ask any question of the witness.

Defendant: Thanks, your Worship. (*To witness*). What's your name?

Complainant: Short.

Defendant: All right. I'll soon make *short* work of you.

(*Roars of laughter, in which the magistrate joined*)

Complainant: (*indignantly*). I don't consider this a case for joking, your Worship.

Mr Bowers: You are right there; but I can't, in justice, rebuke a man for joking, when I've been doing it myself. Therefore, I'll adjourn the case for a week, by which time, I hope, we shall all be in a more serious mood."

But with two men such as himself and George Grossmith around to keep the quips flying, that awful possibility seemed mercifully remote.

III

For those ten *Punch* sketches, which ranged in length from around seven to thirteen hundred words, Grossmith was paid three guineas apiece, no insubstantial fee at that time.[9] They were in fact his second contribution to the magazine, the first having been another – single – sketch entitled *The Society Dramatist* which had appeared the previous April. To have work in *Punch* – even when knowing the editor[10] – is an achievement to be prized by any humorist; and for Grossmith this represented an important landmark in a writing career (creative, imaginative writing, that is, as distinct from straight journalism) which was by that time well established. The writing habit had initially taken hold of him halfway through his teens when, helped and encouraged by his father, he had begun turning out snatches of sketches and songs. Then at Bow Street, on those days when he had time on his hands, he

[9] Eight (? nine) of them were illustrated with one or more drawings by a regular *Punch* illustrator, Harry Furniss.

[10] See page 164.

was soon experimenting further. One day – or week – or month – he would be engaged on "the opening chapters of three-volume novels"; another day – or week – "extra verses to comic songs". The novels were never finished, the verses never sung. But every writer has to begin somewhere.

Now came another phase through which many writers pass: the desire to publish their own work. In Grossmith's case desire was translated into reality. Before long he was producing a paper or magazine which he called *Ourselves at Home* and of which he had fifty or a hundred copies printed at a time. Two of his friends each contributed half a crown a week towards the cost in return for having their own literary efforts included. Their money, he considered, was more valuable than their articles, though as these were "not so bad as mine, no complaint was made". The results of such ventures, though, are always liable to disappoint their instigators, and this case proved no exception. It is one thing to produce a magazine, quite another to persuade people to read, let alone buy it; and at length, after thirteen issues, *Ourselves at Home* "died a natural death".[11]

That was in March 1867. But it was all valuable experience, and soon his writing career was moving on to its next – and this time more successful – stage. Encouraged now by John Courtenay, who would read, criticise and help him revise anything he cared to show him, he began trying his hand at humorous verses and short articles for submission to editors elsewhere; and every so often, to his delight, one of these efforts would be published. What any of them were and in which magazines they appeared is, once again, impossible to say – if only because, thanks to the practice of the time, most would have been printed without a by-line.[12] During the 1870s he was to publish a number of songs.[13] But these come into a somewhat different category, and the piece that must serve as an example of his early work (even though it slightly postdates his Bow Street period) is a poem that appeared in the first – and in the event only – issue of a new "holiday" magazine, *Ours*, in May 1878. It is a light, amusing trifle, whimsical in idea and neat in execution, even if the punning on which it relies for its principal effects does seem a little forced.

---

[11] And went to an unknown grave. All trace of it has long disappeared.

[12] It will be gathered from what has already been said that nothing of his during these years got into *Punch* – even assuming he submitted anything to so lofty a periodical thus early in his career. Nor, it seems, did he have anything in what was then *Punch*'s chief humorous rival, *Fun*.

[13] See pages 54–5.

Mrs and Miss Mirror:
a reflection by George Grossmith, jun.

"Young Mrs Mirror has a notion that her only child
Is without an imperfection, so the girl is growing wild.
She's ignorant and unrefined, and noisy now and then;
Her voice is always forte, though the maid is under ten.

"The progress in her learning one can very plainly see,
She almost knows her alphabet as far as letter D.
She owns, with her calligraphy, she cannot get along;
And when she does begin to write – her letters are all wrong.

"At dinner time upon her best behaviour she is seen;
She has three plates of soup, then throws her spoon in the tureen.
Her mother will not look at her, nor cast a little frown;
Her way to bring her daughter up – is not to put her down.

"Miss Mirror learned some needlework of Madame Sowanso;
She very often went to class, and yet it was no go.
She could not hem, she could not stitch, and in her wildest dreams
She never hoped to sew a simple border, so it seems.

"Her brows are always cloudy, though her eyes are ever fine,
And when she has a wish to storm there is a little shine.
She cries for every mortal thing – 'tis part of her design;
She cannot beg a glass of port without a little whine.

"These little whims and errors all escape mamma's detection,
Because the daughter of the mother is the true reflection.
Young Mrs Mirror has few friends; the reason why is plain –
They suggest a 'mild correction', and they don't get asked again."

But it was not only as a writer that "George Grossmith, jun." established himself during his Bow Street period; something else, by no means unconnected and even more significant in terms of his career as a whole, was happening during these years too. Throughout, he had remained his father's son; and just as George senior managed to combine journalism with lecturing, so increasingly had *he* been combining it with his own brand of public performing. First as an amateur, before long turning professional, he had meanwhile become – a fully-fledged musical entertainer.

45

CHAPTER THREE

Piano Entertainer, Part I

The Royal Polytechnic: "Mr George Grossmith the younger follows with an illustrated fairy tale, and he really entertains his audience." (*The Times*, December 27th, 1870)

"To entertain is difficult, as everybody knows,
You have to sing and play the piano well, and to compose,
To act a bit, invent, and write in verse as well as prose –
    Oh! the trials of an entertainer."
(George Grossmith – *The Trials of an Entertainer*)

It had all started in effect with those appearances at "penny readings" referred to at the end of chapter one. Penny (or occasionally sixpenny) readings had first come into vogue during the late 1850s; and in the decade that followed they had gained firm popularity throughout the country. The initial idea behind them was eminently worthy: that they should feature for the most part readings and "recitations" from contemporary or near-contemporary English literature, to the moral benefit and intellectual uplift of both readers and listeners.

But – perhaps inevitably – they by no means always lived up to such high ideals and hopes in practice. Rather they were seen increasingly as a cheap form of pure entertainment, sentimental, lighthearted and even downright comic by turn; and an entertainment, moreover, that could be enjoyed without guilt or qualms, for almost always they took place under the auspices of the local clergy.

Equally, since they were in essence entertainments given by amateurs, the standards of performance varied no less than the content. And the result, to anyone with the least discrimination, could at times be agony. The comedian W. S. Penley, to be best known in due course as the creator of Lord Fancourt Babberley in *Charley's Aunt*, described one such "reading" at which he found himself while staying with a clergyman uncle in Suffolk. The event was held in the parish schoolroom:

"First of all, my aunt and the doctor's wife tried over a pianoforte duet which, I should say, neither of them had ever set eyes on before. The audience, not knowing any better, applauded their failure with amazing enthusiasm; and they were not less complimentary when my uncle read two or three chapters

47

out of *The Pickwick Papers*. The good man could not read for nuts, but as he was the vicar they seemed to be afraid to 'goose' him. Quite late in the evening, when a succession of maddening recitations and excruciating songs had worked the audience into a delirium of enjoyment, I was asked if I could not do a little something. Ever ready to oblige, I started upon *What Could the Poor Girl Do?*, a poem which has invariably met with approval when I have recited it in the drawing-rooms of Belgravia or at the camp-fire during my yearly soldiering at Aldershot. I had hardly started on the second verse when one of the most important – or at any rate the bulkiest – parishioners gave a scream and without any more ado went off straight away into hysterics. I thought it better not to persevere with my recitation and escaped from the schoolroom as quickly as I could . . ."

Shades of George Grossmith senior and that "not very intelligent" old lady at his Dickens lecture. And shades too, if not to quite so dramatic effect, of George junior's debut at his own local "readings". These were held in a schoolroom close to the parish church which he had attended for many years both as a member of the congregation and, on occasion, as a choirboy. He was thus a familiar figure there; and, naturally enough, with his parental and musical background, it was not long before the vicar, as chairman, called upon him to make his first active contribution. He was bursting with confidence, was more than willing to oblige. No penny reader, he laughingly admitted later, "ever had such an exalted opinion of his own talents as I had of mine". Performing for him, of course, meant the use of the piano. Taking his seat, he plunged without hesitation into a popular comic song. It was the story of that juvenile party again – or almost. Maybe this particular song was not actually risqué; but each time he reached the refrain, the "noisy portion" of the audience joined in. The dignity of the proceedings was threatened. Disapproval hovered in the air. So thereafter he settled for readings from Dickens, Thomas Hood and other writers "which I cribbed from my father's repertoire", and other comic songs of a "milder form".

But whether such songs were really milder or not, his further contributions as a performer on these occasions continued in demand. And at length a suggestion was put forward that he and his friends present the *Hamlet* burlesque that had gone down so well at private parties. But when, on the evening fixed for this, the group of them turned up with several bags of costumes, the vicar was horrified and refused to allow the performance to take place. Costumes! Costumes were what actors wore in theatres – on the stage! And to all right-minded clergymen of the 1860s the stage and everything connected with it was *ipso facto* steeped in sin. The audience, however, was disappointed and made that disappointment plain. With visible reluctance the vicar agreed to their giving the performance on a future occasion, but – emphatically – no costumes. Grossmith, as leader of the cast, refused to accept this edict, and eventually, after a protracted discussion, a compromise was reached. He, as Hamlet, was to be allowed to wear a makeshift cloak; the Ghost might sport a tablecloth; while Weedon, when being Ophelia, might even appear in a muslin bodice and skirt. Presumably at his age – ten or twelve at most by this time – the disease of theatrical contamination was not considered infectious.

The performance, however, ended in hilarious fiasco. The cause of the trouble was the lad playing the Queen, a substitute who had had to be brought in for this one occasion. Aged about seventeen and with a perceptible moustache, the latter "had never acted before"[1] but was a performer nonetheless with a mind of his own. First, without telling Grossmith or anyone else, and to the vicar's annoyance, he togged himself up in a servant's frock and a "carrcty" wig. And then at the end, as they went into their final snatch of song, he suddenly became seized with uncontrollable excitement and began dancing and kicking wildly in the air. The audience, crammed inside the room, laughed and clapped with delight. The vicar tried to silence them by standing and raising his hands, but to no effect. He motioned to the cast to leave the platform, and they all did so with the exception of the moustachioed Queen who, positively frenzied by now, seized the reverend gentleman by the arms and swung him right round two or three times. And "that", records Grossmith, "was my last appearance at those particular penny readings".

Penny readings constituted the first – the amateur, though for all their vagaries, far from valueless – stage in Grossmith's development as an entertainer. But all the while, thanks particularly to the contacts and friendships he made with the many writers, actors and entertainers who were such frequent visitors at home, he was becoming known as a young performer of talent. With their advice and encouragement to spur him on, the second stage of his development – his breakthrough into professional entertaining – could not be long delayed. Through a Dr Croft, one of the directors, he was introduced as a potential entertainer to the Royal Polytechnic Institution in Regent Street. This was in many ways, as its name might imply, a serious educational establishment. But somehow – and it was far from being alone among places of its kind in this respect – it had also managed to acquire a reputation as a venue of entertainment. The Polytechnic was then headed by one John Henry Pepper, "Professor" Pepper as he was generally known, a showman of affability and unshakable bounce. He took to Grossmith immediately;

[1] "And in all probability has never acted since."

49

and on November 11th, 1870 Grossmith gave his first "trial" entertainment – his first performance as a professional – under the professor's auspices.

For this he presented a sketch entitled *Human Oddities*, lasting about forty minutes. *Human Oddities* was the joint creation of himself and his father. The latter, having written the words, was responsible for the bulk of it. But he was, it seems, no musician and in consequence George junior had his first real chance to try his hand at musical composition by setting music to the songs the sketch included. Presumably it went down well, for in December, as a Christmas entertainment, he was giving another sketch, *The Yellow Dwarf*. This *Yellow Dwarf*, which he wrote entirely by himself (and later dismissed as "exceedingly puerile") was put on in conjunction with a showing of "dissolving views", which were included because Pepper had something of a fixation with them; but Grossmith learned a lesson from that. "Dissolving views" meant a darkened room, and he found he did not in the least enjoy being stuck at his piano in a corner in complete darkness. To be any good at all, he rapidly decided, he needed to be seen. And so he was unashamedly delighted when, after a month, he was allowed to revert to *Human Oddities* and no more dissolving views or other extraneous makeweights.

This time *Human Oddities* ran for about six months. And then that summer, 1871, another opening for his talents presented itself: an invitation to participate in a seaside tour in the concert entertainment of Mr and Mrs Howard Paul. He accepted with relish; it was an opportunity not to be missed. The Howard Pauls were a significant force in the entertainment world.

Howard Paul himself had been born in Philadelphia, and was a prolific writer of plays, sketches, songs and other comic material, and a comic performer of some finesse. His wife,[2] born (at Dartford) Isabella Featherstone, was in her way equally versatile. A skilled actress and a singer with a rich and quite remarkable range of voice, she could cope with pretty well anything from contralto up to tenor, and in her early years had made a particular name for herself playing Captain Macheath – no less – in *The Beggar's Opera*. The two of them had got married in 1857; and the following year they embarked on the performance and management of their own entertainment.

This they called *Patchwork*, and it was hailed by one critic as "a clatter of fun, frolic, song and impersonation, carried on by performers of unfailing dash". Their success, in both London and the provinces, was immediate and considerable. In 1869 Mrs Paul returned to the stage to

[2] The eventual Lady Sangazure in *The Sorcerer* (see pages 5–6).

play Lady Macbeth (doubling with Hecate) at Drury Lane. But in due course she was back at her "entertainment" once more, and casting out her net for supporting artists. Which was where Grossmith came in.

That 1871 tour lasted several weeks; and while it was on, Grossmith, in the manner of his father on other occasions, cheerfully abandoned Bow Street to the current deputy. The experience, he found, proved a splendid way of "combining business and pleasure"; he enjoyed particularly "a delightful week at Scarborough". The *Scarborough Gazette*, in a brief review, seemed equally delighted with their whole programme:

> "*Mr and Mrs Howard Paul*. These admirable entertainers have given two representations of their popular songs and impersonations at the Spa Saloon to brilliant and fashionable audiences. Their last performance in Scarborough will take place tomorrow (Friday) when, in addition to a varied programme of characters, Mrs Howard Paul will give her astounding photograph of Mr Sims Reeves[3] and sing *My Pretty Jane* and *Love's Request*. Mr Geo. Grossmith, jun., who has appeared in conjunction with [them], is an artiste of the John Parry school, and his *Human Oddities*, given with immense facial expression and admirable by-play, excited roars of laughter. He will appear tonight with the Howard Pauls at Whitby."

The tour over, Grossmith returned once more to Bow Street and, soon afterwards, to a new season at the Polytechnic. And this time his act at the latter featured a sketch that over the next few years he was to give again and again in a variety of surroundings: *The Silver Wedding*. *The Times* (more or less favourably) described the first or an early performance:

> "Mr Adolphus de Browne, arriving at the twenty-fifth anniversary of his marriage day, celebrates the occasion by giving an evening party. Each of his many guests displays some marked peculiarities of character, and it is for the purpose of delineating these peculiarities that Mr Grossmith comes forward. That he is not unequal to the task may be safely affirmed. His voice and elocution, indeed, are somewhat against him, but a nice perception of what is striking in character, a faculty of fairly individualising the personages he represents, and, lastly, a power of embodying his ideas with a whimsical effect, enable him to redeem all disadvantages. He met with an excellent reception."

> "It was not a fashionable party. It was a *comfortable* party. That is to say, there were more chairs than guests."
>
> (George Grossmith – *The Silver Wedding*)

And into *The Silver Wedding*, which again he otherwise wrote by himself, went another song of his father's that rapidly became one of the most popular numbers associated with his own performances. That

---

[3] John Sims Reeves, the most celebrated English tenor of the period. Though as for that "astounding photograph", this meant, alas, no more than an astounding impersonation.

song was called *I am so Volatile*. The lyric had an incisive, rollicking, irresistible rhythm:

> "My name is Nimble Dick,
>   I was born in a caravan;
> In a couple of months I stood alone,
>   And in fourteen weeks I ran.
> And the people came around
>   Having walked for many a mile,
> All to see this boy, his mother's joy,
>   Who *was* so volatile.

> "I went to the village school,
>   And I proved so uncommon quick
> That I gallop'd all thro' my geography,
>   And I skipped my arithmetic.
> And my writing was 'up and down'
>   In a new and original style,
> And I jumped clean over the globes, I did –
>   I *was* so volatile."

The tune with which George junior clothed this lyric had a no less irresistible lilt.

Odd though it might now seem from some of the activities it countenanced, the Polytechnic was a place of prestige; and before long, as a result of his regular appearances there, George junior's fame began to spread. Soon he found himself receiving invitations to give entertainments at similar institutions in the provinces and at branches of the YMCA. A number of these he accepted – those at places within a short distance of London, to ensure there would be no problem about his getting back to Bow Street the morning after. The pattern of these solo entertainments (or, as he called them at times, "recitals") he had already largely formed.

Solo entertaining in this country has had a long and vibrant history, with a variety of celebrated practitioners both before and after Grossmith's time.[4] But the father and prototype of what might be termed the Victorian version was, unquestionably, a man named John Parry. Parry has been called the original "society entertainer". Born in 1810, he began his career as a serious concert singer, and discovered his true métier somewhat improbably while studying singing in Italy. After a spell on the stage, he eventually went over to solo comedy performances in 1850. Retiring through ill-health in 1853, he re-emerged seven years later under the umbrella of Thomas and Priscilla German Reed at the

---

[4] An earlier exponent was of course William Robert Grossmith, the "Young Roscius" himself. Its most prominent exponents in recent years have perhaps been Victor Borge and the late Joyce Grenfell.

Royal Gallery of Illustration, a place of London entertainment that was in fact a small theatre, but not called such in order to circumvent the anti-theatrical prejudice that was so much part of the mid-Victorian ethos. His chief accomplishments were on the one hand genuine musicianship exemplified by a virtuoso touch on the piano and, on the other, superb skill as a parodist and mimic, the ability to imitate almost any sound from the drawing of a cork to the chords of a violoncello and a mastery of patter equal to that of any conjurer. His act was built around sketches on contemporary fads and foibles. It also included comic songs. The comic song, frequently – though not invariably – topical, has been an ageless vehicle for amusement; but it is surely the case that the nineteenth century was the period of its popularity *par excellence*. The comic song as Parry treated it, wrote one commentator, "ceased to be musical buffoonery and became a comedy scene with musical illustrations". And in that description lay the key to his whole style. Refinement and finesse were his hallmarks; subtlety the core of his humour.

Parry was to have a number of disciples and successors; but of them all Grossmith was generally considered the closest to him in basic style. The mention of Parry's name in that *Scarborough Gazette* report was only one of many such mentions to be found in descriptions of his own work. During his teens he had watched Parry several times performing at the "Gallery" and was greatly influenced by what he saw and heard. Certainly he was happy to acknowledge his debt to the older man and was delighted on one later occasion when, filling in at the Gallery for another entertainer, he was able to use the very piano on which Parry had played.[5]

Each of his own entertainments, as with Parry's, was made up of a combination of sketches and comic songs, and all centred round that vital piano away from which, when performing, he rarely strayed. "A perfect master of the instrument, he makes it talk, laugh, sing, do everything that is human but sneer," as one writer put it. His voice at all times had a pleasant, easy quality. And if he had started his career as a performer by drawing on material written by other people, so the material he now used, both words and music, was all – or nearly all – written by himself. During the 1870s sketches (a combination of songs and spoken passages with, in performance, mimicry, wisecracks and *ad lib.* chat) and single comic songs poured from his pen. Their subject matter was impressively varied. Of one of his early sketches, *Our Choral Society*, he summarised the component elements thus:

[5] In 1899 he was to purchase the original – presumably handwritten – scripts of some of Parry's sketches when these were put up for sale; to the pleasure of the latter's daughter.

"Musical movement in Moreton-super-Mire; great excitement, local and vocal; Moreton acquires a choir; formation of the Society; the pleasure of singing (and the pain of listening); the patroness, Lady Alum Gargle; her harmonic triumphs, past and present; the Society gets up a public bawl for the benefit of a private charity; a polite conductor; Mr G. Sharp composes a new cantata, *The Penitent Pilgrim*; the *Pilgrim* undergoes a trying rehearsal; the concert!; marvellous effect of an indistinct *Reapers' Chorus*; breathless effect of the long runs; the secular music; pianoforte solo by Miss Spikes; manufacture of Italian songs; grand finale, *Lightly Tripping o'er the Hills*, by Mr and Mrs Hoggsedd."

And, as indicated in the previous chapter, some of his songs were now being published, including – first, it seems, of all of these – *I am so Volatile*.

"*I am so Volatile*. Composed and also sung by Geo. Grossmith, jun[r] (of the Royal Polytechnic Institution)" and "sung applausefully by Mr Howard Paul in his popular entertainment."

"*Too Slow!* An amusing song for the drawing-room, written and composed by George Grossmith, jun[r]," and "sung by him with great success[6] in his popular entertainments." The theme of *Too Slow!* was effectively that of *I am so Volatile* in the opposite, the first two verses here running as follows:

"To greatness I was really born some forty years ago,
But greatness has deserted me because I am *so* slow.
I did not cut a tooth until I reached the age of three;
My mother lost her patience and observed one day to me:
    'You really must get on a little faster, Sir!
    You're all behind, I grieve to tell you so, Sir.
    But to a very ordinary mind 'tis clear
    You're born to be a little bit too slow, Sir.'

"To play with me a game at cricket none could see the fun,
Because it always took me such a time to score a run.
The cricket ball would pass me in a tantalising way,
And as it reached the wicket first it almost seemed to say:
    'You really must get on a little faster, Sir!
    You're all behind, I grieve to tell you so, Sir.
    But to a very ordinary mind 'tis clear
    Your *running* is a little bit too slow, Sir.'"

But probably the most pungent and diverting of all his songs of this first prolific decade was *The Muddle-Puddle Porter*, the idea for which came to him while waiting nearly an hour for a train at Bishopstoke in Hampshire and listening to an aged porter calling out the same string of station names over and over again:

[6] Anything for a variation.

"There was a railway porter on the North South Eastern Line,
Whose intellect was limited, whose age was forty-nine.
His post was situated at the Muddle-Puddle Junction;
The stations' names he called out indistinctly – but with unction.
And all this porter had to do thro' morning, noon and night
Was to waggle to and fro a wretched bell with all his might;
And shout this sentence in a manner which you all must know –
'Change here for London, Chatham, Peckham, Brighton, Margate, Bow.'

"He thought in all his thirty years of service it was strange
His wages never were increased. 'Twas time to make a change.
He meant to try another calling earlier or later,
So went at once to Spiers and Pond who turned him to a waiter!
But in his new vocation he in trouble quickly got:
The first old gentleman who came required a dinner hot,
And asked, 'What are the joints?' He said, 'The joints, sir, yes sir, oh!
The joints are London, Chatham, Peckham, Brighton, Margate, Bow.'

"He got dismissed and went away in misery and pain,
Determined that he never would a waiter be again;
Such tax upon the intellect would surely make life shorter –
He'd still remain the Muddle-Puddle Junction railway porter.
And having got his berth again, his spirits did revive;
With pride and joy he waited till the first train did arrive.
He rang his bell and shouted out with vigour and with ease:
'Two beefs, a kidney and potatoes, jelly and a cheese.' "[7]

"It is not only the drollest but the most innocent comic song of the season," declared one contemporary commentator. "Unlike many comic songs it is funny. Wherever it is heard people *must* laugh."

In addition, as he had started his composing career by putting music to words written by his father, so he was also to set the occasional number for other writers of lyrics.

"*The Perpetual Hop.* Written by Wyke Moore. Composed by Geo. Grossmith, jun. Sung with immense success by Wyke Moore."

II

Entertaining at the Polytechnic; with the Howard Pauls; on his own at YMCAs and literary institutes – his experience was growing weekly. Now came a suggestion from his father that would widen that experience still further: why shouldn't the two of them combine their talents and

[7] The three verses that follow, in which the porter next became a cabin boy and finally man on the door at the Westminster Aquarium, were written, according to the score, by one James McCraw (also given as "junior"). Which seems odd; for Grossmith was not in the habit of writing only half his songs. And who, anyway, was James McCraw?

try an entertainment together? Accordingly they worked out a programme. And on May 8th, 9th and 10th, 1873 they gave their first joint recitals in the Masonic Hall, Birmingham.

The reaction, both of audience and press, was encouraging; unmistakably so. And the upshot was a decision to undertake a joint tour of other provincial institutions to start, it was hoped, in the autumn. A tour on these lines would mean of course their abandoning Bow Street once more. But against that could be set three other considerations, each no less important. First, it would serve for George junior in place of the Polytechnic, his association with the latter establishment having come to an end eighteen months or so earlier. Second, if he branched out too obviously on his own, it might look as though he were deliberately attempting to set himself up as his father's rival, which was something he had not the least wish to do. And third, he needed the money. For he was just about to get married. His wife-to-be was Emmeline Rosa Noyce, daughter of a North London doctor. He had originally met her many years previously at one of those juvenile parties to which he was then being so frequently invited. They had talked, had been mutually attracted at once. "She flattered me by approving of my comic songs"; while "I was immensely struck with her power of conversation, which was unusual for one so young." They had danced every dance together. But they then saw nothing further of each other until three or four years later when they met at *another* crowded function, and this time they danced *nearly* every dance. And this time too contact must have been maintained. The wedding took place at the parish church of St Stephen's, Camden Town, on Wednesday, May 14th.

> "I first met my love at a juvenile party,
> Such beauty I'd never beheld.
> I found myself staring at her all the evening;
> My heart, how it beat and it swelled."[8]
>
> (George Grossmith – *Tommy's First Love*)

For the start of their honeymoon they went to Leamington in Warwickshire. On May 17th their names were recorded in the *Royal Leamington Spa Courier* as among the latest arrivals at the town's Regent Hotel. But within a few days they had moved out from there and into rooms over a chemist's shop. The reason was shortage of money. But why had they – or, rather, he – chosen Leamington for the occasion? It was another instance of his mixing business with pleasure. Some time previously he had received a communication from a friend of his there suggesting he

---

[8] Not, strictly speaking, that this was a fair analogy. For not only was "Tommy" in the song a mere nine years old; but his ladylove was twenty-eight.

give a solo recital at the end of his stay, and the friend would ensure that the fact of his being on his honeymoon in the town was suitably publicised. It was an idea that more than paid off. For the result was "a crowded room", the takings from which helped materially to defray the cost of what he called his "pleasure trip" away.

In the days that followed they toured around, before winding up with a week or so at Aigburth near Liverpool, staying with one of Rosa's[9] relations. But again this was not purely a pleasure visit; there was a business motive here too. For it so happened that Mrs Howard Paul was performing in Liverpool at the time in question, and he was able for that period to team up with her once more and, by so doing, recoup for a second time some of his holiday expenses.

The honeymoon at an end, the newlyweds returned to London and settled in a house in Blandford Square, Marylebone. But it was not long before they experienced their first parting, for about three months later George was off with his father on that initial provincial tour. They started in Devon and Cornwall and were away from London for a fortnight. Thereafter, they normally got home at weekends. But with regular (or near-regular) engagements from Monday to Friday right through each week and for about seven months in each year, it meant that he and Rosa saw much less of each other than they would have liked; and, as with her mother-in-law, Rosa had to get used to life with a husband who was forever tearing about the country (*his* phrase). All too often, indeed, whether in conjunction with his father or on his own, he found it impossible to arrange his itinerary with any reasonable geographical logic. Thus one night he might be appearing somewhere in the Home Counties, the next in South Wales and a third somewhere up north, on occasion travelling back to London between each performance.

The two Georges billed their joint venture as a "Literary and Musical Entertainment" and arranged each of their programmes so that they alternated their turns. For these performances they used neither costumes nor, in general, properties or any other aids (apart from, in George junior's case, that all-important piano) but obtained their effects entirely by voice, facial expression and gesture. Of their success as performers there could be little question; of their popularity socially there was even less. And as George senior had always been welcomed as a guest by local dignitaries and other worthies wherever he lectured, so now George junior found that hospitality extended to him too.

---

[9] "Rosa" or "Rosie" – rather than Emmeline – was the name by which the new Mrs Grossmith tended to be known. And in this she followed her mother-in-law, who seems always to have been known by *her* middle name – in her case actually Emmeline (see page 25).

For the most part their entertainments were patronised by what he called the "more serious" – by which he presumably meant the more literate – section of the public; and again, as with penny readings, the arrangements were more often than not in the hands of the clergy. And what with this, not to mention his own single-handed YMCA engagements, he came to regard himself with some amusement as a sort of "religious comic singer". His YMCA evenings nearly always began with prayers; sometimes too there would even be a short sermon. Once in a London schoolroom when engaged to entertain a parish group that proved to consist largely of mothers with babies, he was pulled up by the vicar in charge just as he was about to begin. Could he, the vicar asked, slip in a little reminder impressing on those mothers that they should come to church on Sundays at least occasionally. Grossmith refused. Coming from him, he remarked, the audience would think the exhortation part of the entertainment and probably receive it with roars of laughter. The vicar saw the point, and thereupon launched into that exhortation himself. "I hear too often from you," he complained,

> "that you cannot leave your babies. Mrs Brown says she cannot leave hers, and Mrs Jones tells me she cannot leave hers, and so it goes on. But you can befriend each other. Mrs Brown can mind her own babies as well as Mrs Jones's for one Sunday, and Mrs Jones can do the same for Mrs Brown the following Sunday. You would then be able to come once a fortnight at all events. Remember this, my friends, you *must* try and come to church. Mr Grossmith will now sing *I am so Volatile.*"

But if literary institutes, church and religious groups provided him with the bulk of his engagements at the outset, it was not long before he was attempting to draw a quite different set of audiences into his net. This new development resulted from a chance meeting towards the end of 1873 with another young entertainer of similarly growing popularity, Richard Corney Grain.

Corney Grain – it was, improbably, his real name – was another of John Parry's most distinctive successors. Born in 1844 he had, like Grossmith, turned his thoughts initially towards the Bar, and unlike him had actually practised for a time. A tall man, slim and lanky in early life, he later developed a huge, rotund figure guaranteed to make him stand out in any company. But from the first his real inclinations had lain in the dispensing of amusement rather than advocacy. In May 1870 he joined the Reeds at the Gallery of Illustration, making his debut there with a sketch called *The School Feast*, and before long he had become the mainstay of the whole establishment. In the years ahead he and Grossmith were to become staunch friends. But as yet they were on less familiar and hence more formal terms.

58

Fig. 5a. Rosa Grossmith, Grossmith's wife.

Fig. 5b. Grossmith in the 1870s – the "religious comic singer".

On this occasion they came face to face in a ham and beef sandwich shop on the corner of Bow Street; and in the course of their conversation Grain happened to mention that he was preparing a repertoire of sketches which he intended giving professionally at private houses. Grossmith was immediately interested. He had, he said, no idea such openings existed. He plied Grain with questions. "Were the people nice?" "Very," said Grain. "Was the work agreeable?" "Very," said Grain again. "And, what is more important, it pays well." He also mentioned that John Parry had sung professionally in this way. And that, says Grossmith, decided him. He made up his mind he would try something of the sort on his own account at the first opportunity.

That opportunity presented itself surprisingly quickly – no more, indeed, than a few evenings later. He was due to go to a large musical party somewhere near Harley Street; and he decided that, if asked to perform, he would not give the single comic song he might otherwise have contributed but the full sketch of *The Silver Wedding*. The hostess, when the time came, expressed herself delighted with the idea. The grand piano was turned just as he wanted it; two or three small properties he needed were placed in readiness at his side. All these preparations only increased the interest; and the result left him astonished. Despite the sketch lasting a full half hour, he was asked at the end if he would give another. Not daring to ride his luck too far first time, he said no. But the bug had bitten him. At the next parties to which he was invited he gave another two of his Polytechnic sketches with the same result. And meanwhile, following Grain's example, he started to prepare some new sketches to be used at similar gatherings in the future.

His next step was to visit the offices of George Dolby, the man primarily responsible for organising the later reading tours of Charles Dickens. Dolby showed immediate interest. Without hesitation he told Grossmith he could in all probability secure for him a batch of private engagements during the following June and July which, he explained, was the busy time for parties of the sort at which entertainment was often required. He was as good as his word; the invitations came in.

But at first Grossmith found the whole business "terribly uphill work". It was one thing to sit at a piano; it was quite another to get anybody to listen to him while he was playing and singing. The more fashionable the people who were – theoretically – his audience, the more likely they were to chatter in loud voices throughout his performance. On each occasion, out of courtesy or genuine interest, a few would listen, and for those few he would resolutely try his hardest. But several times he came away from such engagements so disheartened as to be almost ready to throw this side of his work right up. The turning point, however, was to come, and it came just when he had reached his nadir. Singing at the residence of the Duchess of St Albans on March 6th, 1875 and failing to make himself heard above the noise of conversation, he broke down in despair. But suddenly the crowd around him parted; and there, coming towards him, was Alexandra, Princess of Wales. The Princess took a seat close by him with the clear intention of listening to what he was doing. Her action revived his spirits immediately. Drawn by her example, the rest of the company listened too. More, they obviously liked and enjoyed what they heard. His popularity in fashionable drawing-rooms, it was later written, may almost be said to have dated from that night. Gradually over the following years he built up his connections. People giving parties began to write to him personally – the best sign of all that he was becoming known.

The types of such parties varied considerably. There were the four-to-seven afternoon parties. There were parties held to celebrate birthdays and other special occasions. There were the "smart" London evening parties which started late and finished later. With lengthened experience he would take each one as it came in his stride. And, in consequence of all this, he started to think of himself not merely as George Grossmith the musical entertainer but – in the phrase he was to use some years later as the title of his first volume of reminiscences – as George Grossmith the "society clown".

III

Then in 1876 came another venture still. The high point of his association with the literary institutions seemed to have passed. The number of engagements they were now affording him had unquestionably declined; so had the fees offered by those that still wanted him. The number of his "society" engagements too, while growing, did not as yet provide sufficient work or income in compensation.[10] It was by no means surprising, therefore, that his reaction should be favourable when Dolby proposed that he undertake a joint entertainment tour with a lady named Florence Marryat.

If Mrs Howard Paul was a remarkable and versatile woman, Florence Marryat, then in her late thirties, was a figure of still more wide-ranging achievement. Marrying twice, she produced by her first husband eight

---

[10] A year or two earlier, nonetheless, he had felt obliged to turn down a prolonged engagement with Mrs Paul, on the ground that it would have taken him away from London for months at a time. But presumably he now felt that London – and, in particular, Bow Street – would simply have tó do without him.

children. A daughter of the novelist Captain Marryat, she was a more than prolific writer herself, publishing over the years close on eighty novels and other books of her own, and was also at various times a writer for magazines and newspapers, a magazine editor, manager of a school of journalism, playwright, operatic singer, actress, lecturer and – of most significance here – a solo entertainer. Galleon-like in appearance and movement, she had a presence that, to put it at its lowest, commanded attention.

She and Grossmith now devised a programme with which they planned, in the manner of the Howard Pauls, to appeal to a wider section of the public than that which patronised the entertainments toured by himself and his father. They gave their show a title, *Entre Nous*, a phrase suggestive of cosy intimacy. The items that made it up comprised a mixture of Grossmith's piano sketches alternating with scenes and recitations in historical costume. And it was rounded off by a twenty-five minute "satirical musical sketch", in effect a short play, written and composed specifically for the pair of them by Grossmith himself. The piece in question was called *Cups and Saucers*. There were just two characters:

Mrs Emily Nankeen Worcester (*a china maniac*)
and
General Deelah (*another*)

She is a middle-aged widow waiting for him to propose; *he* is a hearty, grey-haired bachelor. *She* fears he may only be interested in her because of what she believes is a valuable old saucer she has secretly in her possession; *he* is determined to avoid committing himself to her until he knows for certain whether she has it or not. The whole thing, though, is really no more than an extended piece of nonsense. Here, for instance, is Mrs Worcester at the beginning absorbed in a book, *Crackwell on Old China*:

> "Now let me read this most interesting and curious statement once more. 'All that remains of Julius Caesar's favourite tea-service is one little blue and white saucer. The remainder of these celebrated cups and saucers came to a melancholy end in consequence of a little dispute between Julius Caesar and his mother-in-law who, self-invited, had been spending three months with him and showed no disposition to terminate her visit.' How inconsiderate of her! 'Hence the origin of the term *break a brick*, now called *bric-à-brac...*' "

And here is part of the conversation that ensues on the entrance of the General:

General: How fine it was today.
Mrs Worcester: It was.
General: It was.
Mrs Worcester: Yes, it was. (*Pause*)
General: And yet yesterday was wet.
Mrs Worcester: (*quickly*). It was.
General: It was.
Mrs Worcester: Yes, it was. (*Another pause*)
General: Have you ever noticed –
Mrs Worcester: Oh, I have!
General: So have I, frequently! How much we are alike. But although the rain is disagreeable, yet I always think it makes the grass and the fields and flowers look – look wet.

And, needless to say, the piece ends with the two of them agreeing to get married, and singing the last of four lighthearted musical numbers.

For all their hopes, though, the results of *Entre Nous* proved somewhat varied. It was more an artistic success, Grossmith considered, than a financial one. They did well, for example, in Scotland. But in Dublin, where they played for a month, the hall they took in the "Antient Concert Rooms" was by contrast rarely more than half-full. Even so, it was a month he enjoyed, finding the Dubliners most hospitable and being a guest on several occasions at lavish parties given by the actor Henry Irving who was also in the Irish capital at that time. (Grossmith had come to know Irving originally, as he had so many other celebrities, through the latter's friendship with his father; and despite the disparity in their ages – Irving was all but ten years his senior – the actor became one of his own closest friends). But Dublin left an impression on Grossmith in another way too. Their journeys around the city were made in what Florence Marryat referred to as an "outside *kyar*", "to keep on which, when guided by a wild Irishman, is an education of itself". One day, riding on one of these vehicles, Grossmith was jerked right off. He came to no harm; but there he sat in the road and had to be rescued, a pitiful object, caked in Dublin mud, mud that was warm and greasy, mud – as his partner later wrote – that vied only with Canadian mud after a thaw.

Back in England and Scotland too the pair of them had other experiences to cherish and remember. Travelling somewhere by train one day, they found themselves in a carriage dominated by a loquacious sermoniser. The latter began the journey by haranguing the rest of the compartment on the evils of intemperance and the blessings of prayer – evils and blessings, fumed Florence Marryat, "of which we were all perhaps perfectly well aware but did not choose to have expounded to us by an impertinent stranger". Clearly what that stranger needed was a gentle but firm puncturing; and, happily, that was what he got:

> "Catching sight of a furtive smile on Mr Grossmith's face, the man (partly, I expect, as a vent for his own irritation) seized hold of the knees of that gentleman's trousers and exclaimed: 'There's not much wear here, sir! I fear that they are not often bent in prayer.' But if he thought he would raise a blush or provoke an argument, he was very much mistaken. George proved himself quite equal to the occasion. Looking down on his condemned trousers with his own peculiar expression, he quickly replied: 'You are right, sir. I always take them off before I say my prayers.' "

Collapse of the whole compartment into roars of laughter. And – even more to the point – withdrawal of the sermoniser into merciful silence.

The year 1876 drew to a close. 1877 began with *Entre Nous* still pursuing its varied course. At Cardiff at the end of January Florence Marryat was suddenly taken ill and Grossmith had to appear without her, his own efforts being supplemented instead by a local amateur entertainer, a friend of his father, who convulsed the audience with a skilful imitation of George senior giving a recitation or lecture. But even with his partner's return it was obvious the show would not survive much longer, and some time during the spring or summer they brought it to an end. Its conclusion, though, left Grossmith with a problem. Where should he go from there? The only answer seemed to be a return to entertaining at the institutions and elsewhere, whether alone or with his father, on the lines of what he had been doing before, taking up as many offers as still presented themselves. In mid-September, for example, he was performing for a week at the Assembly Rooms, Margate.

> Mrs Obbs: Our two 'usbands seem to be getting on very well together.
> Mrs Ibbins: Well, my good man always 'as such a lot to talk about, and makes friends so easy. Everybody knows 'im in Margate. We go there every year.
> Mrs Obbs: Well, I don't think Margate so cheap as men make out. Last year we were only there for a fortnight and we made a fiver look simply silly.
> (George Grossmith – *Seaside Society*)

A small number of other engagements followed. And then, one day in October,[11] he received a letter that was to change the whole pattern of his life for several years. That letter was addressed from London's Beefsteak Club.

---

[11] November, according to his narrative in *A Society Clown*. The letter as he reproduces it is dated simply "Tuesday night". But as other evidence adduced in the next chapter will make clear, it must have been written sometime during that earlier month. Tuesday, October 23rd is the likeliest date.

"Dear Mr Grossmith [it ran],

Are you inclined to go on the stage for a time? There is a part in the new piece I am doing with Gilbert which I think you would play admirably. I can't find a good man for it. Let me have a line, or come to 9, Albert Mansions tomorrow after four or Thursday before two thirty."

The letter was signed "Arthur Sullivan".

PART TWO

WITH GILBERT AND SULLIVAN,

1877–1889

CHAPTER FOUR

The Sorcerer, H.M.S. Pinafore, The Pirates of Penzance

He read that letter through. He read it again; and again; and again. Its import took some time to sink in. An offer of a part on the stage. In itself, as he had to admit, this was not a new development; he had had a number of stage offers before, and always he had turned them down. But ... an offer of a part in a piece by Gilbert and Sullivan, a piece that was the talk and speculation of all musical and theatrical London; that, surely, was different. He was thrilled. More, he felt intensely flattered.

And yet, as with those others previously, it was an offer he could not accept – how could he? What, to take only the most obvious point, had he behind him by way of stage work before? The answer, from a professional standpoint, was nothing. Even as an amateur he had done little. Yes, but looked at another way – did not that little, taken now as a whole, seem to represent something of a pointer?

Nine years earlier, in June 1868, he had taken a leading part in a production of a then popular comedy, T. W. Robertson's *Society*, at the Royal Gallery of Illustration. To one of the two performances had come a dramatic critic from a magazine called the *Illustrated Times*. And writing under the pseudonym "The Theatrical Lounger", that critic had said:

> "Mr Grossmith has comic powers of no mean order, and his idea of John Chodd, carefully modelled on Mr Clarke,[1] had, nevertheless, an amusing originality of its own."

[1] John Clarke, a leading burlesque and comedy actor of the period.

The programme also featured a burlesque written by his father, in which again, declared that same critic, he distinguished himself.

That critic, "The Theatrical Lounger", was none other than W. S. Gilbert.

Two years later Grossmith gave a repeat performance of his *Society* role, played in a "burlesque comedietta" of which this time he was himself part-author, and took the title-role in another popular nineteenth century comedy, *Paul Pry*. Then in March 1877 he appeared as one of the jurymen in a benefit performance of Gilbert and Sullivan's own *Trial by Jury*. And not long afterwards, in another amateur production of the same piece, he was cast as the Learned Judge, the chief comic part, and put through his paces for this not by some unknown hopeful but, as director of that particular production, by Gilbert himself.

Gilbert indeed he had first met back in his teens at the house of a schoolfellow. Sullivan he had also met previously, the first time – a brief handshake – on the stage at that first *Trial by Jury*, the second soon afterwards at a dinner party. And that dinner party had proved of more than passing significance for, perhaps in consequence of a song or short sketch he had contributed to the post-prandial entertainment, he was one of a group the composer invited back to his rooms to round off the evening when the main affair broke up. The group included Sullivan's fellow-musician Alfred Cellier and another John Parry-style entertainer, Arthur Cecil. It was a fascinating experience. Everybody played and (or) sang and chatted till something like four in the morning, with Grossmith as a "new man" in this particular circle being (as he put it) especially "drawn out".

And he must have made an impression. For while it would not have been entirely surprising after that second *Trial by Jury* had his name occurred as a possibility for the new piece to *Gilbert*, it seems clear that the initial invitation to play in *The Sorcerer* came purely from *Sullivan* – and, in effect, on the strength of that one evening. It appeared that the composer had happened, quite incidentally, to mention to Arthur Cecil his lack of success up to that point in finding anyone suitable for the main part. Cecil had responded almost by reflex: "I wonder if Grossmith . . ." And before he could add another word, Sullivan had exclaimed: "The very man!" And so the letter to Grossmith had been written and sent off.

But . . . there still seemed so many buts. His initial thrill at receiving that letter soon gave way to a period of "awful anxiety" as he tried to make his decision: to accept the offer – or not. To accept would mean cancelling the engagements he had made with various institutions. Few though these engagements now were, they could at least be counted on;

whereas *The Sorcerer*, however promising the omens for it might be, could not. And were those omens so promising anyway? Wasn't the Opera Comique a notoriously unlucky theatre? He talked over the offer with his father, whose judgment he valued. The latter was firmly against it. George junior, he said bluntly, did not have the voice for stage work. Nor, going by what he had seen of him as an amateur, did he have much opinion of his ability as an actor. Others to whom he talked were equally discouraging. And, most worrying of all, if he were to appear on the professional stage just once, no YMCA group, no group associated with the church would ever – would they? – offer him an engagement again.

And yet ... there could be no harm, surely, in going round to see Sullivan as the composer had suggested, to find out a few details about the part in question. The interview was short and splendidly to the point. Sullivan went to the piano, struck a note and said, "Sing that out as loud as you can." Grossmith obliged. Sullivan looked up with, recorded George, a most humorous expression on his face – "even his eyeglass seemed to smile" – and he simply said, "Beautiful!" Then he sang through the patter song *My Name is John Wellington Wells* and, at the end, asked him:

"You can do that?"

Grossmith nodded. "Yes. I think I can do that."

"Very well," said Sullivan. "If you can do that, you can do the rest."

Clearly his voice – or lack of it – appeared to present no problem. Spurred on by his interview with Sullivan, he now went to see Gilbert. In the meantime Sullivan must have obtained approval of his offer to Grossmith from his partner. At all events Gilbert, when Grossmith called, greeted him affably. He sat him down and read out to him Wells's long opening speech: "Yes, sir, we practise necromancy in all its branches," etc.[2] Grossmith was much amused. The part of Wells, Gilbert told him, had developed considerably greater prominence than he had visualised for it when he began writing the piece. Another hurdle was falling. The more Grossmith heard about the part, the more it appealed to him. But there was one thing that puzzled him; and it was a point that might as well be cleared up straight away. Conscious of his slight figure, his lack of inches, he remarked: "For the part of a magician I should have thought you required a fine man with a fine voice."

The reply was typical Gilbert. "No," said the librettist emphatically, "that is just what we *don't* want!" He also had the answer to Grossmith's worry about the YMCAs. "Go on the stage," he told him, "and you'll

[2] See page 6.

71

make such a success as to render yourself quite independent of them."
But even with this to fortify him, Grossmith still felt anxiety. He now
went to see Richard D'Oyly Carte, manager of the company that was
backing *The Sorcerer*, to ask for – and be granted – a further day or two
for deliberation.

By now, though, news of the offer to him had reached the ears of the
press. On October 28th a reference to it was made in the *Era*, the leading
theatrical journal of the day. On November 3rd it was noted likewise
in the *Tatler*. And, in the end, the positive arguments overcame everything. The advantages to be gained publicity-wise from being per-
manently in London (not to mention the chance of a more settled home
life), the benefits to his career as a whole in being associated with both
Gilbert and Sullivan, the appeal of the part itself were – taken altogether
– too great to be ignored. With hope and self-confidence returning, he
wrote to accept. And, as though to underline the rightness of his decision,
he received at this point a letter from Mrs Howard Paul, urging him at
whatever the sacrifice to do just that. "If I have any influence with you,"
she went on, "now's the time to prove it."

It was a letter that came, he admitted, as a "great comfort"; and not
only to himself but, he seems to suggest, to his father and the rest of
his family as well. And an evening or two following – Guy Fawkes night,
Monday, November 5th, as it happened – he, Mrs Paul and a few others
celebrated the forthcoming production of the new opera with a firework
display in the back garden of her house out at Turnham Green. The
date indeed is important. For *The Sorcerer* which, for various reasons,
had been postponed at least twice, was now definitely due to open just
twelve days later – on Saturday the 17th.

Next he went to see D'Oyly Carte again, to settle the financial side
of the engagement. Carte meanwhile, and unknown to him till later,
had been backing his candidature on his own account.[3] One of the
manager's co-directors had sent him a telegram: "Whatever you do,
don't engage Grossmith!" But Carte was not the man to be swayed or
browbeaten by injunctions like that. Carte was the man who, effectively
on his own, had brought Gilbert and Sullivan together; and if "G. &
S." wanted Grossmith, "G. & S." should have him. That was one thing;
but giving Grossmith all he asked for in terms of salary was quite another.
A first month's money guaranteed – yes, fair enough. But the actual
amount Grossmith specified – no, he couldn't run to that. And then
suddenly he (Carte) suggested the two of them go out to lunch.
Grossmith agreed, unsuspecting. It was a decision he regretted ever

---

[3] He too had seen Grossmith perform on at least one occasion – at a party in 1870.

after. Lulled by the effects of oysters and wine he accepted Carte's terms – three guineas a week less than he had requested – without further demur.

Then, after a journey up to the Midlands for a final solo entertainment at Dudley, it was back to London again the following morning to take part in his first rehearsal at the theatre and to meet all the rest of the company. Though cast for the leading role he was also – as he must have felt – very much a newcomer. But this mattered little; since it was not as if he were joining a company already established. For in choosing the players for their burgeoning venture, Gilbert and Sullivan had deliberately avoided going for well-known London stars. They saw *The Sorcerer* as something new in entertainment, different on the one hand from the excesses of contemporary burlesque and on the other from the posturings of Italian opera. Their aim was to find a fresh, pliable, youthful team they could mould to their own ideas;[4] and considered from this point of view the rest of his fellow-players were as much novices as Grossmith himself.

That first rehearsal in which he was involved was held in the theatre refreshment saloon (without refreshments, as he commented wryly). But this drawback apart, things now went briskly and smoothly. If Gilbert and Sullivan had definite ideas as to the type of actors they wanted, they were no less clear about the dramatic and musical effects they were aiming at, right down to the last gesture, the last nuance of speech, the last note of music. Their imposing reputations as playwright and composer gave them authority over their young cast immediately. Yet at the same time everything was encouragingly good-humoured. One day, when rehearsing the first act finale, Sullivan made the whole company advance to the footlights, raising their arms towards the gallery "*à la* Italian method" as they stood there. But the result did not satisfy him at all. Screwing his eyeglass into his eye, he said, persuasively:

> "Don't you understand? I want you to think you are at Covent Garden Opera, not at the Opera Comique. I want you, Miss ——, to imagine you are Adelina Patti. And you, my dear Grossmith, are dreadful. There is not enough Mario about you."

"I saw what he meant," acknowledged Grossmith, "and exaggerated the Italian mode, and nearly fell over the footlights into the orchestra. Sullivan

---

[4] The youthfulness of *The Sorcerer* cast is a point that can hardly be overstressed. Grossmith himself was still a few weeks off thirty. Richard Temple, the opera's elderly baronet, was just nine months older, Harriet Everard was thirty-three, Rutland Barrington a mere twenty-four. At forty-four Mrs Paul alone could fairly be termed anything like middle-aged. Nor were "G. & S." themselves exactly ancient. Gilbert would celebrate his forty-first birthday on November 18th; Sullivan was thirty-five; D'Oyly Carte younger still at thirty-three.

with a smile said: 'Ah! That's better. Capital! Do even more. You needn't consider your safety.' "[5]

And so, after a final dress rehearsal beginning at seven thirty the evening before, to the eagerly awaited first night. All the cast, Barrington later suggested, felt confident of success. But it is doubtful whether even the most optimistic of them can have anticipated just how great that success would be or to what other, still greater successes it would eventually lead in turn.

The particular excitement and tension of that opening night behind them, the players began to settle down, with the prospect before them of a substantial run. But they did so with no sense of complacency. When the *Era* critic revisited the opera on December 3rd, he found it quite apparent that a large amount of extra work had been put into it by everybody during the previous two weeks. "Much as we[6] admired the new comic opera, *The Sorcerer*, on the night of its first performance," he confessed, "we were not prepared for the refined, finished, exquisitely humorous and altogether admirable performance we saw on Monday evening last"; and he went on to devote a full paragraph to each of the principals individually. Of Grossmith he wrote:

"Nobody seeing Mr Grossmith representing the Sorcerer would imagine that he only appeared on the stage for the first time a few nights ago ... His conception of the [part] is downright comical, whimsical and original. The dry, odd manner with which he recommends the 'love-at-first-sight' potion as his 'leading article' paved the way for that irresistibly droll burlesque incantation scene upon Sir Marmaduke's lawn; the features of the wild music in *Der Freischütz* and the mysterious scene in Meyerbeer's *Robert le Diable* being amusingly caricatured by the composer. Mr Grossmith fills in the details with the most laughable effect. His imitation of Bertram and Caspar, Mephistopheles and other fiendish personages must be seen to be appreciated; and his comic locomotion[7] is rewarded with roars of laughter. Mr Grossmith sings the patter songs[8] assigned to the character so amusingly that he is every night encored."

---

[5] Did this incident occur in connection with *The Sorcerer* rather than at some other time? In the interview in which he related it Grossmith is quoted as saying merely that he *thought* it did; and this may for convenience be accepted. But *The Sorcerer* was not the only G. & S. piece in which Sullivan sought to parody the conventions of Italian opera. He was to do so again two years later in *The Pirates of Penzance*; given which, therefore, it is at least feasible that it took place instead during the run up to that latter production.
[6] The use of "we" rather than "I" as the personal pronoun in criticism and reporting was for decades – if not centuries – a common journalistic affectation. Unfortunately.
[7] ? his railway engine gag (see page 8). Grossmith himself referred to this on at least one occasion as his "teapot dance".
[8] "Songs" in the plural? Hardly.

Grossmith's John Wellington Wells "was a far more entertaining person on the fiftieth night than he had been on the first," wrote another commentator several years later. It would have been surprising – more, it would have been a matter for concern – had this not been so. Clearly he was learning fast. Clearly too he had made the transition from entertainment platform to stage with the minimum of difficulty, and without overtaxing himself either mentally or physically. He played Wells every night of the run.

Nor was this his only contribution to that run, for in January he was rounding off each Saturday matinee performance with one of his piano sketches, *A Christmas Pantomime*. On three equivalent occasions in February he gave another: *The Puddleton Penny Readings*; on three more in March a third: *Amateur Theatricals*. Then on March 23rd, *Dora's Dream* and a further curtain-raiser having been withdrawn, *The Sorcerer* was joined as an afterpiece by *Trial by Jury*, thus making an entire programme of Gilbert and Sullivan. And in *Trial by Jury* Grossmith played his second professional G. & S. role, the Learned Judge, the part he had already played for Gilbert as an amateur. Once more, as in *The Sorcerer*, this provided him with the most lively, most dynamic song in the piece, in this case a meaty "autobiographical" number:

"When I, good friends, was called to the Bar,
    I'd an appetite fresh and hearty,
But I was, as many young barristers are,
    An impecunious party.
I'd a swallow-tail coat of a beautiful blue –
    A brief which I bought of a booby –
A couple of shirts and a collar or two,
    And a ring that looked like a ruby!"

Previously, at the end of February, *The Sorcerer* had notched its hundredth performance; on April 25th, with *Trial by Jury* now equally well established, it reached performance number one-fifty. There had been two brief periods early in the new year when, for no obvious reason, bookings had temporarily dropped, and D'Oyly Carte's fellow-directors, a syndicate who had backed the opera solely for the money they hoped to make from it, had sought to have it taken off; but, considered overall, *The Sorcerer* had pretty well fulfilled its first night promise. Yet even before Christmas, before its run was five weeks old, Gilbert had begun work on its successor. On December 27th he had sent Sullivan a "sketch plot" of the new piece. Already too he had ideas on its casting. "Barrington will be a capital Captain and Grossmith a first-rate First Lord." Sullivan's response was enthusiastic. Gilbert went eagerly ahead. *The Sorcerer*'s successor was to be called *H.M.S. Pinafore*.

75

H.M.S. Pinafore was put into rehearsal early in May. And while the company were playing *The Sorcerer* in the evenings, they were simultaneously preparing the new opera during the daytime. Or, rather, most of them were; for, perhaps inevitably, there were certain changes of cast, if principally on the female side.[9] On the male side, though, things were much as before, and Grossmith's success as John Wellington Wells ensured he would again be offered the chief comic part.[10] This, as Gilbert's comment a few lines above will have indicated, was to be the First Lord of the Admiralty; by name Sir Joseph Porter, K.C.B. The opera is set on board the ship, which Sir Joseph is preparing to visit in company with an "admiring crowd" of female relatives – "sisters, cousins and aunts" – who, explains one of the other characters, "attend him wherever he goes". Again, as in *The Sorcerer*, he was the last person to appear, with all the advantage of build-up a delayed entrance provides; and this time he would announce himself thus:

> "I am the monarch of the sea,
>   The Ruler of the Queen's Navee,
>   Whose praise Great Britain loudly chants"

moving promptly thereafter into an autobiographical song of distinct kinship to the one he was currently singing in *Trial by Jury*:

> "When I was a lad I served a term
> As office boy to an attorney's firm.
> I cleaned the windows and I swept the floor,
> And I polished up the handle of the big front door.
>   I polished up that handle so carefullee
>   That now I am the Ruler of the Queen's Navee!"

The dialogue exchanges that followed and the briefest of musical exits completed his contribution to Act I. Act II gave him a scene that included a lively trio at roughly the same place in the opera as his "family vault" scene with Lady Sangazure in *The Sorcerer* and a return a short while later for an important share in the opera's dénouement. In addition – and this gave the part further spice – the character could be seen as a take-off of the then First Lord of real life, W. H. Smith of the famous newsagent and bookselling firm. Gilbert had, on the surface at least, been at pains to dispel the idea that any such connection had been in his mind. "The fact that the First Lord in the opera is a radical of the most pronounced type," he had explained to Sullivan, "will do away

---

[9] Among the players not retained for *Pinafore* – though the circumstances of her departure are by no means entirely clear – was Mrs Howard Paul.

[10] He was also given a new and, presumably, more lucrative contract.

with any suspicion that W. H. Smith is intended" (Smith being a Conservative). But whether he meant this seriously or not, nobody was to be fooled for a moment. Though in an attempt perhaps to confuse the issue further, Grossmith was to be made up with whitened hair to resemble portraits of Lord Nelson.

On May 24th – a Friday – the company gave their one hundred and seventy-eighth and last performance of *The Sorcerer. Pinafore* was to open the next day. If time had not been quite so short as during the rehearsal period of that earlier piece, this was to some extent counterbalanced by Gilbert rewriting parts of the new one almost up, as it seems, to the very last week. That Friday there was a rehearsal in the morning, followed by a final dress rehearsal after that final *Sorcerer*, which went on, as it obviously had to, long after midnight. But miraculously the whole thing proceeded without a hitch. "Everything smooth; dresses all right," Gilbert recorded with satisfaction in his diary.

A cause for some concern, though, became manifest a few hours later: Rutland Barrington found himself with a severe cold. A printed apology to this effect was inserted in the programme. But it was an inconvenience that dampened the occasion for him alone. The success of *The Sorcerer* ensured that the first night of *Pinafore* would be another "occasion". "Seldom indeed have we been in the company of a more joyous audience," wrote the reporter from the *Era*, "or an audience more confidently anticipating an evening's amusement."

The result seemed to justify all expectation. The laughter was continuous, the encores numerous, the applause immense. Once again at the end, author and composer were called to the footlights to take their bows with the cast. And once again the press were unanimous in praising the latter's performances, the chief comedian firmly among them. "Few theatres can boast of such a trio of genuine humorists as are Mr G. Grossmith, Mr Rutland Barrington and Miss Everard," declared the critic from *The Times*. "Mr Grossmith presents an admirable embodiment of the pompous First Lord," proclaimed his counterpart from the *Daily Telegraph*, a gentleman who was decidedly scathing about certain aspects of the opera itself.[11]

Again, too, with the first night behind them and the accolades for their performances coming in, the players settled down for what they could reasonably anticipate would be a substantial run. "*H.M.S. Pinafore*, the new ship designed by Mr W. S. Gilbert and Mr Arthur Sullivan, sails capitally at the Opera Comique, and the theatre is full every night," the *Era* recorded a week later. But, even so, there had already been

---

[11] A "frothy" production, he called it, "destined soon to subside into nothingness." Ah, well – nobody can be right about everything.

some "disasters on board". Barrington's cold had developed to such an extent that he was off at least a fortnight. Jessie Bond, a new soubrette and a figure who would become in due course one of the most famous names in the company, had also been off "indisposed" for a few days. The voyage of the *Pinafore* (to continue the same overworked metaphor) was for some time to be anything but smooth.

Serious trouble first arose during the last week of June. The reason was the weather. Suddenly London sweltered under an intense heatwave. The effect was predictable. That week box office receipts dropped considerably; the opera actually ran at a loss. And as before, when bookings had dropped for *The Sorcerer*, D'Oyly Carte's co-directors became alarmed. The theatre, they insisted, must be closed; *Pinafore* taken off. Gilbert, Sullivan and Carte himself were determined it should stay on. The cast were caught in the centre of the tussle. They too had faith in the opera's future. That week they all – principals and chorus – voluntarily offered to take a substantial cut in salary for nine weeks to see things through the summer. But, even though this offer was taken up, they were nonetheless wondering as late as the Friday whether the next night's performance would not be the last.

In the event, the heatwave passed with the weekend. The following week bookings began to revive; to the extent, at least, that the opera once more covered its costs. The directors relaxed. But then, in mid-July, the whole brouhaha was gone through again. Another hot spell, with poor audiences and receipts showing a loss, and again the directors wanted the theatre closed. But again the crisis soon passed; and this time the upturn in *Pinafore*'s fortunes that followed proved to be lasting. Suddenly the opera seemed to be attracting some highly distinguished visitors. On July 27th the Prince and Princess of Wales came to see it.[12] On August 6th it was the turn of Lord Beaconsfield, the Prime Minister. Three days later, as though to acknowledge that the gloom had finally lifted, the directors ("generous souls!" one of the chorus was sarcastically to comment) took Gilbert, Sullivan and all the cast on a river outing to Cliveden. By the middle of the month at the latest, *H.M.S. Pinafore* was playing to packed houses every night.[13]

---

[12] They had also been at least once to see *The Sorcerer*.

[13] Traditionally (to use a word beloved in G. & S. circles) it has always been believed that *Pinafore* was saved from early withdrawal by Sullivan including a selection from the opera in the promenade concerts he was conducting that summer at Covent Garden. But these concerts did not begin till August 3rd; and *Pinafore* did not feature in them till the 24th, which is to say, all but a month after its second bad spell and a fortnight after the picnic. The saving of the opera, in other words, had nothing to do with Covent Garden at all. What happened there merely underlined the revival in the opera's fortunes that had already taken place at the theatre.

And once again, as with *The Sorcerer*, Grossmith's contribution to the proceedings was not limited to his part in the main work. On August 6th his play *Cups and Saucers* was added to the bill as a curtain-raiser. *Cups and Saucers*, though written originally for performance in concert rooms and town halls, proved no less successful as a piece for the theatre. Whether by his own wish or that of Carte or Gilbert, however, he was not cast in it himself; the part of General Deelah going first to Richard Temple, with Emily Cross, a newcomer, taking Nankeen Worcester. Instead, as from that same date, he was made responsible for rounding off the programme each evening with one of his solo sketches. The sketch adopted for the purpose this time was called *Five Hamlets*, and concerned a Shakespeare lover who managed (somehow!) to visit five theatres on the same night to find *Hamlet* played in five different ways: seriously, operatically, melodramatically; as a burlesque and even as a pantomime. And this too went down well. "Nearly everybody stays to hear it," proclaimed the ubiquitous *Era*. "The twenty minutes or so occupied in his delivery of the *Five Hamlets* are amongst the pleasantest memories of the evening" – a comment which, however pleasing for Grossmith, may have been read with mixed feelings by Messrs Gilbert and Sullivan. Similar interest greeted him in October when he replaced his *Hamlets* with another sketch, *Beauties of the Beach*, and in February when he was to begin a prolonged spell (ten and a half months in all) rounding off each Saturday matinee performance with *The Silver Wedding*.

Meanwhile, though, the theatre had been temporarily closed on December 24th, ostensibly for redecorating and renovation but also for a relaying of the drains; and for Grossmith this meant his first break from G. & S. since joining the company more than thirteen months previously. As he had not missed a single performance of *The Sorcerer*, so almost alone among the principals he had played in all the one hundred and ninety-five performances to date of *Pinafore*. It was a record he maintained and continued to improve upon when the theatre reopened on February 1st, 1879. He and *Pinafore* passed still more milestones: two hundredth performance, two-fiftieth, three hundredth. And as the opera moved into its second year, it began to seem as though it might go on untroubled for ever.

But there was, as things turned out, one final convulsion for it yet in store. Carte's co-directors were growing over-ambitious. Their rights in the piece so far as the Opera Comique and its company were concerned were due to come to an end that July, and D'Oyly Carte had given notice that he intended thereafter to dispense with their backing and take sole charge of the company himself. But this was not to their liking

79

at all. *Pinafore* was by now far too obviously a gold mine to be abandoned just like that. They decided instead to mount their own production elsewhere. More, they claimed that the scenery used at the Opera Comique was legally theirs and they determined to procure it for themselves. But they went about trying to take possession of it in the most ham-fisted manner imaginable.

It was the last night of their tenure, Thursday, July 31st. The performance (number three-seventy-four) was about twenty minutes from its conclusion. Suddenly the actors on stage were startled by cries of "Fire!" and "Now's the time!" followed, almost simultaneously, by the clatter of feet charging down the stone steps leading from the stage door. It proved to be a gang of "roughs", commandeered and urged on by three of the directors intent on removing the scenery and other effects they wanted. And never mind that the performance was still in progress, they were having it immediately. The stage manager, trying to bar their way, was thrown back to the bottom of those same steps; and in turn a group of stage hands and "supers" rushed to his assistance. The result was a free fight. Much of the backstage area became a battleground.

Many of the cast had heard a rumour that trouble might be on hand, though until the invaders actually materialised they had not taken that rumour seriously. But now, with the battle raging no more than a few yards away from them, several of the chorus ladies became panic-stricken – some even fainted – and within seconds that panic had communicated itself to the audience. Many of those sitting in the stalls began to rise from their places. Alfred Cellier, who was conducting, turned round and begged them to remain seated; a member of the chorus made a like plea to the occupants of one of the boxes. All to no effect. Nothing, not even Harriet Everard as the bumboat woman, Little Buttercup, struggling valiantly on as though things were quite normal, could drown the noise of scuffling and shouting. The audience indeed was beginning by this time to rise *en bloc*. Bowing to the apparently inevitable, Cellier in the pit stopped the performance. Now Grossmith stepped forward to address the moving mass. Speaking with a calm he can scarcely have felt, he explained what was happening: there was a great dispute proceeding behind the scenes but no danger whatever. His manner was somehow reassuring, even though few of those to whom he spoke could have heard anything he said. There was a noticeable relaxation of tension. People resumed their places. As he stepped back there were even a few cheers. Behind the scenes the battle continued to rage for some time until the police arrived and the invaders were finally ejected. On stage the players proceeded to work their way as nonchalantly as they could through the final minutes of the opera and, after some more words of reassurance, this time from Barrington, and a longish interval, the one-act piece that now followed it.

The upshot was the appearance of three of the directors at Bow Street on charges of assault and causing a riot, and further legal proceedings elsewhere in connection with their activities throughout the whole period previously. On one occasion even Grossmith was required to give evidence:

> "Mr George Grossmith was next called and examined as to the condition of the drains in the Opera Comique during 1878. He thought directly the receipts went down, the drains got into a bad condition. He was sure that the run of the piece was broken by what took place in December 1878. He had special reasons for being positive."

Which was gratifying to know. But why he should have been considered a person suitably qualified to testify to the condition of those "Op. Com." drains must remain a minor Gilbert and Sullivan mystery.

Meanwhile, though, legal proceedings or not, the directors had duly opened their own – unauthorised – *Pinafore* at the Imperial Theatre, Westminster on the very day after the fight. But following a few weeks of full houses and even a transfer in September to the Olympic Theatre, almost within shouting distance of the "Op. Com." itself, this rival version folded on October 25th, never to be resurrected. And what the *Illustrated London News* was to call in January the "everlasting" *Pinafore* in the original version still sailed merrily on.

Nor by then was its attraction confined to one mode of performance, for in December the management had mounted a *Children's Pinafore* to be given at frequent matinees, the actors all juveniles of perhaps twelve to fourteen. Grossmith's part was taken by "Master Edward Pickering" ("there was a dainty official dignity about him that was positively side-splitting," declared the *Era*) and Grossmith himself was in on this act as well, supplementing the children's exertions with an appropriate sketch called *A Juvenile Party*. Meanwhile too, Gilbert, Sullivan and Carte had taken a company across the Atlantic to present *Pinafore* in America. And not only *Pinafore* but also its prospective successor. On December 31st that successor opened in New York. Its title was *The Pirates of Penzance*. And just as *Pirates* had replaced *Pinafore* on Broadway, so would it come to replace it likewise at the Opera Comique.

III

Before that happened, though, Grossmith was at last able to take another break. On February 20th, 1880 the adult *Pinafore* was withdrawn at last,[14] the children's version being promoted to evening performances in its place. How should he fill the time? He decided to take his wife on a short visit to Paris, almost certainly the first occasion (if his month in Ireland with Florence Marryat be discounted) he had been abroad. But, even so, he was not allowed to forget *Pinafore* immediately. Comfortably settled on the boat crossing the Channel, he took out his copy of the *Pirates* libretto to study his forthcoming new part, only to find himself distracted by – of all absurdities – a French steward who persisted in humming Little Buttercup's song on and off for the whole crossing. In Paris the Grossmiths stayed at the Hotel Continental, Rue Castiglione; and there George was safe at last. For the French in general, obsessed by Offenbach and the works of their other light comedy composers, had no time for or interest in anything so British as "Gilbert and Sullivan".

The holiday passed. Before long he was back at the Opera Comique, being put through his paces in the daily *Pirates* rehearsals. And in *Pirates* he was cast as Major-General Stanley, an ageing ex-warrior who arrives on a Cornish beach in full uniform on a gloriously hot day apparently (as it later emerges) at the end of February. Again, as with Sir Joseph Porter, there was an element of specific caricature injected into the character, Grossmith being made up (or so it appeared in some quarters) to resemble Sir Garnet Wolseley, the popular hero of the Ashanti War and other campaigns. And since no Gilbert and Sullivan opera could now be regarded as complete without a show-stopping number for its leading comedian, Gilbert had Major-General Stanley introduce himself with a patter song that equalled in intricacy the *tour de force* he had written for John Wellington Wells:

> "I am the very pattern[15] of a modern major-gineral,
> I've information vegetable, animal and mineral;
> I know the kings of England, and I quote the fights historical,
> From Marathon to Waterloo, in order categorical;
> I'm very well acquainted too with matters mathematical;
> I understand equations, both the simple and quadratical;
> About binomial theorem I'm teeming with a lot o' news"

---

[14] Its final total of performances was five hundred and seventy-one. Later Grossmith himself was to put the figure – incorrectly – at "nearly seven hundred"; presumably, after close on two years, that was what it felt like. But in fact he would have to wait until the opera had its first revival seven years later (see page 122) before that figure became valid.

[15] "Pattern" was the word used here originally. But it must have struck Gilbert, Grossmith or one of the latter's successors as unsatisfactory, for it was eventually changed to the alliterative and much snappier "model" which had been used all along at the end of the verse.

– pause (and suspense) while he affects to have great difficulty thinking up the next rhyme. "Lot o' news" – "lot o' news". "Ah!" (*joyfully*) –

"With many cheerful facts about the square of the hypotenuse"

– a line repeated three times by an equally joyful chorus. Then:

"I'm very good at integral and differential calculus;
I know the scientific names of beings animalculous;
In short, in matters vegetable, animal and mineral,
I am the very model of a modern major-gineral."

A late second act appearance in a dressing-gown, clutching a light and singing a mock-serious ballad about the breeze, the brook and the poplars was another highlight in what was again a rewarding part.

And so to another first night: 1880, Saturday, April 3rd. Outside, much of the day had been cloudy and showery, but inside the theatre the atmosphere on both sides of the curtain radiated warmth and unconcealed excitement. As the success of *The Sorcerer* had guaranteed a good send-off for *Pinafore*, so the phenomenal run of *Pinafore*, coupled with the success of *Pirates* in America, virtually guaranteed the London success of this Cornish opera before a single note of it had been played. The laughter, the encores, the applause fully equalled anything that had gone before; and again the press were hugely enthusiastic about the performances of the actors.

Grossmith, declared the *Illustrated London News*, "gave a capital caricature of military sternness combined with dry humour." No one, proclaimed the *Saturday Review*, could have delivered the patter song with "more complete success, with more commendable gravity and absence of exaggeration. He has the rare art of singing admirably without seeming to possess any voice." "Never," enthused (some months later) William H. Rideing in the year's *Dramatic Notes*, "was a major-general more cleverly burlesqued than by Mr Grossmith in his scarlet coat, gold lace and white plumed hat; the ineffable conceit of this character being quite as good in its way as the same actor's impersonation of Sir Joseph Porter."

But *Pirates* had been running just three weeks when, for Grossmith, tragedy struck. It was Saturday evening, April 24th. A messenger arrived at the theatre with an urgent summons from his brother, Weedon. Their father had been suddenly taken ill while presiding at the weekly house dinner of the Savage Club; could Grossmith come at once? He did so, rushing the short distance along and across the Strand to the Caledonian Hotel in Adelphi Terrace where the club then had its quarters.[16] There

[16] An odd point: was he – as is likely – already dressed and made up for the night's show when the summons arrived? And if so, did he change back into normal clothes before dashing off? The answer is nowhere stated.

he found George senior unconscious, with his brother and other club members in anxious attendance.

It had all happened without warning. Through the days and weeks, the very hours and minutes preceding, he had been as lively, as genial, seemingly as robust as ever. He had indeed just finished giving one of his "recitations" when the attack came on. First, so it appeared, he had turned giddy and then, almost immediately afterwards, had fainted. Someone suggested the cause might be smoke, which he was known to dislike,[17] and he was carried to the window for fresh air. But it proved to be something more serious than temporary lack of oxygen. Doctors had been rapidly called. They diagnosed an apoplectic fit. Now his sons sat by him, growing more concerned about him with every minute that passed. But there was nothing they – or anyone else – could do. He never regained consciousness and died about three hours after his collapse. He was not quite sixty years old.

The news of what had happened was brought to his Hampstead home and broken to his wife on the doorstep in a manner that could at best be described as thoughtless. The bearer, a club factotum, first asked her if she was Mrs Grossmith.

"Yes. That's right."

"Well," he went on, without any further preamble, "I've come to tell you your husband's dead, here's the sausages we found in his pocket, and would you mind paying sixpence for having the handkerchief laundered one of the members put over his face."

Had the circumstances not been so tragic, it is likely the family would rapidly have come to see the funny side of this (what on earth, for instance, was George senior doing with sausages in his pocket?). But understandably they were not so much amused as livid. The whole business indeed left Grossmith himself agonisingly distressed. The shock was so terrible, he wrote eight years later in *A Society Clown*, that he wondered whether he had quite recovered from it even then. In only one thing, he seems to suggest, did he find any initial consolation:

"I should like to say that my father was more than astonished at the result of my appearances in *The Sorcerer*, *Pinafore* and *Pirates*, and was extremely proud of [them]. He was easily pleased, no doubt. But it was a great source of comfort to me to know he *was* pleased."

Newspapers all over the country made reference to his death. The post brought letters of condolence. One of the first of these, written the very day after, came from Arthur Sullivan:

[17] According to Weedon he "loathed tobacco".

"My dear Grossmith,

I am most shocked and pained to hear of the great loss you have sustained. Pray believe in my most heartfelt sympathy. I have suffered the same grief as yourself,[18] and I know that time and work are the best healers.

When I say work, you will, I am sure, not think that I am speaking from a personal point of view, or that I am swayed by a selfish interest. I do honestly believe that a speedy return to the daily routine of one's life is the best distraction one can have in great trouble – distasteful as it may be to make the effort."

Sullivan was right, of course. The funeral took place at Kensal Green on the Thursday;[19] and Grossmith – now officially for the first time without his "junior" – was back in *Pirates* the following Monday. But a return to work at this juncture did not mean merely his reappearance at the Opera Comique. It also meant a renewal of his acquaintance with Bow Street. He had given up – or thought he had given up – that side of his career finally and completely when he accepted a part in *The Sorcerer*. His father's death, however, left a vacuum there which he felt obliged to fill, even though there was almost certainly no reason why the reigning deputy could not have filled it just as adequately instead. The intention was praiseworthy, no doubt; but with his nightly appearance in G. & S., coupled (as will be seen from the next two chapters) with a substantial number of other "performing" engagements, it is not surprising to find him somewhat less than punctilious about his duties as a reporter. Five years later he was to receive a letter from the current *Times* manager, John C. MacDonald, making it plain that that paper at least regarded his more recent efforts as far from satisfactory:

"The sub-editor draws my attention to the enclosed case omitted from your Saturday report; and he tells me that this is not the first occasion on which he has had cause of similar complaint. If anything of the kind should occur again, I fear it will be necessary at once to transfer the reportership of the court to other hands."

It was a letter which, it seems reasonable to suppose, forced Grossmith to review the whole situation. Soon afterwards he took the only sensible decision and once more gave up – and this time really for good – all connection with the court and its reporting. And thereafter his professional life was devoted exclusively to what Bow Street chronicler Percy Fitzgerald happily called "increasing the gaiety of the community" through his true occupations of acting, humorous writing and entertaining.

[18] His own father's death (1866) had also come suddenly.

[19] The principal mourners included William Robert Grossmith, the "Young Roscius", who was to live right on till 1899.

CHAPTER FIVE

Patience, Iolanthe, Princess Ida

The run of *Pirates* was as calm and uneventful as that of *Pinafore* had been full of tension and incident. And for George Grossmith it also, in terms of his own contribution, found him with noticeably less to do. Apart from five weeks or so beginning just before Christmas when he complemented a series of revived matinee performances of the *Children's Pinafore* with a new sketch called *A Musical Nightmare*, he was not required to provide any additional solo entertainment, but concentrated exclusively on his portrayal of Major-General Stanley. He was to play that part, in fact, for exactly a year; at which point, after three hundred and sixty-three performances, *Pirates* was taken off and replaced three weeks later (April 23rd, 1881) by *Patience*, a brilliant G. & S. satire on the excesses of the Victorian "aesthetic" movement.

The story of *Patience* revolves round the rivalry of two poets. And dressed in a tight green velvet suit that incorporated the knee-breeches associated with Oscar Wilde, and with, on his head, an unkempt wig in which was featured the single white lock affected by the painter Whistler, Grossmith played the first of these, Reginald Bunthorne. It was a part substantially larger than any of the three he had created previously; indeed John Wellington Wells and Major-General Stanley especially can be seen on analysis to be surprisingly small. Then again, Bunthorne is a much more fully drawn character than any of those others – arguably as fully drawn and developed a character as Gilbert ever conceived. Described in the *dramatis personae* as a "fleshly"[1] poet, he is by his

---

[1] A "meaningless and offensive epithet", remarked *The Times*, which Gilbert should have avoided.

own admission an "aesthetic sham", a poseur who has taken up the poetic cult simply to attract and retain the worship of a group of tenaciously clinging "love-sick maidens". Yet while he shows himself effeminate, petulant and posturing on the one hand, he possesses on the other a mordant streak of determination. When his poetic rival, Archibald Grosvenor, appears and the maidens switch their clinging allegiance to the latter instead, he makes it clear he will go all out to win their attentions back.

Grosvenor was played by Rutland Barrington, whose position in the company and in Gilbert's scheme of things was for the most part second only to that of Grossmith himself. Like Grossmith a protégé of Mrs Howard Paul, his initial success as the vicar in *The Sorcerer* had equalled if not surpassed Grossmith's own initial success in the same opera. As a pair of comedians they formed the classic contrast, the one (Grossmith) short, wiry, mercurial, light on his feet, busy and chock-full of energy, the other (Barrington) the "heavy" man, taller, more solidly built, placid, avuncular, suave, unctuous. Only in *Pinafore* had Gilbert as yet had them on stage jointly for any length of time; but now in *Patience* he brought them together towards the end of the opera for a splendid confrontation and sprightly duet.

No less effective, in Grossmith's case, was another scene earlier that same act, this time with Lady Jane, the solitary "plain" one among the maidens. Lady Jane was played by Alice Barnett, a contralto who had come into the company during the run of *Pirates*. Alice Barnett was a large woman, with voice to match; and the contrast between her "majestic figure" (as the *Era* described it) and the diminutive Grossmith provided obvious possibilities for comedy:[2]

> Bunthorne: Everything has gone wrong with me since that smug-faced idiot came here. Before that I was admired; I may say, loved.
> Jane: Too mild. Adored!
> Bunthorne: Do let a poet soliloquise! The damosels used to follow me wherever I went. Now they all follow him!
> Jane: Not all. *I* am still faithful to you.
> Bunthorne: Yes, and a pretty damosel *you* are!
> Jane: No, not pretty. Massive!

Cue – a few moments later – for another lively duet. And in addition, of course, Grossmith was provided with a solo number, though one very different from any of those he had been given to sing before:

---

[2] The same basic contrast had also been capitalised on by Grossmith and Mrs Howard Paul in their second act scene in *The Sorcerer*.

Fig. 6. Grossmith and Alice Barnett in *Patience*.

"If you're anxious for to shine in the high aesthetic line as a man of culture
rare,
You must get up all the germs of the transcendental terms, and plant them
everywhere.
You must lie upon the daisies and discourse in novel phrases of your compli-
cated state of mind,
The meaning doesn't matter if it's only idle chatter of a transcendental kind.
And everyone will say,
As you walk your mystic way,
'If this young man expresses himself in terms too deep for *me*,
Why, what a very singularly deep young man this deep young man must be!' "

The first night of *Patience* proved an occasion of virtually unqualified triumph for all concerned, the "extravagant humour" of the piece, in the words of the *Musical Times*, drawing forth "both applause and laughter such as is rarely heard in a theatre." The principals took curtain calls not only at the end of the evening but at the end of Act I as well. And how did Grossmith cope with the greater demands of his new character? "Mr G. Grossmith was richly comic, in make-up and manner, as the atrabilarious Bunthorne"; thus the *Illustrated London News*. "Mr Grossmith was amply funny, and passed from lackadaisical affectation to most exaggerated melodrama with humorous effect"; thus the *Saturday Review*. His "comic grimness" – thus the *Daily News* – contrasted admirably with the "mild simplicity" of Barrington.[3]

Which seems fairly conclusive; even allowing for the tendency of critics to write favourably about any theatre's leading actor. And if he pleased the press it was even more certain he delighted the wider public. "I am coming up to London tomorrow for one night and wired for a *Patience* stall on Saturday, so I hope to see you in full force on that evening," wrote one admirer a few months later. "As it is always a pleasure to see you 'chez vous' and in your own element, I will try to find you between the acts . . ." Or, to put all this another way, he had become a star. And it was perhaps a further measure of his stardom

---

[3] In a book published forty-five years later, A. H. Godwin, a journalist and ardent G. & S. fan, was to be found enthusing still more rapturously over Grossmith's performance in this role. Bunthorne, he wrote, was probably the actor's "finest achievement". It was "a sheer revelation . . . In a sense he was assisted by his figure, by his little artifices of manner and by his dilettantish ways. But it should be remembered that this was a part in which ordinary comedy methods, or the obviously funny methods, did not apply. Bunthorne is a humorous figure because he is unconscious of humour and because his egotism veils his own realisation of his absurdity. Grossmith's dry humour carried him through what, from his point of view especially, was a very difficult part." But Godwin, not born until 1889 or thereabouts, could not possibly have seen him play the part in person; and it may be salutary, therefore, to balance his own second-hand eulogy with a comment made by a still later and, overall, more perceptive writer on G. & S., Audrey Williamson. It is difficult, *she* suggests, "to imagine Grossmith as Bunthorne at all."

that he acquired, around this time, a generally recognised nickname. That nickname was the happy and obvious one: "Gee-Gee". It was to stick with him for the rest of his life.

Throughout that summer, 1881, *Patience* ran blissfully and cheerfully on. But as the weeks passed there was growing excitement in the company. Way back in July 1878 – if not before – D'Oyly Carte had decided that the Opera Comique was too small and otherwise unsatisfactory for the size and type of audiences Gilbert and Sullivan were attracting. More, he wanted a theatre entirely of his own. And now this ambition was approaching fulfilment with the building of the Savoy, situated in a prime position not half a mile from the "Op. Com." but on the other – the Embankment – side of the Strand. *Patience*, it was eventually announced, would transfer to the new theatre in the autumn.

In the event, the actual date of the changeover was altered at least four times. But at last, on Monday, October 10th, the Savoy opened in a blaze of incandescent glory with the auditorium lit (the first time the magical new invention had been used in any theatre) by electricity. Other innovations included the adoption of a queue system for the unreserved seats and free programmes for the whole house, while for the actors there was a new feeling of spaciousness, a comfortable green-room and for Grossmith (though for him alone) a dressing-room to himself. Then at the end of December electric lighting was ready for the illumination of the stage itself. The performance chosen to inaugurate this was, strangely, a midweek matinee; and, strangely too, it proved to be a performance for which Grossmith for some reason was "off". It was the first performance of *Patience* he had missed.

But it was not, as it happened, to be the last. For just as tragedy had struck early in 1880 with the death of his father, so now, not two years later, came a second misfortune, and once again he was away from the theatre a number of nights as a result. On February 27th, 1882, after a prolonged illness, his mother died. Something of a shadowy figure compared with the three men in her family, the first Mrs G. G. – or so Grossmith tradition has it – had been very much in command at home. And part of the reason for this, no doubt, was that the men, with their varied outside commitments, were forever coming and going; whereas she was there, entrenched as it were, in effect the whole time.

As was the case much of the time with its three predecessors, *Patience*, first night and matinees apart, had been played from the start with a curtain-raiser. The first of these, carried over from the *Pirates* run, was a piece most notable for its offputting title: *In the Sulks*. But within days of *Patience* opening, *In the Sulks* had been returned, so to speak, to its corner in favour of a one-act "operetta" called *Uncle Samuel*; libretto by Arthur Law, music by George Grossmith. Law, son of a vicar, one-time soldier, a member for nearly four years of the German Reed company and now for a short time with D'Oyly Carte, was becoming known as a prolific writer of such pieces. Grossmith no doubt had been greatly encouraged by the reception given to *Cups and Saucers*. *Uncle Samuel* was played with the evening performances at the Opera Comique right through that first *Patience* summer.

Later on, Grossmith was to have periods when he gave his piano sketches at the Savoy as he had earlier given them at the former theatre. One of these that would provide particular amusement was called *The Drama on Crutches*, incorporating as it did a skit on Gilbert and Sullivan opera itself, in which he made much good-natured fun of the "highly trained" Savoy cast and chorus and the individual quirks and mannerisms of the leading members of the company. But whether his sketches were at any one time required – or not required – by D'Oyly Carte, they had all the while been in demand for any number of the benefit and charity matinees at other theatres and elsewhere that were an ever-recurring feature of London life at the time. These matinees, patronised by a cultured, leisured public, were as often as not extended affairs of four packed hours and more; the participants with endless willingness and generosity giving their services free and, naturally, being chosen with a sharp eye to their popularity and drawing-power. It was thus yet another measure of the mark Grossmith had made in G. & S. that, right from the beginning of his stage career, his own popularity and drawing-power proved such that his presence seemed nearly as essential on these occasions as it was to the perfect enjoyment of an evening at the Opera Comique or the Savoy.

II

The first such matinee in which he appears to have taken part was one organised on behalf of the Stafford House Fund on Wednesday, February 6th, 1878. The other performers on that occasion included Arthur Cecil, the comedian J. L. Toole, the actor Beerbohm Tree and a Hungarian tragedian with the improbable name – for a Hungarian – of Maurice Neville. Grossmith's contribution to the afternoon was, first, a piano sketch illustrating the progress of a Lord Mayor's Show seen – or, rather, heard – through a fog. The details of this sketch had been graphically described on a former occasion as follows:

"The bells of St Clement's ring out in the wild-fog, to which the three bells of another church seem to offer in their melancholy tones the sad, importuning remonstrance, 'Do leave off'. Both are interrupted by the military band, at

92

first heard in the distance and gradually brought near, the whole reaching a grand climax with the arrival of the hero of the day, when the martial strain *See the Conquering Hero Comes* is blended with the joyous peal of St Clement's and the doleful 'Do leave off' of the despondent trio in a manner as musically marvellous as it is ludicrously amusing."

He followed this with his *Five Hamlets* and a song, *He was a Careful Man*, his whole performance being attended by "cheers and merriment".

It was an auspicious start. Thereafter the list lengthened at frequent intervals. Here is a table, impressive but, even so, far from complete, of other matinees in which he featured over the next few years:

March 4th, 1878: a benefit for F. B. Chatterton, manager of the Theatre Royal, Drury Lane – for which he was also on the organising committee.

May 4th, 1878: an entertainment of "readings and music" at Willis's Rooms, King Street, St James's.

May 25th, 1878, the very day, that is, of the opening of *H.M.S. Pinafore* (and only a few hours, therefore, after that opera's final rehearsal): a benefit for the manager of the Globe.

May 27th, 1878: an entertainment at St George's Hall, Langham Place, in aid of the vicarage fund of St Michael and All Angels Church, North Kensington.

June 22nd, 1878: an entertainment, one of two given that day at the Park Theatre, "with a view of recouping the management for the long continued series of losses sustained in endeavouring to establish the drama in Camden Town."[4] On this occasion the names billed included George senior.

May 7th, 1879: an entertainment at the Gaiety in aid of a fund for the support of the families of the soldiers killed fighting the Zulus that January at Isandhlwana and Rorke's Drift.

September 10th, 1881: an entertainment at the Polytechnic, Regent Street given, sadly, to mark the closing down of that illustrious establishment.

May 4th, 1882: a benefit for Kate Vaughan, a popular contemporary actress, at the Gaiety.

May 22nd, 1882: a benefit for Nellie Farren, an even more popular ditto, at the same place.

Nor were his contributions to such matinees always confined to performances of his own songs and sketches. In many cases the programme took the form of drama, with anything from one-act plays to single acts of longer plays, and full-length plays given complete; and from time to time he featured in these too. In May 1878, for example, he took part at the Gaiety in a performance of *Society*. In March 1883 he played a lead in a production of one of Gilbert's blank verse comedies, *The Palace of Truth*, at the Savoy. While on at least two other occasions he appeared in a new dramatisation of the trial scene from *Pickwick*. "Great laughter," recorded the *Era* of the first of these (December 1879) "came of

---

[4] Some people will endeavour to establish the drama *any*where – even in places where it is patently not wanted.

93

the Nathaniel Winkle of Mr George Grossmith, jun. who, by the way, was tempted to make some references to Mrs Bardell as 'Little Buttercup'. All the nervousness of Nathaniel Winkle, who puts the court in a fog as to whether he is Daniel Nathaniel or Nathaniel Daniel, was displayed most amusingly."

But most noteworthy from the standpoint of his career as a whole were a number of appearances he made during these years in another short piece equally suited to a varied bill: *Cox and Box. Cox and Box* was an adaptation made in 1866 by the playwright and humorist F. C. Burnand of a straight farce, *Box and Cox*, by another nineteenth century dramatist, John Maddison Morton, and had been Arthur Sullivan's first venture into the field of light operatics. A one-act piece with just three characters, it concerned two men unwittingly and, at first, unknown to each other, sharing the same room: Cox, a hatter, sleeping there by night, Box, a printer, using it during the day; the third character being their landlord, Sergeant Bouncer.[5]

The first time Grossmith took part in this was in June 1879 at a charity matinee at the Lyceum. He was cast as Cox, and in that role he had to reel off a patter song no less intricate than those provided for him by Gilbert:

> "My master is punctual always in *business*;
> Unpunctuality, even slight, *is in his*
> Eyes such a crime that on showing my *phiz in his*
>   Shop, I thought there'd be the devil to pay.
>   Yes, I thought there'd be the devil to pay.
>
> "My aged employer, with his physiognomy
> Shining from soap like a star in astronomy,
> Said, 'Mister Cox, you'll oblige me and honour me
>   If you will take this as your holi*day* –
>   If you will take this as your holi*day*.' "

With Arthur Cecil to spar with as Box and Corney Grain trying to keep them both in order as Bouncer, the whole performance went with a swing that was marred only by the absence through illness of Sullivan, who was to have conducted. The three players, all natural comedians, established an immediate stage rapport. Then at the Gaiety in July 1880 they again obliged with the piece at a benefit organised on behalf of Morton himself, and this time Sullivan did conduct. Again the comic rapport of the three of them communicated itself to their audience, and when Grossmith (fairly revelling, as the *Era* put it, "in the fun of the part of the hatter") reached the patter song quoted above, the applause

---

[5] In Morton's original Sergeant Bouncer was a woman: *Mrs* Bouncer.

94

was so great that Sullivan unhesitatingly granted him an encore, for all the world as though it were a first night at the Opera Comique or the Savoy. Nor were they allowed to leave the piece there, for they did it on at least two other occasions, once at Cromwell House, South Kensington, and another time (March 1884) at St George's Hall.

That Grossmith's presence on a platform or stage was now recognised as an unfailing guarantee of amusement and laughter virtually all theatrical London was ready to attest. But what of the man away from the footlights, away from the public eye? Was he still to be relied upon to provide amusement when, so to speak, off duty? He himself had strong feelings on at least one aspect of this. "Any hostess who asked me to her residence in the expectation that I should gratuitously amuse her guests would find me particularly prosaic." He could, he claimed, be a very rational being when he chose.

Well, yes. But if he was not always willing – as a matter of deliberate determination – to play the clown or comedian in private merely because he was a humorist by profession, that in no way ruled out his doing so spontaneously and, as it were, informally when the mood took him. Fun and humour for him would out whether he wanted them to or no; and – to consider just one facet of this for the moment – should anything in the nature of a practical joke be suggested or instigated when he was anywhere around, there was no one more ready to fall in with what the joker required. The joker, moreover, might be anybody; and here, as proof that he was entirely unfussy in this respect, are three quite separate anecdotes that make this same point. The first comes from a fellow-actor, entertainer, comic singer and spoofer extraordinary, Arthur Roberts.

It was early one afternoon. The two of them were walking near Cavendish Square behind Oxford Street after lunching with some "titled folks" when they passed a house that was obviously undergoing extensive alterations. Glancing at it with interest, Roberts suddenly said:

"Let's ask if the foreman is on the premises."

"Why?" enquired Grossmith, immediately curious.

"Wait and see," laughed Roberts, and promptly led the way inside.

The foreman, it transpired, was not in and would not be back that day. Roberts acknowledged the information complacently.

"We'll have a look round," he said.

And, with that, he beckoned Grossmith to follow him down to the basement. There they found a man putting a sash into a window. Straight-faced and businesslike, Roberts gestured to him.

"You must stop that!"

The man looked surprised. "What do you mean?"

"That window is not large enough. Not sufficient light. This is to be the billiard-room. You will have to get fresh plans for that window."

"All right, sir."

The man left off his job. They were evidently people with authority – sons of the owner, perhaps?

Next they found a man installing a stove, and now it was Grossmith, fully grasping his companion's idea, who took the lead.

"This is not what we ordered."

"I think it is, sir."

"No, no – that's for the bedroom. Take it up at once, please."

"I can't do that, sir. The foreman . . ."

"I know. We've just left him (!). Take that stove upstairs."

It was taken up.

Then Roberts put in another spoke.

"You're wrong," he told Grossmith, "that stove is for the room where he was fixing it"; and Grossmith in response called to the man to bring the thing back down again.

"We disorganised everybody on the premises," Roberts continued. "We stopped paperhangers because doorways had to be built through the walls they were engaged on. We wanted windows bricked up, and a kitchen range placed in the drawing-room. 'Father always gets so cold on winter nights,' we said. We wanted a conservatory on every landing and a mosaic pavement in the dining-room. And when every man was so bewildered that they did not know their heads from their heels, we told them all to leave work at four o'clock and spend a little beer-money that we offered in grateful recognition of their labours on behalf of our comfort."

But even that was not quite the end; for some months later Roberts, on his own this time, passed the house again, though being careful as he did so to keep on the opposite side of the road. The alterations, he noted, were "still unfinished".

The second story comes from the reminiscences of Rutland Barrington, and had to do principally with Richard D'Oyly Carte. Carte, it appears, was contemplating buying a houseboat near Henley. Would Barrington go down there with him one day to see what he thought of the boat in question? Yes, certainly, said Barrington, he'd be delighted; and "with a view to some fun" asked if he might bring Grossmith along as well.

The day having arrived, the two of them wasted no time. They started their "fun" in the train by addressing Carte as "Pa", much to the amusement of the other passengers in the compartment; an amusement only increased by the exasperation of Carte himself which culminated in his telling them to "Shut up, you fools!" Then, when they got out at Shiplake, Carte made the mistake of pausing to talk to the stationmaster, leaving the two jokers to go on ahead towards the river.

"The way to the waterside lay through the meadows, and we had to pass through a gate which we carefully shut and then waited for Carte. As he came up, we yelled playfully, 'Gate's locked, Pa, you've got to get over,' and to our delight he believed us and clambered on to the top bar, by which time we had, of course, opened the gate and were gently swinging it to and fro. The remarks he made to us and the intentions he expressed were so forcible that we had to bargain for immunity before letting him get down. For a short time we then displayed an exaggerated deference, which worried him a good deal; but the climax of our fun was to come at lunchtime. Carte, having ordered it, went to the station to enquire for telegrams, and as George and I both felt that he ought not to be disappointed of a message, we went quietly to the post office and sent one off to Shiplake Station, to be sent on. It arrived during lunch, and it was worth all our trouble to hear D'Oyly's pleased 'At last!' The messenger claimed eighteenpence for porterage, which rather annoyed him, but he paid it, opened [the envelope] and read: 'Come at once – baby much worse.' For a moment he was completely puzzled, then he turned to us and – we both went quietly but quickly out."

If the butts of the joking in these two instances had been other people, in the third case the joke rebounded on himself. He told the story with much relish in *A Society Clown*.

"I was coming up with a party of friends from Ascot, and we were journeying by one of those delightful trains on the South Western Railway which not only stop at every station, but between each station as well. We stayed at one place a particularly long time; and as a serious-looking stationmaster faced the window of the carriage in which we were, one of the ladies begged of me to 'chaff' him about the slowness of the train. Chaffing is a vulgar habit. But, unfortunately, it is a habit to which I am occasionally addicted . . ."

As a candidate for chaff the "serious and stolid" official seemed eminently promising material. The only trouble was that he (Grossmith) did not really feel in the mood for taking him on. But in deference to the "general wish" of his fellow-travellers, he agreed to have a go. And so – his account continues – he addressed the stationmaster as follows:

"I say, stationmaster, you ought to be ashamed of this line."
The serious official replied:
"So I am."
This scored the first laugh against me. Some of the ladies encouraged me and said: "Go on – go on. Get a rise out of him." I tried again, and this time observed weakly:
"Why don't you get something better to do?"
My victim, never changing his serious aspect, replied:
"You mean, why don't *you* get something better to do?"

97

This was a real knock-down blow. I came up staggering and a little dazed. My victim, seeing his chance, led the attack.

"Anything more to say?"

I feebly answered:

"No. Have you?"

He said:

"No – except that you act a good deal better here than you do at the Savoy."

And back at that same theatre, *Patience*, after a total run of five hundred and seventy-eight performances which thus eclipsed even *Pinafore's* figure, had given way to a successor at last. That successor was *Iolanthe*, a Gilbertian mingling of politics represented by the House of Lords and fantasy in the shape of some very human and not all sylph-like fairies; and, as in *Patience*, so now for a second time, Grossmith had a large part: the leader of the Lords, the Lord Chancellor. The part included no fewer than three solo numbers, the most remarkable – and challenging – of which was what came immediately to be christened the "nightmare song" midway through the second act:

"When you're lying awake with a dismal headache, and repose is taboo'd
by anxiety,
I conceive you may use any language you choose to indulge in, without
impropriety;
For your brain is on fire – the bedclothes conspire of usual slumber to plunder
you:
First your counterpane goes, and uncovers your toes, and your sheet slips
demurely from under you;
Then the blanketing tickles – you feel like mixed pickles – so terribly sharp
is the pricking,
And you're hot, and you're cross, and you tumble and toss till there's nothing
'twixt you and the ticking.
Then the bedclothes all creep to the ground in a heap, and you pick 'em all
up in a tangle;
Next your pillow resigns and politely declines to remain at its usual angle"

etc. etc. for a further twenty-two lines of the same length and a final, still more frenetic wind-up at the end.

The part as a whole may be aptly described (to use two epithets much beloved by the press of the time) as "quaint" and "whimsical". The Lord Chancellor is "a clean old gentleman", a "highly susceptible" widower whose romantic fancy has lighted on Phyllis, a ward of court. After much comic verbalising, he finally persuades himself that he is effectively engaged to her. But no sooner has he reached this conclusion than he is stopped short by Iolanthe, one of the fairies, pleading that her own son Strephon be allowed to marry Phyllis instead – and suddenly the whole mood of the opera changes. The Chancellor turns her down abruptly; and thereupon she reveals herself as his wife, whom he has

98

Fig. 7. Grossmith as the Lord Chancellor.

99

not seen for years and had believed dead. The ensuing scene, though brief, is both musically and dramatically moving, demanding from the two players a genuine depth of feeling. Jessie Bond, who played Iolanthe, an oratorio singer by training and an actress with an ability to conjure up the soulful without difficulty, could take this in her stride. But depth of feeling on stage was something that had not been required of Grossmith before, was not in his normal repertoire as a performer at all. How, then, did he play the scene? Did he achieve the pathos the words and music seemed to demand? Or did he alter mood scarcely at all, but treat it in the same lighthearted vein as the rest of the part? It is a question that must be asked, if only because questions as to his interpretation of a scene of still greater pathos and intensity were to arise in connection, six years later, with *The Yeomen of the Guard.*[6] But equally it is one that cannot be answered with any certainty, for the reviewers were curiously silent on the point. If anything, this absence of comment suggests he may have taken the second course.

> "Mr George Grossmith as the Lord Chancellor (declared – for instance – the *Era*) brings all his comic talent and skill to bear upon one of the drollest impersonations imaginable. A Lord Chancellor making love is comic enough in itself, and Mr Grossmith's method of delineating the effect of the tender passion is humorous in the extreme. His wonderful facility in delivering the greatest number of comic lines in the shortest possible time, and yet making every word distinct and intelligible, calls for hearty admiration, and was rewarded – if reward it could be called – with enthusiastic encores. The dry, precise, legal, formal and sententious way in which the Chancellor treats the question of proposing to Phyllis would make the gloomiest visitor break into a broad grin. Too much praise could hardly be awarded to this characteristic impersonation."

The question of that one short scene aside, though, there is no doubt that once again Gilbert had provided him with a role admirably suited to his personality and aptitudes; and the Lord Chancellor joined Bunthorne and, above all, John Wellington Wells as his favourite parts so far. It was, too, no less a favourite with his public. A photograph showing him bewigged and with his eyes twinkling behind his Lord Chancellor pince-nez or spectacles, enjoyed a record sale.

III

Iolanthe ran for three hundred and ninety-eight performances,[7] thus achieving third place in the G. & S. league table to date. It was succeeded

---

[6] See pages 123–4.
[7] November 25th, 1882–January 1st, 1884.

on January 5th, 1884 by *Princess Ida*, Gilbert's "respectful operatic perversion" of a poem by Tennyson and a rehash with new lyrics of an earlier play of his own. *Princess Ida* came in three acts,[8] the only one of the operas to do so, and Grossmith appeared in only the first and last of these, not being needed for the second, longest and (unfortunately from his point of view) the best. In consequence, and perhaps as some consolation, life for him was less strenuous than usual during the period before the opera opened – although for a time it seemed this was not to be the case at all. But then, at one of the early musical rehearsals, he got his break. They were going through, as they had been for some time, the whole of the concerted music for the first act, his part in which music consisted of two lines of recitative precisely:

King Gama (*Grossmith*): Must we, till then, in prison cell be thrust?
King Hildebrand (*Barrington*): You must!
King Gama: This seems unnecessarily severe!

To turn up time and again just to contribute these two lines seemed ridiculous. And at last he asked Sullivan with (to judge from his own account) a trace of irritation:

"Could you tell me, Sir Arthur,[9] what the words 'this seems un-necessarily severe' have reference to?" (The company had not yet had the full libretto read to them, so they might – theoretically – have referred to anything.)

Sullivan replied:

"Because you are to be detained in prison, of course."

It hardly seemed an adequate response. "Thank you," said Grossmith, "I thought they had reference to my having been detained here three hours a day for the past fortnight to sing them."

His comment went home. For Sullivan immediately took the point, excusing him forthwith from the remainder of those particular rehearsals.

For all that his part in *Princess Ida* was relatively small, however, it was not by any reckoning negligible. "Royal Gama", as the chorus refer to him, is a character of considerable power. A grotesque, hunchbacked figure walking with a stick, he would introduce himself on first entrance with a song of searing venom:

"If you give me your attention, I will tell you what I am:
I'm a genuine philanthropist – all other kinds are sham.
Each little fault of temper and each social defect
In my erring fellow-creatures I endeavour to correct.
To all their little weaknesses I open people's eyes;
And little plans to snub the self-sufficient I devise;

[8] Originally categorised as two acts and a prologue.
[9] The composer had been knighted the previous May.

101

I love my fellow-creatures – I do all the good I can –
Yet everybody says I'm such a disagreeable man!
And I can't think why!''

It was, considered Grossmith, one of the best songs Gilbert ever wrote.[10] But at the same time he could not help wondering: was the librettist having a dig with it at *him*? At length he took the plunge to ask whether this was so. The answer was happily reassuring. ''Certainly not,'' said Gilbert. ''I meant it for myself. I thought it my duty to live up to my own reputation.''

That song alone was almost sufficient to ensure that, come the first night, Grossmith's performance would once again make an impact. He ''so played an ungrateful part as to show power unsuspected perhaps by many present,'' declared the *Musical World*. ''A Richard the Third in body and a misanthrope at heart, Gama was elaborated by Mr Grossmith to the point where a complete picture is the result.'' The *Observer* spoke enthusiastically of his ''malignant impishness''; the *Era* of his ''strange angular attitudes''. But, of course, that impact could have been greater, as was pointed out by *The Times*. The ''exigencies of the story,'' wrote that paper's reporter, ''exclude him from the stage for a long time, and prevent the character from gaining that importance which no doubt would have been given to it had the play been designed for the present cast.'' It was a comment that had to be made.

This and certain other reservations apart, though, the first night of *Princess Ida* seemed the usual brilliant G. & S. première. But it ended for the players – as for everyone else concerned in it – on a note of some anxiety. Sullivan, who had conducted for the occasion as usual, had been ill all through that day, and after he had taken his curtain call at the end of the evening he fainted. He remained confined to his room for at least a week, and during that time Grossmith must have written to him to express sympathy, for a few days later, on January 15th, Sullivan penned the following reply:

''My dear Grossmith,
Many thanks for your very kind letter. It is pleasant to be thought of when one is ill. And it is also pleasant to know that one's works are in the hands not only of artists, but of *friends* like yourself who bring something more than a mere professional interest to bear on their work.
I have had a very sharp and severe attack;[11] but, fortunately, a short one. I have been out three times for a drive, and today go into the country till Friday. My kind remembrances to Mrs Grossmith.''

[10] It is also worth mentioning that he (along with others in the cast) considered *Ida* the best of the operas musically.
[11] The cause was kidney trouble from which he suffered at various times during his adult life.

It was a letter that indicated in striking terms just how close had become the relationship between the two of them since that evening seven years or so previously when Grossmith had first been admitted to the composer's circle as a "new man". Sullivan, he later suggested, was "the most amiable and charming professional man and musician" he had met in his life. He was also an inveterate giver of parties, and Grossmith was frequently among his guests on these occasions, along with other leading musical and theatrical celebrities and "society" figures of the day. Nor were his invitations confined to London and parties, as would be evidenced by another letter written by him that August from Stagenhoe Park in Hertfordshire:

"I am here" (Sullivan began) "for a few weeks, instead of going abroad. Will you and Mrs Grossmith come and spend a week or so with me?

Name your own time, as soon as you like, take a train from King's Cross to Hitchin, let me know beforehand, and I will send to meet you. I have two or three people whom you know staying here, but we are very quiet, and our greatest dissipation and excitement is lawn tennis."

If Sullivan had been smiling or chuckling to himself as he wrote that last sentence, it would have been very much in character. From the first, Grossmith made clear, he had been struck by the "intense humour" in the composer's face. "He was indeed a wonderfully humorous person." He was also a great tease. There was, for example, one evening during the run of *Patience* when Grossmith went through the performance suffering agonies from a badly swollen left cheek. During the interval Sullivan appeared in his dressing-room, avowedly to offer condolence. Grossmith replied that he didn't mind the pain; he was more concerned that he looked an awful sight. Sullivan smiled disarmingly. "Not at all, my dear Gee-Gee," he told him. "I assure you it is a great improvement. You never looked better."

But if his relationship with Sullivan was relaxed and warm, what of his relationship with Gilbert? Here things were undoubtedly less easy. The reason for this stemmed at least in part from the fact that he had very much more to do with the librettist at the Savoy itself. For whereas Sullivan over the years spent remarkably little time actually at the theatre (the bulk of the musical rehearsals for each opera being taken by the musical director, François Cellier) Gilbert was there on hand as producer, drill-master, benevolent uncle and even – where he deemed it necessary – guardian of morals if not every day then certainly to a vastly greater extent.

Gilbert was a man who invariably knew his own mind, a martinet with a fierce will and an iron determination to come out on top in every situation. That he could be touchy, difficult, quick-tempered at times, that he would grow more touchy, more difficult as the years progressed, there is no dispute. When he was in a bad mood, nobody was safe from his tongue; and one day during the run-up to *Princess Ida* it had been Grossmith's turn to suffer his sarcasm. The spark for this had been a rare expression of exasperation he (Gee-Gee) had vented on his own account.

"I've rehearsed this confounded business," he snapped, "until I feel a perfect fool."

"Ah," retorted Gilbert. "Now we can talk on equal terms."

A few moments later there was friction again.

"I beg your pardon?" said Grossmith wearily, not having caught something the librettist was telling him.

"I accept the apology," snapped Gilbert in return. "Let's get on with the rehearsal."

This exchange (variously quoted by various writers) soon went the rounds and shows the librettist in a somewhat unsympathetic light. But if Grossmith was moved at times to irritation or resentment at Gilbert's treatment, it was not in his nature to blazon that irritation in print himself. The only time he came anywhere near an adverse comment was to refer to him in one section of *A Society Clown* as a "perfect autocrat", rigorous in insisting that "his words should be delivered, even to an inflexion of the voice, as he dictates." Yet even here, a reading of the passage as a whole leaves a strong doubt whether Grossmith really meant this as a criticism (the word "autocrat" to a nineteenth century mind did not necessarily have the same pejorative connotations it has today); and, moreover, had he seriously been seeking to imply that Gilbert was as objectionable as has sometimes been made out, he would surely not have remained in the Savoy company so long.

The bad moments indeed were rare, and Grossmith comments on, for instance, the "great patience" Gilbert displayed time and again with actors who found difficulty following his instructions. "The performer," he wrote, "frequently gets the credit which is due to Mr Gilbert, and to him absolutely." He made up a hilarious dialogue sequence in which Gilbert, clearly struggling to keep his temper, is trying to show a hopeful but increasingly nervous (imaginary) member of the chorus how to act the small part and speak the one line allotted to him. He fails. An explosion is averted only narrowly.

> Mr Gilbert: (*bottling up his fury*). We won't bother about your scene now, Mr Snooks. [We'll] get on with the next. Grossmith! Grossmith! Where's Mr Grossmith?
> Mr Grossmith: (*a very small man with a still smaller voice*). Here I am.

Mr Gilbert: Oh, there you are. I'm sorry to have kept you waiting. We'll go on with your scene. Do you want to try your song?

Mr Grossmith: Not unless you want to hear it.

Mr Gilbert: No, I don't want to hear it. (*Roars of laughter from the company*). Do you?

Mr Grossmith: No!

And thereupon, for the rest of the rehearsal, "good humour" prevails.

Nonetheless, while there can be little doubt that Grossmith genuinely – and deeply – admired Gilbert as a writer and producer, it seems also to have been the case that he could never quite relax in his company, that he retained to the end a certain awe of him, may even have been more than a trifle scared of him.[12] And this applied not only to their relationship *in* the theatre but when they were together outside it. Like Sullivan, Gilbert entertained; and Grossmith found himself on several occasions a guest at *his* home too, both in London and later (after he had left the Savoy) at Grim's Dyke, the country house the librettist was to buy at Harrow Weald. He mentions being shown the model theatre used by him to work out in advance of production the stage movements of all his characters for each of the operas in turn; and in a magazine article written after Gilbert's death[13] he told how he had been among those roped in to help amuse the youthful guests at one or more of the children's parties the Gilberts were so fond of giving. "All the great charm of this great genius – this great man – lay in his own home. He was a marvellous host." True, that article was in the nature of an obituary. True, too, their feelings towards one another were to go through a definite stormy-cum-icy patch some years afterwards.[14] But even allowing for all this, things can hardly have been – in general – too terrible.

Meanwhile at the theatre *Princess Ida* was proving something of a disappointment, and it became clear as 1884 progressed that its run would be, in G. & S. terms, relatively short. It survived a month's break between August 16th and September 15th when Carte for the first time closed the Savoy; but thereafter its days were obviously numbered. The break, though, gave Grossmith a rare chance to take a holiday and he spent at least part of the month in North Wales. It was all the more unfortunate, therefore, that his return to the theatre should have been marked by a mishap that must to some extent have counterbalanced the benefits of the break. The *Era* reported on September 27th:

[12] "Gilbert was kindness itself to me, though he seemed to terrify my father," wrote the third George Grossmith many years later.

[13] See page 195.

[14] See pages 150, 195.

105

"Mr George Grossmith and Mr Rutland Barrington have been poisoned by oysters. They partook of a few 'natives' for luncheon after rehearsal last Thursday week (September 18th) and the next morning both were seized with cholerine. Mr Grossmith, who was at Datchet[15] at the time, was so seriously indisposed that he could not play at the Savoy Theatre either Friday or Saturday . . ."

It was perhaps lucky, therefore, that those new rehearsals in which he was now involved were again, from his angle, relatively undemanding. For the situation that autumn had caught Gilbert and Sullivan on the hop. A new opera had been started, but was nowhere near ready for production and, as a result, Carte had decided to replace *Ida* with a revival of *The Sorcerer* and *Trial by Jury*.

For this first reappearance, *The Sorcerer* underwent a number of textual changes. Grossmith, for instance, lost eight lines of recitative at the end of his Act II scene with Lady Sangazure, but in compensation gained a trio with Alexis and Aline at the beginning of the act that helped to give his small part a little more body. Could Gilbert have taken *The Times* and other comments on his lack of opportunities in *Princess Ida* to heart? If so, it was only curious that he was not asked to be in *Trial by Jury*, the part of the Judge which he had previously played going this time to Barrington.

At all events, when the revised and revived *Sorcerer* opened on October 11th, it was received with unmistakable acclaim from the start. That night was like the original first night in 1877 all over again, only more so. For whereas on the earlier occasion the opera's success had inevitably been to some extent in the balance, now "Gilbert and Sullivan" was an established form of entertainment, with an immense following. And whereas Grossmith's own success on that initial occasion had been in similar balance, now he weighed into his old part with the confidence gained from all but seven years uninterrupted stage experience. And he was still some weeks short of thirty-seven years old.

[15] In Buckinghamshire on the Thames. It became his habit to rent a small cottage there for the autumn each year.

CHAPTER SIX

The Mikado, Ruddigore, The Yeomen of the Guard

The revived *Sorcerer* ran for five months. It might, had necessity demanded, have run still longer. But early the following year, 1885, Gilbert and Sullivan at last had their new opera ready. That new opera opened on March 14th before an audience keyed up to the pitch of anticipation and eager to laugh and applaud at the slightest opportunity – and provided for Grossmith the most miserable evening of his stage career to date.

"The first night of *The Mikado*," he wrote in *A Society Clown*, "I shall never forget the longest day I live. It must have appeared to all that I was doing my best to spoil the piece." He was, thought the *Evening News*, "so imperfect in the knowledge of his part that it would be unfair to judge him by the first performance." The climax of his distress came during what should have been a sparkling duet in the second act[1] when he stumbled and fell right over on to the stage; and the fact that the audience assumed this fall to have been deliberate, and had not only roared with delight in the wake of it but clamoured for an encore for the song as he made his exit at the end, only made things worse.

Any actor can have a night when everything goes wrong. But from that evening there arose the belief – a belief fostered largely by himself – that his performances had been similarly calamitous on other first nights. "All my first appearances are completely marred by uncontrollable nervousness. I am more than nervous; I am absolutely ill." The

---

[1] *The Flowers that Bloom in the Spring – tra la.*

stage director, he claimed, was wont to refer to him on these occasions – and with reason – as a "lamentable spectacle".

All this, though, was written in retrospect, and after one more traumatic first night,[2] and gives rise to an odd query. For if he had experienced that "uncontrollable nervousness" on first nights before, at least a hint of it would surely have been manifest here and there among the earlier press reviews, and of such a hint there is no sign. Possibly, therefore, it was not so uncontrolled as he imagined, and in fact the extent of it was by no means apparent to what he called those "terrible rows of critics" as a whole even as regards *The Mikado*. Thus, for instance, the *Musical World*: "Somewhat tame at first, Mr George Grossmith ... finally warmed to his work and raised the accustomed laughter." Or again, the *Globe*: "Mr Grossmith seemed scarcely at home in the dialogue, but sang his two songs with infinite humour." While others still, most notably the *Era*, appeared not to be conscious of anything untoward or wrong at all.

But whether it showed or not, of his nervousness on this occasion there can be no question, and it stemmed in all likelihood from two factors. First, Gilbert was nervous too. The relative failure of *Princess Ida* had gnawed at and bothered him. In consequence he was doubly anxious to ensure that *The Mikado* should go well. And when Gilbert was anxious, his edginess rubbed off on everyone around him. To satisfy Gilbert in this frame of mind through one long rehearsal after another (and while still playing John Wellington Wells in the evenings) was a wearing task, and Grossmith, with his spare physique, found himself for the first time in his life drained of energy.[3] And second, the part for which he was cast was, to use his own description, his "heaviest" so far.

That part was Ko-Ko, Lord High Executioner of Titipu, the imaginary Japanese town where the action takes place. And Ko-Ko is the figure around whom the opera's whole fantastic plot revolves. Following an early first entrance[4] he was on stage as much as he was off it, the centre of the action for most of the time. But if the part was a heavy one, it was also one of splendid potential. From start to finish a jaunty, engaging character, Ko-Ko has about him something of the schoolboy, something too – and in both respects this made the part unlike any of those he had previously played – of the clown. It was this combination of clown plus

---

[2] *Ruddigore* (see page 113).

[3] The dress rehearsal the evening before the first night should have been a warning of what was to come. Grossmith (Sullivan noted in his diary) had been "ill, nervous" then.

[4] In which he carried a genuine Japanese executioner's sword; the very sword that, hanging on the wall of Gilbert's library or falling off it at an inspired moment, had sparked in the librettist's mind the whole idea for the opera.

Fig. 8. Grossmith as Ko-Ko.

109

his first night uncertainties that clearly inspired the following review in *Punch*:

"*The Mikado* promises to be all that its successful predecessors have been, though the first performance, which would have been good enough anywhere else, was not quite up to the Savoy mark. It broke upon many of us there, as quite a revelation, that our George Grossmith's real humour had hitherto been less in his face and voice than in his legs. Throughout the first act his legs were invisible, and the audience felt that something was wanting; they didn't know exactly what it was, but their favourite was not being funny. He didn't even look funny. He had a good song; he got flustered in the words; was nervous; but all this could have been forgiven him if he had only been funny – just once. But no, the act went on, and all Mr Grossmith's admirers were what Jeames called 'nonplushed'. Suddenly in the second act he gave a kick-up, and showed a pair of white stocking'd legs under the Japanese dress. It was an inspiration. Forthwith the house felt a strong sense of relief. It had got what it wanted, it had found out accidentally what it had really missed, and at the first glimpse of George Grossmith's legs there arose a shout of long pent up laughter. George took the hint; he too had found out where the fault lay, and now he was so pleased at the discovery that he couldn't give them too much of a good thing ... And the audience shouted, applauded, encored and actually joined in the action, unconsciously kicking up their own legs in their irrepressible delight, much after the manner of a less aristocratic and well-bred audience which gives vent to its feelings by chorusing a popular tune sung by one of its favourites.
"From that time to the end of the piece there wasn't a dull minute ..."

Which, under the circumstances, was hardly surprising. And indeed, rehearsals and that agonising first night behind him, Grossmith settled into this latest part in his normal relaxed manner, working it up to his usual high standard, and making it ultimately perhaps his biggest success of all. A song in Act I, in which he mentally lined up candidates for possible execution, became one of the most famous numbers in the G. & S. repertoire:

"As some day it may happen that a victim must be found,
    I've got a little list – I've got a little list
Of society offenders who might well be underground,
    And who never would be missed – who never would be missed!
There's the pestilential nuisances who write for autographs –
All people who have flabby hands and irritating laughs –
All children who are up in dates, and floor you with 'em flat –
All persons who in shaking hands, shake hands with you like *that* –
And all third persons who on spoiling *tête-à-têtes* insist –
    They'd none of 'em be missed – they'd none of 'em be missed!"

A few days, a couple of weeks, a month perhaps at the most, and it became clear *The Mikado* would fulfil all Gilbert's hopes for it; a long run on the scale of those of *Pinafore* and *Patience* seemed assured. But long runs, however gratifying in themselves, do give rise to certain problems for the actors involved in them. "Mr George Grossmith, on being asked whether he considered long runs conducive to madness," reported the *Era*, "made this characteristic reply: 'In a run, say, of six hundred nights, my experience is that the last five hundred and ninety-nine do *not* affect the nerves; but the first one does – very much indeed.' " In *A Society Clown* he took up the point more seriously. Long runs, he suggested there, did not so much affect the nerves as they affected the performance:

"Constant repetition begets mechanism, and that is a dreadful enemy to contend against. I try hard to fight against it personally, and believe I succeed. There is one thing I always do – I always play my best to a bad house; for I think it a monstrous thing that an actor should slur through his work because the stalls are empty, and thereby punish those who *have* come for the fault of those who have *not*."

A long run, too, can lead to slackness, to carelessness and over-confidence. But with Gilbert likely to be alerted to the slightest deviation either from his script or from the lines and details of production he had laid down, slackness, carelessness of any kind were rarely to be found at the Savoy. Above all, he would tolerate no gags, no new business of any kind being introduced into his works without his express consent. Any such additions suggested by his players that seemed to him legitimate he would sanction; any he thought silly, irrelevant or detrimental to the action as a whole, he would reject. Grossmith himself had not (so far as can be judged) ventured anything unauthorised – or, at any rate, blatantly unauthorised – since his "locomotive gag" on the first night of *The Sorcerer* (a piece of business to which Gilbert had instantly given approval). But now in the second act of *The Mikado* there was a scene during which he, Jessie Bond and Barrington were required to kneel together side by side, heads down, on the floor. One night at this point Jessie Bond gave him a push; and responding instinctively to her press-ure, he rolled – as he put it – "completely over". The reaction of the audience was all he could have desired; he – and she – duly repeated the business in the performances that followed. But then, before long, notice of it was brought to the attention of Gilbert; and Gilbert immediately asked him to cut it out. "Certainly," Grossmith replied, "if you wish. But I get an enormous laugh by it." Gilbert's reaction was typically pungent. "So you would," he retorted, "if you sat on a pork pie." In consequence: end of roll, end of pork pie. End too of all discussion.

111

The Mikado ran in the end not far short of two years: six hundred and seventy-two performances, a total that not merely challenged but beat unassailably all the other totals for the series, both previous and to come. Yet even *The Mikado* could not go on for ever, and in mid-December 1886 stage rehearsals began on its very different successor. That successor, billed as "A New and Original Supernatural Opera", was a burlesque of old English melodrama. It was called *Ruddygore*.

In *Ruddygore* Grossmith found himself with another "heavy" part; heavy as much as anything in this case because the role was in effect a dual one. He appeared first as Robin Oakapple, a shy young farmer. But Robin Oakapple is really a baronet in disguise: Sir Ruthven Murgatroyd, scion of a line condemned by a curse that compels its current representative to commit a crime a day for life. His identity revealed, he is obliged to resume his baronetcy, a sudden and complete transformation of status which called for a no less sudden and complete transformation of outward character. But as a "bad bart" he has no stomach for what he has to do; and his eventual decision to defy his ancestors who have sought to enforce the curse leads some way towards the opera's conclusion. And even more important: it provided the excuse for the now all but mandatory patter song – or rather, for once, patter trio – in which he himself cast off thus:

> "My eyes are fully open to my awful situation –
> I shall go at once to Roderic and make him an oration.
> I shall tell him I've recovered my forgotten moral senses,
> And I don't care twopence halfpenny for any consequences.
> Now I do not want to perish by the sword or by the dagger,
> But a martyr may indulge a little pardonable swagger,
> And a word or two of compliment my vanity would flatter,
> But I've got to die tomorrow, so it really doesn't matter!"

It was a song which, in both style and sentiment, was typically and uniquely Gilbert. But, by contrast, the opening dialogue between Robin and the heroine Rose Maybud contained a distinct echo of the opening dialogue Grossmith had provided for himself and Florence Marryat eleven years earlier in *Cups and Saucers*.[5] Robin is eager yet desperately hesitant:

Robin: Mistress Rose!
Rose: (*surprised*). Master Robin!
Robin: I wished to say that – it is fine.

[5] See page 63.

Rose: It is passing fine.
Robin: But we do want rain.
Rose: Aye, sorely! Is that all?
Robin: (*sighing*). That is all.
Rose: Good day, Master Robin!
Robin: Good day, Mistress Rose!

The opening performance of *Ruddygore* was billed for Saturday, January 22nd, 1887. It proved, however, not quite a vintage G. & S. first night. Though for the most part the audience seemed enthusiastic enough, the closing moments were disturbed by some hissing and other unmistakable signs of dissatisfaction; with the result that, the following morning, the whole cast were called for an extra rehearsal to learn that G. & S. had made various changes and cuts. Within a fortnight too they had modified the title, the emotive *y* in the middle giving place to a supposedly more innocuous *i*.

Grossmith, it seems reasonable to assume, almost certainly went through agonies again that first night. After his unnerving experience with *The Mikado*, the fear of a repeat disaster on this next equivalent occasion must have been at the back of his mind the whole time. In a biography of Gilbert and Sullivan published during the 1930s, the assertion was made – though on what evidence the author, Hesketh Pearson, did not specify – that to keep himself going he had resorted to taking drugs.[6] But even if this *was* the case, those drugs were not strong enough to conceal his nervousness altogether.[7] Some critics noticed it, in particular Clement Scott in the *Illustrated London News*. Yet, as with *The Mikado*, others seemed totally oblivious. To quote the *Era*: "Mr George Grossmith did everything in his power to make Robin Oakapple acceptable"; the *Musical Times*: "Mr George Grossmith, in the character of Robin, has a part rather out of his usual line – but which, however, he plays with his customary tact and ability." And, most lyrical of all in this instance, the *Daily Telegraph*: "Let a special word be said for Mr Grossmith. He was seldom off the stage, and whatever he did when on it was done with every help from an artistic nature and consummate skill. His Robin will have a conspicuous place in the gallery of Grossmith portraits."

Yet whatever he went through that first night was this time as nothing to what he then went through almost immediately afterwards. On the Friday of the following week he began to feel groggy. On the Saturday

[6] He was certainly a smoker and possibly a heavy one. But that, no doubt – as all smokers would say – is a different matter.

[7] Not that he was the only member of the cast to be badly affected by nerves on this occasion. Two of the female principals were also off form that night for the same reason.

he was seriously unwell. Somehow he got through the two performances that day, but he arrived home in a state of collapse and over the next few days his condition became still worse. Confined to bed, scarcely able to eat anything, he was in such a bad way there were even fears he might not live.

But then, as violently as the illness had struck, so almost as dramatically he began to recover.[8] On the Thursday afternoon of that same week his doctors issued a bulletin: "Mr Grossmith's condition is considerably improved. He has passed a fair night and is freer from pain." And by the Saturday it was even being suggested he might be back at the Savoy in about a fortnight.

Which seemed optimistic; and yet, remarkably, it was a forecast that proved in the event to have erred on the side of caution. For he was off *in all* just two weeks and two days – and that included a period of convalescence at Brighton. Nor could he have wished for a friendlier welcome than he received on the night of his return. Making his initial entrance, he was greeted, reported the *Era*, "by a cordial outburst of feeling from every part of the crowded house." The warmth of it all, indeed, momentarily overcame him. But rapidly regaining his composure, he was soon playing "with all his wonted briskness, gaiety and lightness of touch."

In his absence his part had been taken by a young actor with the then stage name of H. Henri, later to be much better known as Henry Lytton. Lytton's G. & S. career had begun three years earlier in the chorus of one of D'Oyly Carte's provincial touring companies. But then had followed a break, and he had been re-engaged – and appointed Grossmith's understudy – only a matter of days before *Ruddigore*'s opening. On the Monday morning following Grossmith's collapse he was told he would be on that night. It was, he realised, his big chance. But on his own first entrance he was met not by any "cordial outburst of feeling" but, instead, a chilling silence. The audience wanted Grossmith, not this – Lytton's description of himself – "unknown stripling". He worked through the opening lines of dialogue with Rose Maybud and the duet between them that followed. But already the audience was warming to him. The applause at the end of that duet was sufficient to merit an

---

[8] The very speed of that recovery, though, bearing in mind the state of medical science at the time, gives rise to some doubt as to what his illness had actually been. According to *The Times* it was a severe cold that turned to inflammation. According to the *Era* it was a liver and digestive complaint. Simple exhaustion, and possibly some sort of reaction after the strains of the *Ruddigore* rehearsals and first night – he had had at least one other day off unwell back in December – may also have been a factor. In later years it became – in two books – peritonitis. But this, to judge again from the speed of his recovery, was one thing it was almost certainly not.

encore. Disappointment at Grossmith's absence was gradually swallowed; by the time the evening's performance was halfway through it was clear the young man had made his mark. It was an impression amply confirmed in the performances that followed. At length, as one of the first things he did on his return, Grossmith called him into his dressing-room and presented him with a signed photograph as a memento of his success.

Lytton was in fact his third understudy, with a public career to be confined to the stage. By contrast, the two men who had understudied him previously had at times worked, like himself, on the entertainment platform. Understudy number one was a man named Frank Thornton. Thornton, Grossmith believed, had all but been appointed originally in his own place, and from the first had been desperate to go on for him. Nightly at the start of *The Sorcerer* run he had appeared in his dressing-room enquiring how he was feeling; trying to persuade him he did not look well; that he needed a break, a change; and finally he even urged on him a suspicious looking pill. All to no avail. Grossmith refused to take either break or pill, and Thornton had to content himself with parts in certain of the curtain-raisers (which included his replacing Richard Temple as General Deelah during the run of *Cups and Saucers*) until Grossmith was off for the first time more than two years later following the collapse and death of George senior early in the *Pirates* run. But though he performed then with much credit, and though too he was later given a small part of his own in *Patience*, his opportunities in G. & S. were clearly limited, and he left in 1882 to be replaced by Eric Lewis, another actor and entertainer of talent. Lewis substituted for Grossmith on occasion as King Gama and Ko-Ko, while for a period in 1884 he combined a part in *Trial by Jury* with a nightly appearance in place of a temporarily indisposed Corney Grain at the German Reed establishment. One of his items there, a comic song "in which a vocalist singing *Happy be thy Dreams* is interrupted by a parrot," was, the *Era* correspondent considered, among the funniest things of its kind he had ever heard. But, like Thornton, Lewis must have realised how limited were his opportunities at the Savoy, and at or near the end of *The Mikado* run he too left to pursue a long and varied stage career with more fluid managements elsewhere.

During his illness Grossmith had received a flood of telegrams and letters of sympathy and anxious good wishes, and then, following on, a number of others expressing relief and gratification at his return to health. Among those who had been particularly solicitous in their concern was Gilbert, who had enquired after him every day and had actually gone down (with D'Oyly Carte) to cheer him up while he was at Brighton.

115

Enquiries had even come from members of the Royal family, including – no less – the Prince of Wales. Both the Prince and his wife were avid theatregoers, with G. & S. high on their popularity list. After watching a special performance of the *Children's Pinafore* in February 1880, they had made a particular point of complimenting Grossmith on his accompanying sketch. He and the Prince had been fellow-guests at several parties given by Sullivan and others, and it was this ripening acquaintance that led to his being one of a select company of "representatives of the theatrical profession" entertained by the Prince to a widely talked about private dinner in February 1882. It was, considered one of the non-theatrical notables present, a "dullish evening"; but that it was a signal mark of honour to those invited there could be no doubt. It was too, in a more general way, a mark of the fact that the theatre, for so long regarded by so many as synonymous with wickedness and sin, was becoming respectable, and that actors were now being fully accepted into "society".

But if Grossmith felt increasingly at home in the company of royalty (and there were to be other invitations from the Prince in the years that followed) he was even more firmly established in society as a whole. By the early 1880s he knew and was known by pretty well everybody who was anybody in London: peers, politicians, bishops, actors, singers, musicians, artists. Time and again his presence was requested at receptions, at parties, at an endless assortment of other gatherings. Again, gregarious and sociable by nature, he had become a member of two London clubs:[9] the Beefsteak (to which he had been elected in 1878 or '79) and the Garrick (1883). His profession in the latter's records was given as "comedian".

Nor was society slow to court him in his professional capacity. During these years invitations to give entertainments at parties and other social events came flocking in. Relishing the work, he accepted as many of these as he could ("He is amusing – but much too vulgar" was the surprising comment one such performance evoked); although with his nightly commitment to G. & S. he was obviously limited on the one hand to those functions being held in or around London, and on the other to performing either in the afternoon before the theatre or very late in the evening after it. But for all that, the number he undertook

[9] Or was it three? – for he seems to have been at one time a member of the Green Room Club. Or four? – for there were also the Savages. According to Grossmith family legend, he (though not Weedon) resigned from the Savage Club in protest at the way things had been handled there the evening his father died. Certainly he was no longer a member by the turn of the century. But equally he is recorded as having taken part in an after-dinner entertainment put on by the Club in February 1882. Perhaps, therefore, his resignation for some reason came later.

appears to have been extraordinary. The people who engaged him ranged from dukes to businessmen, from ladies titled and ladies elderly to ladies untitled and ladies not so elderly, and any number of them, he makes delightedly clear, had their foibles. There were, for instance, innumerable variations in the way he might be paid:

"I have frequently been amused at the amount of diffidence displayed by people when handing me the honorarium. Sometimes the hostess will thank me profusely and, in shaking hands, squeeze the little envelope into my palm.

"Some ladies will say loudly: 'Goodbye and thank you so much.' Then, softly: 'I will write you tomorrow.'

"Some ladies will whisper mysteriously: 'You will hear from my husband tomorrow.' This at first sounds rather awful; but the husband's communication is pleasant and most welcome."

Furthermore, on top of all his private entertainments he was still taking part in innumerable benefit and charity matinees. Here again is a table of these, again incomplete, continuing that given in the previous chapter:

February 1884: a "recital" at the residence of a Mrs Du Pre Porcher, Connaught Place, Hyde Park, for the benefit of the charities administered by St Barnabas Church off the Edgware Road.
July 10th, 1884: a matinee at St James's Hall in aid of the School of Dramatic Art, which included himself and other members of the Savoy company presenting items from G. & S. under Sullivan's own baton.
January 20th, 1885: a matinee at the Court Theatre, in aid of a fund set up to relieve cases of extreme poverty in Chelsea.
February 12th, 1885: a matinee at the Gaiety in aid of the building fund of the Royal Hospital for Diseases of the Chest, City Road.
May 5th, 1886: a benefit for Fred Leslie, one of the comedy stars of the Gaiety.
May 18th, 1887: an extra matinee performance of *Ruddigore* at the Savoy, in aid of the Actors' Benevolent Fund.
March 7th, 1888: a matinee at the Haymarket that included a performance of Sheridan's *The Critic*, with Weedon and Barrington also in the cast. "Mr George Grossmith as the Earl of Leicester sat on his spurs and scuttled about *à la* John Wellington Wells,"[10] recorded the *Era*.
October 24th, 1888: a benefit at the Savoy for Henry Bracy, a singer who had played the tenor lead in *Princess Ida* and who was now going out to Australia; and a programme that found Grossmith (and Arthur Cecil – though not this time Corney Grain) playing yet again in *Cox and Box*.

For all facets of his solo entertaining, private, charity and otherwise, Grossmith had continued as before to write and compose all his own material. And if his output had been prolific during the 1870s, the 1880s saw him more productive still. Songs of his dating from this decade

[10] At the same time?

included *The Duke of Seven Dials*; *The Lost Key*, a parody of the best known song of the whole period, Arthur Sullivan's *The Lost Chord*; and perhaps his most famous composition of all, one that is said to have earned him a thousand pounds or more in threepenny royalties, and a song that is still remembered – and occasionally played or hummed – to this day, *See me Dance the Polka*:

> "You should see me dance the Polka,
>   You should see me cover the ground,
> You should see my coat-tails flying
>   As I jump my partner round.
> When the band commences playing,
>   My feet begin to go,
> For a rollicking, romping Polka
>   Is the jolliest fun I know."

Nor was he content with single songs and sketches but, following his collaboration with Arthur Law on *Uncle Samuel*, he also composed the music for three other one-act theatrical pieces by the same author. First of these (1882) was a "musical farce", *Mr Guffin's Elopement. Guffin* had its first performances in Liverpool and was then transferred to Toole's Theatre in London, the year's *Dramatic Notes* describing Law's libretto as "bright enough" and Grossmith's music as "tuneful". Their next collaboration, two years later, was called *A Peculiar Case* and concerned a doctor specialising in curious cases of mania; while their final one, early in 1885, came at the time when London was in the midst of its craze for things Japanese. G. & S. were cashing in on this with *The Mikado*; G.G. & L. may well have hoped to cash in likewise. The result was an even more pseudo-Japanese piece called *The Great Taykin*.[11]

Then in 1886, reverting to his earlier, single-authorship formula of *Cups and Saucers*, Grossmith came up with a piece called *The Real Case of Hide and Seekyll*, a skit with songs on Robert Louis Stevenson's recently published *Strange Case of Dr Jekyll and Mr Hyde*. *Hide and Seekyll* was first alluded to in the *Era* on May 22nd that year. But it had to wait for actual production until September 3rd, 1888 when (coincidence!) it was put on at the Royalty Theatre a month after a straightforward dramatisation of the novel had opened at the Lyceum. At that time the Royalty was under the management of Lionel Brough, an actor who over the years made extensive use of Grossmith's songs as an entertainer and who now threw himself with zest into the double-character title-role of this latest Grossmith stage work. "Mr Stevenson," the *Era* explained after seeing the piece, "has powerfully shown the

[11] Or *Taykin*; or *Takin*; or *Taykins*; or *Tay-kins*; a question of takin' one's pick.

fatal consequence of inventing a potion which enables a man to be two distinct persons. It is the aim of Mr Grossmith and Mr Brough to show the disastrous effects of leaving such a draught about. It *is* 'left about' and, by a revengeful mixing and ministering, Seekyll's page-boy causes some curious transformations." A nautical character, for instance, becomes a "smart volunteer rifleman"; an old butler a "boy in buttons". The whole skit or "travestie", the paper proclaimed, was "undeniably humorous" with "not an atom of ill-nature in it" – even if, as *The Times* suggested, it had "no literary or musical pretensions to speak of".

And, not content with everything else, it was in this latter year (1888) that Grossmith produced his first volume of reminiscences: *A Society Clown*. The book was commissioned in January or February and published that August by J. W. Arrowsmith of Bristol as number thirty-one of a shilling octavo series called "Arrowsmith's Bristol Library".[12] In his opening pages the clown of the title summed up his hopes for what he had written:

> "My first desire in producing the following sketches of my life is to benefit others, by making an hour pass pleasantly in the library or in a railway carriage. My second desire, which goes without saying, is to benefit my publisher and myself."

With chapters on his boyhood and his Bow Street days to preface those covering his career to date as an entertainer and actor, *A Society Clown* could fairly be classed as an autobiography. But that having been said, there are certain qualifications that must be made. First, the book dealt no more than incidentally with his private life. Nor, though he had experienced – or claimed to have experienced – "many small troubles and some sorrows", would he deal with these "shadows".[13] For, quite simply, he wrote to entertain: the quirkish conversation, the amusing incident, the anecdote was everything. And in line, as it were, with this, the narrative was not altogether free from factual inaccuracies. For most of it he had relied purely on memory; he had never, he explained, kept a diary. But what he *had* kept were a great many letters, some loose, others pasted in a book; and in the final chapter, with disarming snobbery, he ranged through these in the order he turned them up, naming the people who had sent them, quoting a number of them and incorporating further anecdotes about some of the writers and the matters

---

[12] The series in later years also included the reminiscences of Arthur Roberts and W. S. Penley, from which quotation has been made in previous chapters of the present book, and of George Thorne, an actor who during the 1880s and '90s played Grossmith's roles for D'Oyly Carte in the provinces.

[13] Hence, no doubt, the omission of any reference to that short-lived sister (see page 27).

Fig. 9. Grossmith in the 1880s – the "society clown". Drawn by "Spy".

to which they referred. And if some of the anecdotes seem to modern taste a trifle lacking in punch, the book as a whole still – after more than ninety years – makes an enjoyable read.

Nor, even more to the point, was there any question as to its reception back in 1888. "It is one of the most difficult things in the whole range of literary effort to write an autobiography," pronounced the *Era*. "And that Mr George Grossmith has succeeded in 'doing' his, without either being dull or offensive, uninteresting or egotistical, is another proof of his innate tact and cleverness." Still more convincing proof that the book had succeeded in its aims came from the letters he received about it personally. Among them was one from the celebrated beauty and actress Lillie Langtry, who read it not in a train but on a voyage to America, and who was delighted to find it "so entirely free from affectation and the self-conceit common in memoirs." Equally flattering was reciter Clifford Harrison. To *him* the book was "charming - unaffected and admirable". More, it was "a long way the best thing of the kind that has appeared – even counting the reminiscences that have taken the formidable form of two volumes." And if *that* was not a case of giving its author ideas . . .

III

"It was during the run of *Ruddigore*, in which I played Dame Hannah." The writer here was Rosina Brandram, the company's principal contralto following the departure of Alice Barnett late in 1883. "In the second act I had to fight Robin Oakapple (Mr G. Grossmith) with a poignard," which was normally placed prior to performance in her dressing-room. But one night when her cue for it came, there was a hitch: the "wretched thing" was nowhere to be found, and (her account continues) "I absolutely refused to go on, as without it, it was quite impossible to play the scene.

"Everyone urged and implored me, and Mr Barrington, seeing the stage wait, went into the property-room and brought out something [which he] thrust into my hand, at the same time giving me a push which caused me to appear in sight of the audience; so, *nolens volens*, I had to proceed, knowing that in my hand I carried an insignificant gas key. I did the best I could to conceal this fact, and went on with the business. I had to rush and snatch a large dagger from a figure in armour and fling my supposed poignard to Mr Grossmith, exclaiming: 'Harkye, miscreant! You have secured me, and I am your poor prisoner; but if you think I cannot take care of myself you are very much mistaken. Now then, it's one to one, and let the best man win.' Imagine my consternation when I saw by the expression on Mr Grossmith's face, as

121

he stooped to pick up the key, that he meant mischief; my heart went right into my shoes, but I did not think he was going to give me away in the manner in which he did, for, holding up the gas key to the audience, he said: 'How can I defend myself with this?' Of course there was a laugh; my feelings may be better imagined than described. If ever I contemplated murder it was at that moment. I would willingly have slain both Mr Grossmith and Mr Barrington . . ."

Ruddigore, then, had its lighter side. And, in the wider sense, it came neither into the category of failure which in some quarters it was labelled, nor yet – going by previous G. & S. standards – into that of total success;[14] and after eight months or so the signs were clear it would soon have to come off. Once again, though, as had happened following the withdrawal of *Princess Ida* three years previously, no new opera was ready. This time, indeed, no new opera had even been started; worse, for several months it remained questionable whether there would be a new opera at all, for Gilbert and Sullivan were going through one of their disgruntled and non-productive periods, as had been the case that previous time too. So once again Carte fell back on a revival, in this instance *H.M.S. Pinafore*. In *Pinafore* Grossmith of course played his old role; and he also, for much of its run, accompanied the opera with another sketch: *Homburg; or, Haunted by The Mikado*, a "personal reminiscence". The sub-title of this sketch provided the main theme of its content: since the production of the Japanese opera he had not been able to escape from it anywhere. Even when he had "fled" to Homburg[15] there it was still, its tunes played by German bands, whistled by German boys. But he did not dwell entirely on *The Mikado* in the sketch, for he also used the Homburg setting as an excuse for a lighthearted debunking of things German – including on this count what would become another of his best-known songs, *The Happy Fatherland*:

"The Germans are a noble race, and of that race I'll sing.
They love their Pas and adore their Mas, and they idolise their King.
And these frugal folk are a happy folk, and their life is one long song,
Praising the Fatherland, the Happy Fatherland, which they sing the whole
day long."

Following *Pinafore* came a revival of *The Pirates of Penzance*; and following *that* – to haunt Grossmith anew – the return after only eighteen

[14] Though, oddly enough, it had inspired back in March a full-scale, if not very successful theatrical parody, *Ruddy George; or, Robin Redbreast*. The title was, supposedly, a reference to Grossmith's make-up as Robin Oakapple. Worse still – if possible – the character in the parody is described as "*a gross myth* of the nineteenth century"!
[15] "Fled" equalled a three-week holiday he had taken there the previous year during *The Mikado* run.

months of *The Mikado*. Each of these three operas in turn proved once more the success it had been when performed originally; with the result that by the end of the sequence Grossmith had chalked up close on seven hundred performances of Sir Joseph Porter, around four hundred and thirty of Major-General Stanley and more than seven hundred and fifty of Ko-Ko.

But by the autumn of 1888 a respite from *The Mikado* was at last at hand. For Gilbert and Sullivan had at length resolved their problems and there was to be a new Savoy opera after all. That opera, set in the Tower of London, would ultimately be called *The Yeomen of the Guard*. It was the nearest G. & S. ever came to a straight or serious work, an attempt to portray real people in real situations. The result was an interweaving of the sombre and solemn with much typically Gilbertian humour; and this came out most forcefully in the part assigned to Grossmith: a character by the name of Jack Point.

Jack Point is a "strolling jester" who comes to the Tower with his partner and sweetheart Elsie Maynard hoping to "pick up some silver" by entertaining the local citizenry. They can sing; they claim to dance a variety of dances; while Point's specific qualifications as a jester are, at least in his own eyes, almost unlimited. "Marry, sir," he informs one of the other characters,

"I have a pretty wit. I can rhyme you extempore; I can convulse you with quip and conundrum; I have the lighter philosophies at my tongue's tip; I can be merry, wise, quaint, grim and sardonic, one by one or all at once; I have a pretty turn for anecdote; I know all the jests – ancient and modern – past, present and to come; I can riddle you from dawn of day to set of sun, and, if that content you not, well on to midnight and the small hours . . ."

In the midst of all this unaccustomed Gilbertian seriousness, with anticipated jokes not always forthcoming, "the downright fun of Mr Grossmith" (commented *The Times* after the first performance)[16] "was almost a relief." But the "fun" of Jack Point is very different from the jaunty, inconsequential fun of Ko-Ko or the whimsical incongruities of John Wellington Wells. For as the plot progresses things for the jester go badly wrong. He is obliged to watch helplessly as Elsie is wooed away from him by another man, and the opera ends on a poignant, even tragic note with Point, knowing he has finally lost her, falling "insensible" (as the stage direction puts it) at her feet. But this ending, it seems, bothered Grossmith. He was convinced – and almost certainly warned Gilbert of his fears – that audiences would never accept a tragic finale from him. He was too much the accepted comedian; however serious

[16] October 3rd, 1888.

he tried to be, people would still laugh. It was a valid consideration; Gilbert was quick to see its force, and was apparently quite willing for Grossmith to play the scene with the tragedy toned down.[17]

So far, so feasible. But in later years the idea gained currency that he had not so much toned the tragedy down as turned it into clownish comedy. To quote from the reminiscences of Henry Lytton, he fell down in a way that was "irresistibly funny"; while a story even circulated that as the curtain fell on the first night, the "insensible" jester, lying prostrate in the centre of the stage, raised a leg and waggled it playfully in the air. Lytton's chief concern, though, was to emphasise the contrast between Grossmith's performance and his own unashamedly tragic interpretation of the scene. Moreover, it is questionable whether he actually saw him play the part himself; and his account, therefore, must be weighed against other, more direct evidence. "I saw the piece several times," wrote another G. & S. chronicler, S. J. Adair Fitz-gerald, "and the pathos of Grossmith's final fall struck me as being very fine indeed." True, the *Era*, perhaps a trifle puzzled by the whole thing, could write: "The finale ... ends the opera brightly ... all ends happily." But of far more significance was the fact that if Grossmith in that scene *did* do anything to undermine the characterisation as he had developed it through the rest of the piece, this escaped the notice of the contemporary reviewers entirely. To take the summing up of just one of them, Clement Scott (?) in the *Daily Telegraph*:

"It may be [that Grossmith's] warmest admirers were surprised at the merits of his jester – an assumption of very considerable subtlety, and one in which no ordinary difficulties are surmounted. Whether giving expression to poor Jack's professional wit, or hiding a sorry heart behind light words ... Mr Grossmith was the master of the part he assumed."

Writing on October 7th, a member of the previous night's audience congratulated him on a character that "as conceived and drawn by Mr Gilbert and interpreted by you," was "one of the most admirable creations seen on the stage for a long time." But, of no less significance, it was also to be the last stage part he would play for some time to come. Early in the new year, 1889, he informed D'Oyly Carte he wanted to make a break. It was not a sudden decision; he had previously hinted on a number of occasions that this would come sooner or later. The

[17] Indeed Grossmith's warning (if the fact of it be accepted) may even have come to him as something of a reassurance. For to Gilbert the *Yeomen*, all its solemnity notwithstanding, was still a "comic" opera – he stressed the point in another connection in a letter to Sullivan on the very day of its opening; and whatever Grossmith's concern about the ending, he himself was plagued by the still greater fear that the Savoy public might react unfavourably to the whole work.

reason too was straightforward enough: a call, more and more persistent, back to the entertainment platform. He had of late been receiving offers of engagements from all over the provinces. Whereas back in 1877 he had been keen to settle down and establish himself in London, now he was ready to widen his geographical scope once more. He had by this time all the contacts he needed. His name was well known. His association with "Gilbert and Sullivan", on which at the outset he had hopefully set store, had paid off a thousand times. Nor was it surprising that after exclusively playing works by the same author and composer for so long, he felt he needed a change.

He did not, though, intend the break to be anything more than temporary – six to eight months perhaps, time enough to undertake a substantial tour and still be able to return to the Savoy to take some part in the *Yeomen*'s eventual successor. In addition, he hoped to keep his departure a secret until the last possible moment. But – inevitably – rumours leaked out. Was there any truth, W. Davenport Adams, dramatic critic of the *Globe*, wrote to him as early as February, in a paragraph which had just appeared in a provincial paper to the effect that he was going? "The idea of your leaving the Savoy will be *dreadful* to Londoners!"

But, dreadful or not, it was going to happen, for his initial provincial engagements – if no others – were already being fixed. He would start his tour at the beginning of September. His final performance of Jack Point was given on Saturday, August 17th. Again, he had wanted the fact of this to remain unpublicised. But again the news leaked out. The *Era* reported the following week:

"Mr George Grossmith's temporary adieu to the London public was made with much grace and tact at the Savoy Theatre on Saturday last. [At the end of the evening] he was summoned before the curtain and, a speech being inevitable, Mr Grossmith judiciously made his oration as brief as possible. He said his adieu was not a farewell, but he had received so many invitations to visit the provinces that he felt it would be unpolite to continue to refuse them. He was very 'fit', he said, just then for such an expedition. Here one of the 'gods' called out 'Good old Grossmith!' to which Mr Grossmith cheerfully replied 'Good old Gallery!' and made his exit amidst loud applause ..."

Two prominent members of the audience, the philanthropist Baroness Burdett-Coutts and her husband, Ashmead Bartlett, were afterwards taken behind the scenes by D'Oyly Carte to wish him good luck; another notable face out front that night had been his brother, Weedon. And it was, for all he may have wished it otherwise, an occasion of some emotion. He had a faint recollection, he wrote in after years, of shedding

125

an "extra real tear" during the haunting duet, *I Have a Song to Sing, O*, with which the opera closes.

The rest of the company had wanted to make him a parting gift. Barrington, who had left prior to *Yeomen* to try his hand at theatrical management, had come away with a writing desk; various presentations to other members of the company had been made over the years. But expecting as he was to be back again so soon, he had turned the offer down, and accordingly nothing was done – then. Yet Gilbert at least felt that things could not be left like that; for a short while later he was writing to Sullivan:

> "Don't you think we ought to mark Grossmith's departure by a present of some kind? He is a d----d bad actor, but he has worked very hard for us, and has endeavoured in every way to meet our wishes during the thirteen [sic] years of his engagement. If we presented him with (say) a piece of plate, value about £50, it would be a graceful recognition of his unvarying zeal and good will."

Sullivan must have approved – so too must Carte; for in due course Grossmith received from the "triumvirate" a "genuine big surprise packet". It contained, he later wrote in *Piano and I*,[18] two large solid silver punch bowls, inscribed as follows:

> "To
> George Grossmith,
> from Arthur Sullivan, W. S. Gilbert,
> and R. D'Oyly Carte,
> at the close of his first
> theatrical engagement,
> which lasted twelve years,
> 1877–1889."

"He is a d----d bad actor!" It remains, before leaving this section of his life, to sum up Grossmith's work in G. & S. overall. The verdict will be to a certain extent inconclusive, for the obvious reason that the only truly satisfactory assessment of any performer can come from studying him in actual performance; and after this lapse of time all the evidence is of necessity second-hand. But – "a d----d bad actor!" Was this really Gilbert's opinion of him as a player, and had he only been waiting to see the back of him before giving that opinion voice? The answer – on both counts – is clearly no, but the comment needs amplifying, and Gilbert himself provided that amplification in an interview a few years later:

[18] His second volume of reminiscences, published in 1910 (see page 194). *On Tour; or, Piano and I* was also to be the title of one of his post-Savoy sketches.

"I used" (he explained) "to invent a perfectly fresh character each time for George Grossmith, but he always did it in his own way – most excellent in itself, crisp and smart, but 'G.G.' to the end. Consequently everyone said: 'Why, Grossmith always has the same character'; whereas, if different individuals had acted them, each would have been distinctive. It was no fault of Grossmith's than whom a more amiable and zealous *collaborateur* does not exist. It arose from the fact that his individuality was too strong to be concealed."

The essence of that individuality, and hence of all his playing, lay undoubtedly in his background. He came to G. & S. as a solo entertainer. And the art of the entertainer, though not entirely dissimilar, is overall very different from that of the actor. The actor submerges his own personality in that of other characters; he also has the use of costume, make-up and a variety of properties to sustain him. By contrast, the entertainer of Grossmith's type retains his own character; uses little or no costume or make-up; remains, in a word, himself. Again, as Percy Fitzgerald was to put it in a book on the Savoy operas published in 1894: "Theatrical effects are large, broad and general, whereas those of the entertainer are minute and 'stippled in', as it were." But while this difference of emphasis and approach might have told against Grossmith in any other area of Victorian stage work, it was eminently suited to the style developed at the Opera Comique and the Savoy; for it was just such a passion for minutiae and detail, just that insistence that every action, every gesture, every word spoken should have meaning and relevance that so marked out Gilbert as a producer for the musical stage.

Fitzgerald's references to Grossmith in his G. & S. roles taken individually, *Princess Ida* excepted (his King Gama, he considered, seeming "somewhat after the pattern of monarchs in burlesque") were entirely complimentary.[19] And the press, as the various quotations given in the preceding pages will have made clear, rarely wrote of his performances in terms other than favourable. Of only one aspect of his work was there anything like repeated criticism: his lack of a true operatic voice. The *Musical Times* had drawn attention to this straight away in its review of the original *Sorcerer*.[20] With *Iolanthe* the complaint came in the write-up in the year's *Dramatic Notes*: "Mr George Grossmith acted in his peculiar style as the Lord Chancellor, but his songs would be more appreciated if his voice were better." While for *The Mikado* it was the turn of the *Whitehall Review*: *Titwillow*,[21] that paper believed, "would be a far prettier and more delicate number if someone with a better voice than Mr Grossmith's had to sing it."

[19] Not that this was altogether surprising – he actually dedicated the book to him.
[20] See page 11.
[21] His song in the second act.

All of which was fair enough. Grossmith himself never harboured any illusions as to his power and capacity in this respect. But if vocal capacity *was* his weakness, it was a weakness he minimised with remarkable skill. To quote the *Saturday Review* with regard to *Iolanthe*: "His admirable singing with no voice remains as it has always been – a feat at once astonishing and delightful to all who have any care for phrasing and intonation." And it was, too, a weakness more than offset by the many other – undisputed – qualities he brought to his roles, qualities which likewise had stood out well defined from the first. His exact, incisive diction, exemplified most obviously by the clarity with which he delivered his patter songs; his sense of timing and ability to capture an audience, to hold it and draw laughter from it as and when he wanted; his agility on his feet that showed itself to happiest effect in the comic dances with which he embellished so many of his solos and other musical numbers in which he was concerned; and, most important of all, a dry yet perky sense of comedy and an appreciation, crucial to any actor in a Gilbertian role, of the value of underplaying and of never attempting to force the humour.

That his own success as an individual had been a major factor in promoting and establishing the success of "G. & S." as a whole, there is, moreover, no question. But his contribution to the operas did not end there, for his interpretations of his roles, guided and instructed as he was in playing them by Gilbert himself, have provided a model which has influenced their playing ever since. To this day those roles are referred to as often as not as the "Grossmith roles". For "a d----d bad actor" it was no mean achievement.

PART THREE
LATER YEARS, 1889–1912

CHAPTER SEVEN

Piano Entertainer, Part II

"The well-filled house – the crowded fashionable circles – that greeted Mr
George Grossmith upon his one-night visit on Monday was unmistakable
testimony to the charm which surrounds a talented entertainer."
(*East Anglian Daily Times*, of one of his "recitals" at Ipswich)

Hotel Waiter: (*expecting tip*). I hear you had a very good house tonight, Mr
Grossmith. *I* sent two gentlemen from the Commercial Room. They were
going to see the performing donkeys at the circus, but I said *you* was more
amusing."
(George Grossmith – *The Trials of an Entertainer*)

It is Monday, September 2nd, 1889; the time afternoon; the place
the Portland Hall, Southsea. Inside, Grossmith stands looking around
in a state of near panic. The opening recital of his provincial tour is just
a few hours away. But this is more than a case of first night nerves pure
and simple. For he has expressly stipulated to his agent that he is not
prepared to perform in any hall holding more than four hundred people
at the outside, and this one, it seems, will seat over a thousand. He calls
his secretary over. The latter must send his agent a wire; must tell him
he cannot – will not – go on.

He looks round again. Away at the back he suddenly notices the
figure of a man. The man is moving along the rows of seats, tying a
numbered card to each chair in turn. He watches him, tense and puzzled.
What on earth can this mean? Abandoning speculation, he mounts the
platform and, trying to calm himself, begins running his fingers over the
keys of the piano. At length the man finishes and comes towards him.
He turns out to be the hall-keeper. He says:

"You'll see this hall fuller tonight, sir, than it has ever been before.
The reserved seats are taken right down to where you see those
numbers."

Grossmith nods without conviction, without really comprehending.
He returns, lost in anxiety, to his hotel, bracing himself for the worst.

Seven thirty – seven forty-five. The audience for the evening is starting
to assemble. A large audience, a packed, capacity audience; more, an
audience that is unmistakably fashionable, that includes General Sir
George and Lady Willis from Government House, Portsmouth; Lady

131

Tryon, wife of a vice-admiral; and – more notable still – royalty in the person of Prince George of Wales, the future King George V.

Eight o'clock. Time for the entertainment to begin. But at the last minute there is a holdup. Someone else has inadvertently taken or been given the seat reserved for the Prince and has to be tactfully moved. Grossmith, concerned only to get on the platform, to get the evening over, is kept waiting while things are sorted out. But at length everybody is settled. The moment has come. Immaculate in his evening dress, carnation in his buttonhole, his sleek brown hair well brushed down, the pince-nez he invariably wears fixed firmly on his nose, he makes his entrance and takes his seat at the piano.

He casts off by playing a few instantly recognisable bars from *The Yeomen of the Guard*; then he introduces the sketch that will form part one of the evening's programme. It is called, he says, *Society up to Date*. He embarks directly on his theme. Take first, he suggests, modern men. There on the one hand are the old men, forever trying to appear youthful. And there on the other are their juniors trying no less assiduously to look mature. While as for the ladies . . . See them in the ballroom. Which of them are wearing the low dresses? Why, the elder ones, the matrons, and they alone; quite definitely not their daughters – such styles are forbidden *them*. And when it comes to the dancing itself, which of them are on the floor? Why again, only the older ladies; the younger ones, dance after dance, remaining inactively seated.

Next he moves on to modern music, and the ballads and sentimental songs of the past decade. He surveys his audience with a knowledgeable look. "There is a tendency, ladies and gentlemen, in modern ballad poetry," he says, "to repeat a word frequently and fervently, such as 'Heart of my Heart'; 'Love of my Love'; 'Soul of my Soul'; and, if necessary, 'Heel of my Heel'. As I have no desire to be behind the times, here is a song of my own entitled *Thou of my Thou*. *You* may be able to fathom the depths of its poetical meaning. *I* can't."

"Only once did we meet, only once did we part,
But I loved thee, oh! whole of my heart of my heart.
I've waited for thee on the brow of the hill,
My heart it was aching, and breaking at will.
I saw thee but once, and I heaved but a sigh,
'Twas a heave of a heave, and for thee I would die.
I knew thou would'st come, and we never shall part,
Thou hast come, oh! whole of my heart of my heart."

This song, a parody of a popular contemporary ballad called *The Garden of Sleep*, is received with delight. There has been, indeed, an almost continuous ripple of laughter from the first. Gradually he relaxes, his rapport with the audience increasing every minute. He moves on next to the "modern elocutionist" and gives a recitation, *Brokers Ahead; or, the Old Armchair*, parodying this time a current style of verse. And finally he turns again to the ballroom to discourse on past and present dances, highlighting in particular the old-fashioned but ever popular *Sir Roger de Coverley*. He imitates a middle-aged couple. The lady has not missed the dance for twenty years and she insists that her husband join in it with her now. He immediately protests: it is late; he is tired; he has forgotten the steps. In vain. He is made to get up and partner her, and in a frantic effort to reach the top of the dancing lines, the two of them find themselves at the bottom; and at length, completely worn out with the exertion, he sinks on to the nearest seat. The pianist meanwhile has been pounding away nonstop at the keyboard until his fingers ache with pain, leading him to try playing first with one hand, then with the other. The whole scene, as Grossmith portrays and develops it, is brought to life with ever-changing comic facial expression.

Then he sings his now famous song, *See me Dance the Polka*, and rises. The audience not merely applauds but cheers him loudly. He bows his acknowledgment; bows again; and disappears. Approximately fifty minutes have passed. It is the first interval.

Five minutes later. The audience settles once more. Grossmith makes his second entrance. Part two of his entertainment, lasting about forty minutes this time, is to be one of the sketches he has previously given at the Savoy: *Homburg; or, Haunted by The Mikado*. The sketch has no less appeal here in Southsea than it has had earlier in London. The Hampshire public may never have seen Grossmith himself in G. & S., but his connection with it is well known, and thanks to regular visits and seasons around the county by D'Oyly Carte's touring companies, they are fully familiar with the operas themselves. While his genial taking off of things German – his musical parodies of Beethoven, Mozart, Wagner and Mendelssohn; his singing of *The Happy Fatherland* – is assuredly relished no less.

Another – still briefer – interval. And then part three of the entertainment, an innovation this, for two parts have hitherto been his and every other entertainer's norm. This last, and much the shortest part, is devoted to "Humorous Illustrations and Imitations of our Amateur Singers and Professionals". His mimicry in each case is sharp, pointed – but always good-humoured. The amateurs he takes off include "the comic sentimental man" and "the sentimental comic man", the professionals Corney Grain, Arthur Roberts and Clifford Harrison. His rapport with the audience is now absolute. At the end the applause is deafening. "As an

133

entertainer," declares the local *Hampshire Post*, "he is without doubt the most successful heard in Southsea for many years."

The following evening he presents a quite different programme in the same hall to a still more enthusiastic audience and an even more rapturous reception.

The agent to whom he had entrusted the arrangements for his tour was a man named Narcisso Vert, whose office was in Cork Street near Piccadilly. Agents by this time had come to be regarded as more or less essential for any professional peripatetic entertainer, and he had felt obliged first to sound out the possibility of having in this capacity Richard D'Oyly Carte, who had himself been running a successful operatic and concert agency since 1870. Carte, it appears, would have acted for him in this way if pressed. But always a busy man, he was at this juncture even busier than usual, with two full-scale new projects, a hotel and a second new theatre, engaging his attention besides his normal work at the Savoy. Grossmith therefore asked whether he (Carte) would object to his approaching Vert. Far from it, said Carte, he could not do better.

Vert agreed to take him on, to "pioneer" him round the United Kingdom; though, as Grossmith saw it, he was too well acquainted with the ups and downs of the concert and entertainment business, not to mention the prima donna temperaments of so many of its performers, to do so with any obvious enthusiasm. But from the first their own association proved not only fruitful and profitable but happy and free from all disputes.

His experience at Southsea led him, through his secretary, to inform Vert that objection to large halls was now withdrawn. From Southsea he moved on to other places around the South-East: among them Southampton, Weymouth, Winchester, Eastbourne, Brighton, St Leonard's, Folkestone and Dover. It was an endlessly busy time. Vert, who dealt with all the administrative side of the work, had procured him an engagement every day, afternoon or evening, five or six days a week, right through – with the exception of a three week break at Christmas – to the following May.

By then he had achieved what he had set out to achieve, a provincial tour of several months. It was time, if he were to keep to his original plan, to make his return to the Savoy. But at some point during those months he had reached a new and very different decision: he would not go back to the Savoy at all. There were, it seems likely, three reasons that lay behind this change of heart. First, almost certainly, was the success of the tour itself, a success that had exceeded even his most optimistic hopes. Second, hardly less significant (as he was never ashamed to admit) was the question of money. Already it was clear – if indeed it had not been clear beforehand – that he would find himself substantially better off working on his own. Already his earnings from just those few months[1] had far exceeded the salary (£2,000 or more a year by the end – a substantial sum in itself) he would have received over the same period from D'Oyly Carte. And third was the sense of freedom, of independence, the feeling of being his own master, of being able to let himself go, to do what he liked, after so many years of obeisance, voluntary though this had been, to the will and drill of Gilbert. Accordingly, in the autumn of the next year, 1890, he embarked upon his second solo provincial tour.

This time his itinerary took him before long to Scotland. And while he was in Scotland there came a surprise. He received a command from Queen Victoria to give a recital at Balmoral Castle. He could hardly refuse – not that he wanted to; it was too great an honour – even though it meant cancelling an engagement at Dundee. His acceptance received, Sir Henry Ponsonby, the Queen's secretary, wrote to him concerning the arrangements:

> "As time is precious to you, I may explain that you can come by a train which leaves Aberdeen at twelve twenty – or else somewhere about five – but this latter would not reach Balmoral till past eight p.m. . . .
>
> "We can give you a room here to sleep. But it is possible you may prefer to return to Ballater at night – eight miles – so as to start by the earliest train next morning, as I see you contemplate reaching Inverness – a long journey."

He did, sure enough, decide to settle for a return to Ballater, rather than accept that bedroom at the castle. With all the excitement such an occasion was likely to involve, there was a strong possibility (he was convinced) he would have a restless night afterwards. And given that, it seemed better to be in a place where he could call on his secretary and the hotel landlord rather than risk disturbing the dukes, lords, ladies-in-waiting and heaven knew what other exalted personages who made up the Queen's household.

Soon the great day arrived: Wednesday, November 12th, 1890.[2] Shortly before ten o'clock that evening he took his seat at the piano in the castle ballroom and began. He had settled for giving a somewhat shortened version of his normal programme, merging the first two sketches together to make a more orthodox two-part entertainment rather than his now customary three. And if he had suffered any prior doubts as to how his lighthearted chaffing of society, his gentle satire,

---

[1] £10,000 in the first seven months, according to various reports.

[2] The date had been brought forward a day from that originally fixed – which also meant an adjustment of his other arrangments.

his songs, chat, quips and mimicry would go down in so august an atmosphere, those doubts were rapidly dispelled. "His imitations were wonderful," the Queen wrote in her journal, "and all so well done, devoid of vulgarity. He plays so well on the piano, accompanying himself. We were kept in fits of laughter ... He is a very funny little man."[3] (She laughed so much, he told an interviewer many years afterwards, "she made me laugh too.") When he had finished and had retired to an adjoining room, one of her attendants came round to tell him the Queen "desired" him to return and sing *See me Dance the Polka*. So back he went to comply and in so doing managed to mix up the words of two of the verses.

But even that was not the end of the evening, for Ponsonby now appeared, to usher him into the Queen's presence in the drawing-room. The Queen received him graciously – so graciously in fact, he recorded in *Piano and I*, that for a moment or two he was close to being tongue-tied. And then, seemingly anxious to draw him out, she remarked:

"They tell me you are very much missed at the Savoy."

It was a subject about which he clearly felt a certain awkwardness or embarrassment, a tinge perhaps even of guilt for having deserted the G. & S. banner. The Queen had put the royal foot in it.

> "I felt that horrible choking sensation, and nearly lost my composure again. The Queen, evidently noticing this, asked me if I liked the music of *The Gondoliers*.[4] Of course, I replied truthfully in the affirmative. She said she thought it was extremely delightful, and that she had it played on her orchestra. She talked with me for some little time, and eventually bowed and left the drawing-room accompanied by her attendants. I was much impressed by her quiet, sweet voice and her delightful little smile."

He was asked to sign the royal visitors' book. He also received from her a memento of the occasion: a "watch chain appendage in the shape of a V.R. monogram set in diamonds [and] surrounded with a garter". He chatted with two of her daughters and other members of the court before leaving. Then the following night it was back to normal with an entertainment at Aberdeen (where he had also been on the Monday) and an audience containing a large contingent of university students. "The students have arranged to give 'Gee-Gee', as he is familiarly known to them, a cordial welcome tonight," the *Aberdeen Journal* had recorded of his Monday recital. "Cordial" presumably meant rousing. The rarified air of Balmoral must have seemed like another world.

As his first provincial tour had led to a second, so that second in turn would lead to a third. And in the course of these years and the years

---

[3] *RA Queen Victoria's Journal*, November 12th, 1890.
[4] The successor at the Savoy (December 1889) to the *Yeomen*.

that were to follow, there was scarcely a place of any size in the British Isles that he did not visit at least once. Thanks to Vert, his appearances were regularly advertised in advance in the appropriate local press and nearly always made the subject of a report afterwards. His recitals everywhere became genuine occasions.

Nonetheless, it was inevitable that, from time to time, he would find if not an unenthusiastic house then certainly a house somewhat less than full. In particular, a recital clashing with a production by a local amateur dramatic society (if that production happened to include participants from among the aristocracy) or a matinee clashing likewise with a confirmation service in a cathedral city were sure guarantees of empty seats. Again there were other occasions made less than vintage by some unwonted distraction or discomfort: people arriving late and noisily disturbing him and the rest of the audience; a fire in an adjacent building during one of his recitals at Kilmarnock; the hall for one at Llandudno so cold that the audience began pulling on mufflers, he followed their example by turning up his collar, and everyone including himself was shivering. But, overall, such tribulations and dampeners were rare; though if he ever had moments when success and fame seemed in danger of going to his head, there was usually somebody around to provide the necessary corrective. He reproduced in *Piano and I* the following conversation overheard during the course of his travels:

Lady: Are you going to Mr Grossmith's recital tonight?
Gentleman: Whose recital?
Lady: Grossmith's.
Gentleman: I've never heard of him.
Lady: He used to act at the Savoy Theatre.
Gentleman: I never go to theatres.
Lady: But you may have heard of some of his songs. *See me Dance the Polka*, for instance.
Gentleman: No.
Lady: You must have heard of his book. I saw your own daughter reading it the other day.
Gentleman: Oh, Grossmith! You mean the man who wrote *The Deserted Village*. Of *course* I've heard of him.

But if the work was beyond question enjoyable, it was also beyond question demanding and, in terms of the lifestyle involved, exhausting. In particular, the amount of travelling it necessitated was sometimes colossal. "I always disliked travelling, and suppose I always shall," he had written of his initial peripatetic days in *A Society Clown*. Yet he can hardly have disliked it as much as all that, or he would surely not have subjected himself to it, as he was now doing, week after week, virtually day after day, for eight or nine months every year. As an illustration of the way his itinerary might work out, here is a list of the

137

places at which he would perform during a single fortnight in 1895:

Monday, November 18th: Glasgow
Tuesday, November 19th: Paisley
Wednesday, November 20th: Kilmarnock
Thursday, November 21st: Helensburgh
Friday, November 22nd: Glasgow
Saturday, November 23rd: Galashiels
Monday, November 25th: Newcastle
Tuesday, November 26th: Sunderland
Wednesday, November 27th: York
Thursday, November 28th: Ripon
Friday, November 29th: Darlington
Saturday, November 30th: Stockton

All this travelling and moving around meant, too, many long hours on uncomfortable trains and, with some of his journeys necessitating up to five changes, much hanging about on cold and draughty stations. Not that he was normally on his own; for with him to most places went his current secretary (Heywood Brettell, an old schoolfriend, in the first instance, then for some years a Mr Westropp); a man whose job it was to take charge of the piano;[5] and even, on one tour, his valet. At times he contrived to amuse himself by studying and ruminating on the various railway notices displayed around – as, for example, that instruction "Passengers are requested not to put their feet on the seats." "What man," he argued, "ever does put his feet on the seats? He puts his muddy boots which enclose his feet on the seats." He also drew amusement from some of the hundred-and-one place names he was constantly coming across. "I find on March 4th . . . I am at Shepton Mallet (wherever that may be)" he wrote in a letter to one acquaintance. "I don't like the name Sudbury," he wrote to another. "Do you know why? Because it is exactly like *Sunbury* spoken thro' the nose." Nor was he above coining imaginary place names of his own: "Slosh-in-the-Hole"; "Mudborough"; "Puddleton-on-Swash".

But his tours during these years were not confined to the British Isles, to Shepton Mallet, Puddleton-on-Swash and their innumerable small town and rural equivalents elsewhere in the country, let alone to such bustling centres as Glasgow, Newcastle and, of course, London. For five times he was also to cross the Atlantic, to present his very English entertainment in a variety of the towns and cities, all quite different again, to be found in America and Canada.

[5] Which also normally travelled with him – or, on certain journeys, ahead of him – and sometimes under conditions calculated to do it anything but good.

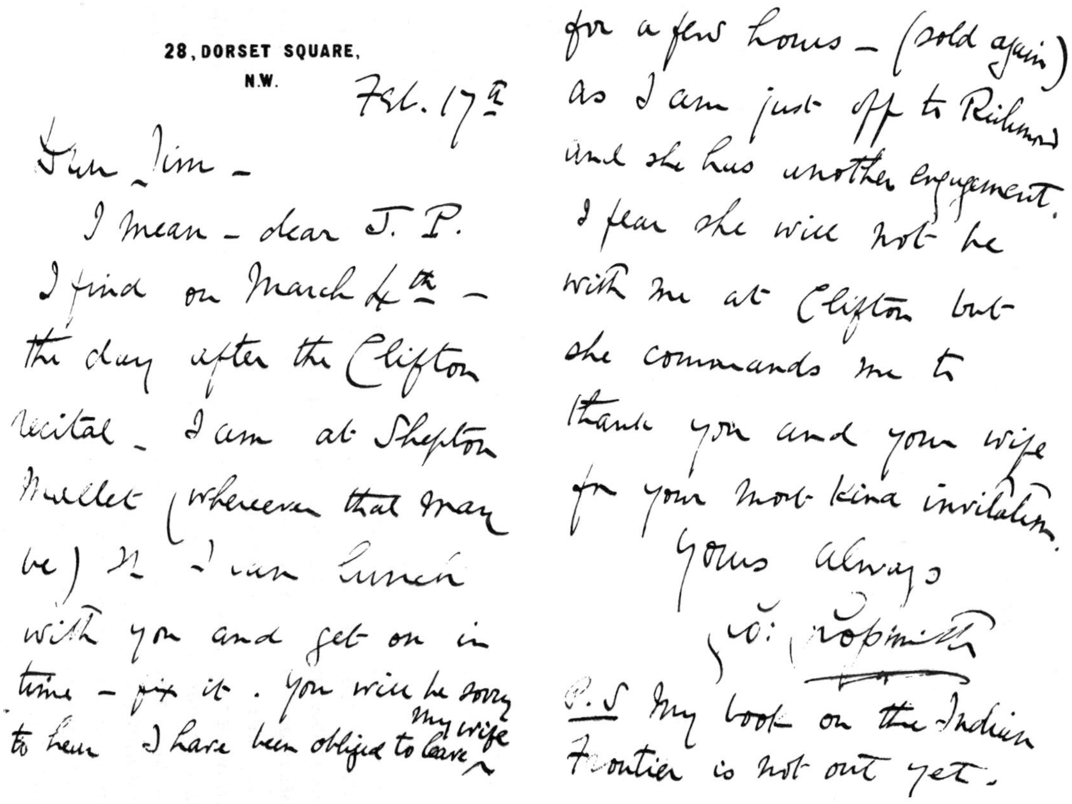

28, DORSET SQUARE,
N.W.

Feb. 17th

Dear Jim –
I mean – dear J.P. –
I dine on March 4th –
the day after the Clifton
recital – I am at Shepton
Mallet (wherever that may
be) so I run down
with you and get on in
time – but it – you will be sorry
my wife
to hear I have been obliged to leave

you a few hours – (cold again)
As I am just off to Richmond
and she has another engagement.
I fear she will not be
with me at Clifton but-
she commands me to
thank you and your wife
for your most kind invitation.

Yours always
(signature)

P.S. My book on the Indian
Frontier is just out yet.

Fig. 10. A letter (characteristically jocular) from Grossmith to Arrowsmith.

The suggestion that he undertake an American visit had been mooted in the early days of his first British tour, and had come, as might be expected, from Vert. He himself, despite some understandable misgivings as to how the Americans would take to him, was ready and willing – but there was one snag. He was determined his wife should go with him; and "Mrs Gee-Gee" dreaded the sea, having in the past suffered intense misery even crossing the Channel on a calm day. But eventually, after the "greatest trouble" on his part, she allowed herself to be persuaded, and it was arranged that they leave from Liverpool on October 19th, 1892.[6]

The ship on which they sailed was the *Teutonic*, one of the largest and fastest liners then afloat; and on board they were treated as celebrities. The purser "paid us every possible attention." He "even offered me a large state-room with a double brass bed in it, but my wife and I decided to keep our cabin with its two small beds." And for some hours, crossing that night towards the south of Ireland, even Mrs Gee was more or less relaxed. Early next morning they docked briefly at Queenstown.[7] But then, as they headed out for the open sea, "the Atlantic rollers introduced themselves in a most unpleasant fashion."

"I said to one of the officers: 'Isn't this a very rough sea?'

He said: 'Oh dear, no, this is nothing.' "

Even so, whether nothing or not, it had already become too much for his wife who, soon after Queenstown, had taken to their cabin, there to stay, visited at frequent intervals by the ship's doctor, for the remainder of the voyage. But for himself, despite a sea that at times was genuinely heavy, he enjoyed the experience enormously, socialising with the other passengers (the smoking-room after dinner, he decided, was "exactly like a club") taking photographs, attending the Sunday morning service (remaining seated throughout the proceedings, it being virtually impossible to stand) and playing a part in the traditional ship's concert. And at last – one day late – they arrived in New York, were shepherded without too much difficulty through customs, then bundled off in a cab to a hotel at the bottom of Fifth Avenue. There in their suite (bedroom and "parlour" – American, as he discovered, for "sitting-room") they unpacked, for they were to stay in New York for some weeks.

---

[6] In *Piano and I* he gave the date (by implication) as early November, one of the few dates he specified in the whole book. But clearly this was a lapse of memory after so many years.

[7] Now Cóbh.

His first recital was to be given on November 15th, at Chickering Hall. Came the day and – inevitably – his now customary first night nerves attacked him yet again. The portents, he convinced himself, were all against him. He was told that the hall itself, situated over the Chickering Pianoforte Warehouse, was a fire trap. An elaborate chrysanthemum show had recently been held nearby; wouldn't he come a poor second to that? In addition, though he was possibly unaware of this, the delectable comedienne and singer Marie Tempest had just opened in the city in a new comic opera. Worst of all the night, when it arrived, proved to be fearfully wet. But fire trap, chrysanthemums, rain – and Marie Tempest – notwithstanding, a large audience turned up, and at the first interval Vert, who had travelled over with him, appeared in his dressing-room confident and encouraging. "You're all right, don't be afraid. Go ahead – you've got 'em!"

The press reaction proved his confidence more than justified. A notable summing up was that of the *New York Herald*. "Two minutes after the dapper little fellow, typically English in manner and voice, but extremely modest and pleasing in his address, had appeared on the stage, a broad smile crept over the faces of his audience. It stayed there all the evening." "Such applause as recalled Mr Grossmith at the conclusion of his second [?] part never before woke the rafters of Chickering Hall," declared a second paper. The professional success of his tour was assured. If in some places people were slow to patronise him at first, once they did come in there was no holding them. American audiences, he came to consider, were the best he ever had anywhere.

And with professional success went immense popularity socially. He had warmed to the Americans immediately and they warmed to him. At the end of that first recital complete strangers came round to congratulate him. People called to see him at his hotel, showered him with invitations and hospitality, sent along their carriages – three or four of these on occasion turning up simultaneously, just to make things awkward – to take his wife for drives while he was giving matinees. Then, too, he was put up for various clubs, among them the Racquet, a "jolly place" where, John Drew, a leading American actor, assured him, he would find "a lot of good fellows". "Dear George," wrote another American, journalist and playwright Stephen Fiske, "will you arrange your engagements so as to be the guest of the Lotos Club at a banquet two weeks from tonight . . . It will be a splendid advertisement for America."

From New York he and his party moved on at length to Boston where they spent a week and where he performed initially in a hall with a seating capacity topping (as he estimated) a staggering five thousand.

141

But if the size of that hall made a lasting impression on him in one respect, so in another, and with even greater force, did the Boston wind. It was his first or second day in the place, a bright day with a pure blue sky, a day, so it appeared, to tempt anyone out of doors. And Grossmith was tempted.

"Being thoroughly heated by radiators in the hotel, I thought I would like to get a little fresh air. [But] as I was passing through the hallway one of the office clerks said:
'Say, Mr Grossmith, you are surely not going out without an overcoat.'
I replied that I never wore an overcoat unless it was quite necessary.
He said: 'But, sir, we have a complaint out here known as pneumonia.'
I answered: 'Oh yes, we have the same complaint in England.'
The office clerk said: 'Yes, but it's not *our* pneumonia. You would know it if you had it.'
I said: 'Well, I think I'll risk it this beautiful morning.' So out I went.
"The flight of steps leading to the pavement was covered in the centre with boards to prevent you from slipping; the unprotected sides of the steps were pure ice. I had on my galoshes, or rubbers, as they call them out there, so I was [confident] of a firm footing. I was mistaken. I was all right until I got to the corner of the hotel, when a hurricane blew round the corner from the opposite street and hurled me completely off my feet. I did not hurt myself, but I got up with great difficulty and sneaked back to the hotel. I was too proud to acknowledge my defeat, and I said to the office clerk:
'I think I will take your advice and put on an overcoat.'
He replied laconically: 'I knew you would.'"

At length, moving west from Boston towards the Great Lakes, he gave a recital at Buffalo. Then, the morning after, it was goodbye temporarily to America as he and his wife took the train crossing the Niagara Bridge into Canada, all the passengers, including himself, rising to their feet and singing *God Save the Queen* as they reached the Canadian side of the border. Settling into their hotel late in the afternoon, however, the Grossmiths found themselves temporarily without their luggage. There was no sign of it at all that day, and when bedtime arrived his wife had to borrow a nightdress from one of the proprietor's daughters while he borrowed a nightshirt – rough in texture and two feet too long – from the hotel "boots". But anything was better than nothing at that moment, for it was the very depth of the Canadian winter:

"The next morning they were airing sheets out of the window. The temperature was below zero, and I was informed they could air sheets as well at that temperature as they could before a burning fire or in hot rooms."

From that first day indeed he always thought of Canada in terms of snow. Not once on any of his visits did he see it other than an unrelieved white.

A day off to look at the Niagara Falls, then it was on to Montreal for his first two recitals in the new country. "There was a very large audience and an equally large welcome, not only for myself but for my work," he wrote; and, as in America, this sort of welcome was his wherever he appeared. From Montreal he went on to Ottawa (where he caught a chill), Toronto, to Hamilton, London (Ontario) and other places until it was time to cross back to America for a further brief spell before at last sailing from New York for home.

So successful and enjoyable, in fact, had the whole tour proved, so much had he taken to the whole "confounded hemisphere" (as he affectionately called it) and its people, that it comes as no surprise to find him repeating the trip early in 1894. The physical problems involved in moving around so vast a landmass seem to have bothered him surprisingly little, even though some of the journeys between different centres, especially where this meant travelling overnight, could be horribly wearing and debilitating. But he had of course accumulated experiences galore and formed ideas of his own about what he had seen, and he would not have been George Grossmith had he not capitalised on such ideas by devising an "American" sketch for this first return visit. That sketch he entitled *How I Discovered America*. It was a take-off of various aspects of American life and society in the same way that most of his other sketches took off aspects of life and society in England.

The principal item he featured in it was, to use his own description, a skit on American comedies of the "old homestead" type. Part of this, a dig at the "modernity" that was so much part of the American ethos, ran as follows:

Pete: (*to his elder brother, who owns the farm*). John, what's all this, anyway? I hear you are going to sell the old homestead. Don't do it, John; don't do it. It will break mother's heart and the heart of everybody who loves the old, old home.
John: Say no more about it. I am going to sell the old home right away.
Pete: (*tearfully*). Don't sell it, John; don't sell it, John.
John: I am going to sell it.
Pete: But John, think, think, think! Remember how very long the old home has been in the family.
John: I can't help it. I am going to sell it.
Pete: (*imploringly*). Remember how long the old home has been in our family. It's been our home now for – for *nearly twelve years*.

Again, he made much of a song he included about the extrovert and emancipated *American Girl*:

"When I go out to dine
I drink no wine,
Yet I never suffer from gloom;

143

> For whenever I talk, or whenever I laugh,
> You can hear me all over the room.
>   My hat you can mark
>   In Central Park,
> As I drive my buggy alone;
>   I can take half a dozen young men to a ball
> And act as their chaperone."

But the whole sketch became a favourite with the Americans, not to mention the Canadians too.[8] He had to incorporate it into every recital he gave, not only on this tour but on all the three that were to follow.

And if his American visits were successful artistically and socially, they were no less so from the financial angle. Returning from the first of them, he could not resist chaffing a group of actors on the ease with which a man could make money single-handed. "You fellows," he said, "have to take out scenery, properties, plays and a large company when you want to perform, while I – look at me. I just landed in New York with my piano and a dress suit and I made £30,000." It may have been true; but as the actors concerned had not themselves had the best of seasons, it was hardly the most tactful of remarks; and back came an answer from Charles Brookfield,[9] a man known for a caustic tongue. "I daresay you did. But *you* have a certain advantage, George. No one else looks so damn funny in a dress suit!" It was a riposte that became possibly the most repeated remark made about Grossmith in his entire career. It may also – in passing – provide part of the key to his whole success as an entertainer.

All this touring – both in America and at home – and the time he had of necessity to spend writing and composing new material each year ought to have kept him occupied at full stretch and more during this early post-Savoy period. But if there was one trait in his character that would never, it seemed, be subdued, it was his readiness, his determination to fill every working moment he could. Thus he continued to fit in the occasional private house engagement and benefit matinee when not touring in the summer; while in the autumn of 1891 he had accepted a commission more time-consuming still. That commission came from W. S. Gilbert.

III

W. S. Gilbert in the early 1890s was a man in search of a collaborator. His long partnership with Sullivan seemed to have ended irrevocably in

---

[8] And not to mention the English either. At a recital he gave at St James's Hall just prior to this second American visit, it evoked "hearty and continuous merriment".

[9] *Not*, incidentally, Henry Irving, to whom it has also been attributed.

consequence of the so-called "carpet quarrel", the bitterest and ultimately the most protracted of all their disputes. His choice had fallen first on Alfred Cellier, and the result of the Gilbert–Cellier collaboration was a comic opera to be called *The Mountebanks*. But meanwhile, with *The Mountebanks* still in the early days of rehearsal, Gilbert – never one to let an idea slip – had prepared yet another work for the stage.

This time the work was an adaptation of a play of his own, *The Wedding March*, written in 1873. *The Wedding March* was itself an adaptation of a French farce, *Le Chapeau de Paille d'Italie* (*The Italian Straw Hat*) and was a rollicking story about a wedding party careering around London, the bridegroom and leading character glorying in the magnificent name of Woodpecker Tapping. Converted into a libretto with lyrics added, Gilbert considered, it might well serve as a new musical piece. But whom should he invite to compose the music in this case? Cellier was still engaged on *The Mountebanks*, and was anyway a sick – indeed, as it proved, a dying – man. So what, Gilbert wondered, about George Grossmith?

The invitation, it seems, took Grossmith completely by surprise; which in itself may be considered no surprise at all. He was flattered; and whatever doubts he felt as to his ability to cope with so substantial an assignment were soon allayed (according to Percy Fitzgerald) by Gilbert himself. With their years of working together in the past, theirs was a collaboration of possible potential. The piece as Grossmith set it contained a variety of musical numbers, all of a carefree and comic nature, one of the happiest being this song for Tapping himself on the subject of his bride-to-be:

> "Maria is simple and chaste –
>   She's pretty and tender and modest –
> But on one or two matters of taste
>   Her views are distinctly the oddest.
> Her virtue is something sublime –
>   No kissing – on that there's a stopper –
> When I try, she says, 'All in good time –
>   At present it's highly improper.'
>   Such virtue heroic I call,
>   To complain were the act of a noodle –
>   She's allowed to kiss no one at all
>   But her cousin – her cousin: young Foodle."

Nor, as things turned out, was Grossmith's involvement in *Haste to the Wedding*, as the piece in its new form was to be called, confined to his own contribution; for its production was to mark the professional

145

stage debut of his elder son, George Grossmith III,[10] as the character alluded to in the last line of that lyric just quoted: the bride's cousin, a "loutish simpleton", young Foodle. Arrangements and rehearsals completed, *Haste to the Wedding* opened on July 27th that year (1892) at the Criterion Theatre. And Grossmith was there, in true composer fashion, to conduct the first performance himself.

The house was crowded, eager not only to savour a new work by Gilbert but also perhaps for the chance of seeing Grossmith in so unexpected, so unaccustomed a role. It was a role, too, that he obviously relished. Jauntily – and seemingly with none of the first night nerves he suffered as a performer – he took his place in the pit. Nor did his behaviour once there altogether accord with theatrical convention. "It may be said," wrote the critic from the *Referee*, "that Mr George Grossmith's manner irritated some of the fastidious in the pit, who did not care to see the conductor of an orchestra on such easy terms with his audience. For my part I think George Grossmith as the conductor of an orchestra was quite as amusing as any character in the play." At the end of the evening he took his call on stage side by side with Gilbert. But whatever might be said of him as a conductor, of the music he had provided for the piece the critics had only criticism or, at best, semi-approval. The tunefulness, the gift of musical mimicry that served him more than adequately for the songs and sketches that made up his solo entertainments, or the occasional one-act skit or operetta, proved insufficient in themselves to sustain a theatrical work of full-length, particularly where chorus writing was involved; though it was not, admittedly, the music alone that came in for censure. The whole thing was summed up scathingly by the *Musical Times* at the beginning of September:

"The public did not care for a good farce spoiled, or for music which had few redeeming features. Apparently it is not enough to be a writer and singer of comic songs in order to blossom forth as a composer of comic opera. Strange that so obvious a lesson could not be learned without the mortification of experience."

That "mortification of experience" had been a short, almost negligible run. For despite a generally spirited production, *Haste to the Wedding* had lasted less than four weeks.

End of the collaboration of G. & G. And, in its place, renewal – against all earlier expectation – of the collaboration of G. & S. The prospect of another opera by the old firm naturally gave rise to much public excitement. It also prompted speculation on an additional score: might this – at

[10] See page 186.

long last – be the medium of Grossmith's return to the Savoy? Gilbert undoubtedly wanted him back for this latest piece. "Come and play in it," he wrote to him early in the new year (1893). "Half a million a week for you and all the net profits if you will."[11] But Grossmith, basking then in the delights of his first American tour, was not to be tempted, at least for the moment, and *Utopia Limited* opened without him the following October.[12] Which might have settled the matter, had it not soon become clear that Gilbert's *Utopia* was going to prove limited not only in name but also in the length of its run. Accordingly it was only a few months before speculation was rife once more. Gilbert, it was believed in some quarters, was already working on a new libretto for Sullivan. *Utopia*, it was believed in others, would be replaced when the time came by a revival of *The Mikado* or *The Yeomen of the Guard*. Either way, it was wishfully claimed, Grossmith this time really had agreed to return. A cartoon in the *Entr'acte* in March (1894) portrayed him as asking Carte: "What do you say, D'Oyly? Shall I come and give you a leg-up again?"

The rumours in this case were to prove both right and wrong. Gilbert was not working on a new libretto for Sullivan. Nor at that juncture were any of their previous operas to be revived. But he *was* working on another libretto; he had found a new musical collaborator in Dr Osmond Carr; and when in due course the cast of this Gilbert–Carr piece was announced, there was Grossmith's name in the list. The new piece was to be called *His Excellency*.

His Excellency was set in Denmark in 1801, and was a work which, though unusually for an original Gilbert libretto lacking any satirical content, was otherwise fashioned in a typically Gilbertian mould. And the part with which Grossmith found himself was a typically Gilbertian character. George Griffenfeld (could the choice of initials have been accidental?) Governor of Elsinore, is a whimsical dignitary whose chief delight in life is to hoax and play practical jokes on everyone around him. Thus he succeeds in making two obscure young men believe they have been appointed to wildly exalted positions at the Danish court at Copenhagen. He causes another character to lose his footing (off stage) on a butter slide. Most effective of all – theatrically speaking – he has

[11] The accepted version of this offer – repeated by more than one writer – reduces the "half million" pounds a week to a mere thousand, and assigns it, moreover, to the time of *The Gondoliers*. But an examination of the letter itself in the "Grossmith Letters" collection (see *Acknowledgments*, page ix) leaves neither the figure nor the date in any doubt.

[12] On stage, that is. He was noted – with his wife – as one of the many celebrities in the first night audience.

Fig. 11a. Cartoon showing Grossmith and D'Oyly Carte.

Fig. 11b. Grossmith as George Griffenfeld.

148

the soldiers of his garrison drilled as ballet girls, making them perform their evolutions in ludicrous fashion to dance steps.

Griffenfeld was thus in more ways than one the chief comedian of the piece, and seemed – on first glance at least – an ideal part for a man given to practical joking on his own account, and an actor whose last stage role had been that other – if very different – Gilbertian jester, Jack Point. But why, after so long a gap, did Grossmith choose this particular moment to make his return to the stage? *His Excellency*, after all, was not "Gilbert and Sullivan"; nor did the Lyric Theatre, where it was to be put on, hold anything like the magic and the glamour attached to the Savoy. The experience of *Haste to the Wedding*, moreover, should have been a warning that the name of Gilbert on an opera or playbill was not necessarily a guarantee of that opera or play's success. But all of this, if he thought about it, he was prepared to discount; for the primary factor that influenced his decision had nothing to do with the piece itself, but concerned instead his own health. The strain of touring had begun to tell. He needed a respite from solo performing wherein agent, secretary and other helpers notwithstanding, the ultimate responsibility was his and his alone. In a stage role, by contrast, that responsibility was shared: with his fellow-players, with librettist, composer, theatre manager, with everyone else behind the scenes. Perhaps too he felt like an excuse to settle in London again, if only temporarily, after five years of being so much on the move. And even if the Lyric was not the Savoy, even if Osmond Carr was not Arthur Sullivan, there were among his fellow-players three familiar faces from those former days, Rutland Barrington, Jessie Bond and the "massive", majestic contralto with whom he had not played since *Iolanthe* eleven years previously, Alice Barnett.

But it was by no means the easiest of experiences going back. The first night (Saturday, October 27th) found him a prey once more to his nerves and – in addition this time – to a strange sense of unreality. "I seemed to feel as if I were myself playing the Governor, instead of being the Governor himself," he told an interviewer later. Nor was he necessarily helped by what *The Times* described as "the extraordinary warmth of the welcome bestowed upon him by the audience at his first appearance." And though most of the critics were not slow to praise ("Mr Grossmith," proclaimed the *Era*, "played the joke-loving Governor in his drollest vein") there were some who had reservations if not about himself then certainly about his part.

Nor – for a different reason – was Gilbert entirely happy with his showing. Within hours of the final curtain falling that same night he had written him a letter suggesting that "doubtless through nervousness –

though you won't admit that you were nervous," his performance in the second act had been "too severe". "There should, I think, be an undercurrent of chuckling impish malignity running through the character . . . You *rehearsed* it with all its proper fun, which convinces me that you thoroughly understand the part." It was a criticism which Grossmith was quite ready to accept, even though, in so doing, he gave evidence that he himself was not altogether at ease with the role; for in the interview referred to above he went on to say: "The Governor is really a very spiteful part to play, and if it weren't treated lightly it would jar upon the audience."

Then in January, following what must have been a complaint that Grossmith had been overacting, Gilbert at his request asked his wife to make a separate assessment of his performance one evening; and in the wake of this wrote to inform him that she had found nothing either "*outré* or extravagant" in his playing. All of which was fair enough. But that, unfortunately, was not the finish of the story, for at the end of March the librettist wrote again, this time accusing him of gagging. It was an accusation made bluntly and in terms almost certainly lacking in tact – and it roused Grossmith's ire. Promptly, if ill-advisedly, he let off steam about it to Nancy McIntosh, another member of the cast and – more directly to the point – a young actress in whom the Gilberts were taking a particular interest. She, no less ill-advisedly (unless – which is unlikely – he asked her to do so) repeated what he had said to Gilbert, who thereupon responded with another letter claiming that he had received reports of his gagging from three sources, including "the official stage manager". This, however, only made things worse, and provoked Grossmith into doing something he had never done before: he retaliated against Gilbert's strictures with an aggressive letter of his own. "I hold a position in my profession which is nearly equivalent to the one you hold in yours, and I expect to be treated with a certain amount of courtesy," he informed him tartly; and he countered the gagging charge head on. "My occasional mild interpolations have been spontaneous, intermittent and seldom repeated." Nor, he maintained, had they ever involved any altering of the librettist's lines.

This counter-blast, it seems (and there was more of it in connected vein) pulled Gilbert up, making him regret his own asperity – though he was still prepared, reasonably enough, to defend his longstanding attitude towards gags. But the damage had been done, and after the withdrawal of *His Excellency* a week or so later (April 6th) Grossmith was never to work with or for him again.

So with a run of less than six months, *His Excellency*, despite good houses for much of the time, had been in the last resort another failure.

But if Grossmith in his post-Savoy period seemed doomed on this evidence to be concerned – in the theatrical field – solely with works that were soon forgotten, it was in this same period that he published in its completed form a book the fame of which lives on to this day. That book was of course *The Diary of a Nobody*. And it was produced – again, as need hardly be said – in collaboration with his brother, Weedon.

CHAPTER EIGHT

Weedon Grossmith and The Diary of a Nobody

It would have been surprising had Weedon Grossmith's career followed lines identical to that of his elder brother – and it did not. But there is little doubt that he was in his own way equally talented. And just as George from an early age had seen himself as an entertainer, so Weedon at a similar age came down, after a certain vacillation, in favour of art; and art, moreover (to judge from his own reminiscences) with an unmistakably capital "A".[1]

If the spur to acting and entertaining derived from their father's side of the family, Weedon's urge to paint came only less obviously from his mother's. The cousin of a distinguished marine painter, Emmeline Grossmith gave her younger son every encouragement. His school career (Massingham House; North London Collegiate – briefly; another small private school in Hampstead; then a larger local establishment, Simpson's School) at an end, he had gone straight away to the West London School of Art in Bolsover Street. And from there, to his great pride, he was admitted at the second attempt – first as a probationer, then after just a few months as a full student entitled to seven years free tuition – to the Royal Academy Schools.

So far he had been working from home, but now, after about a year at the Academy, he branched out on his own, taking a room in a house in Fitzroy Street behind Tottenham Court Road. "I put the shutters up halfway from the bottom and called it a studio," he wrote, "and very soon the smell of tobacco and paint gave it the professional aroma."

---

[1] George too had exhibited what he called – in *A Society Clown* – "a taste for painting" in his earlier days.

153

His ambition was already fixed: to become a fashionable portrait painter. But at the beginning much of his time was spent turning out "pot boilers", in particular small likenesses of children mostly in a romanticised rustic style then in demand; all of which helped to provide him with some sort of an income, while he concentrated his main efforts on the larger portraits with which he hoped to make his name. His first major success in this direction came in 1879 with a three-quarter length portrait of his father reading from *Pickwick*, which was "hung" at the Academy itself, and which brought him as a direct result a commission to paint the then Recorder of Reading.

But this was the prudish and easily shocked world of the Victorians, and in that world the life of an artist could have its complications. One day he was in his studio awaiting the appearance of his mother and one of her friends whom he had invited that afternoon to tea. The time they were due arrived; there was a tap at the door; and on his opening it in walked ... three youngish girls – models! – come to offer themselves for figure work and apparently intent on removing their clothes to show him their figures there and then.[2] Panic! "Oh no, not now – not now," he desperately prevaricated. "Some other time. I'm, er, expecting some friends. I'll take your names and addresses." But no sooner had he done this than, turning round again, he saw to his amazement that they had "slipped off all their things on the floor in a heap" and were "posing in far less than Maud Allan[3] ever left on". And a moment later he heard the door in the hall outside open and his mother's voice saying she knew the way through to his studio. What on earth could he do? Suddenly he had an idea. In the room was another door connecting his studio with that of a fellow-artist, a furniture designer. Going across, he unlocked it, and finding that second studio mercifully empty, pushed the girls inside, bundled their clothes after them and whipped the door back shut. He was just in time; though he hardly bargained for the sequel:

> "I saved the situation for myself, but got my brother-artist into a terrible scrape, for a minute or two later his fiancée and her mother, whom *he* had invited to tea, entered his room and discovered three giggling girls only partially attired. My friend had run short of sugar and had rushed out to buy some. The situation was very awkward for him and he told me it required a good deal of explanation, as a designer of furniture does not need living models of the female form divine, and his engagement was in danger of being broken off ..."

---

[2] In general, he emphasised, models were hardworking and respectable girls; a statement which may or may not have encompassed this particular trio.

[3] A Canadian-born lady who was to create the London sensation of 1908 with a *Salome* dance of distinct flamboyance.

Five months painting with a friend living cheaply in a cottage at Olney in Buckinghamshire, then it was back to London and in due course a move to more spacious quarters in Gower Street. This was, in a sense, a step up; and it was perhaps a feeling of making progress that led him shortly afterwards to embark on one of his most ambitious pictures, "a six foot canvas with nearly a dozen figures in it". The figures in question were George IV "bucks" grouped around a polished table, smoking, drinking and singing, and for whom as sitters he roped in, among others, his father, his brother (whom he had – with impeccable casting – as the musician playing a spinet), Rutland Barrington[4] and the artist–actor Forbes-Robertson. The picture was to be called *Till Daylight doth Appear*, and to achieve the thin blue early morning effect he required, he got up at daybreak for five weeks, with another – professional – model who sat for the costumes, hands and figures, arriving at five thirty, "rather cold". The whole thing took him more than six months to complete.

And all this endeavour availed him – very little. For the Academy, to which the picture had been destined, shattered him by rejecting it. True, it was afterwards hung at an exhibition at the Suffolk Street Gallery, and he did eventually sell it – but only for a price well below half what it had cost him to paint.

Yet this, however much it hurt at the time, was more a passing disappointment than a setback to his career as a whole. Other pictures he submitted, whether to the Academy or – in other instances – the Grosvenor Gallery, were hung. The commissions too were starting to come in with some frequency and, buoyed up with optimism, he moved now (1883) to a house in opulent Harley Street. Here, it seemed, was the ideal place for a fashionable[5] portrait painter to be. But he had been over-confident and before long he found himself trapped in a seemingly endless run of ill-luck. Suddenly the flow of commissions began to dry up. Others, already negotiated (and worth two hundred and fifty guineas in at least one case) fell through. Other pictures still he was obliged to part with to dealers at a fifth or even a tenth of the price he might have expected from a sale made privately.

And meanwhile the rent and the bills, all in the nature of things higher than at Gower Street, were coming inexorably in and his debts no less inexorably were mounting up and up. George helped him out with a small gift or loan; Frank Holl, one of the most prominent portrait painters of the time, and an early and great friend to whom he owed immense

---

[4] A friend of his own no less than he was a friend (and colleague) of George.

[5] And respectable. He set great store by respectability.

help and encouragement, offered to lend him several hundred pounds. He refused; he had already borrowed on his furniture, and that was enough. Determined to remain cheerful and with the need to keep up appearances, he went around as much as he could, "more or less touting for portraits" and making himself particularly agreeable to people of wealth. He even at one time contemplated marrying an older woman for her money. The weeks and months passed; nothing seemed to change his luck. He was close on despair.

But, being a Grossmith, his talents were not limited to one field of activity alone. And just as George had made the change from solo entertaining to acting, so now Weedon began likewise to consider the possibility of the stage. His taste for acting, as previously mentioned, had developed as a boy both at home and at school in emulation of his brother.[6] Having left school, he had indulged on occasion during the intervening years in private theatricals, acting, producing. Nor was this all; for meanwhile his histrionic urge had found another outlet in what he called "music hall imitations". These had begun in a small way, for the casual amusement of friends. But in due course his talents in this direction had become increasingly recognised and several times he was asked to give these "imitations" at parties. His most popular act was a sketch in which he pretended to be a dentist, with George (always willing to be drafted in for any such antics) as his patient with a tooth to be extracted.[7] Things even reached the point where, he convinced himself, he was being invited out solely on account of his capacity to perform; and it was after one of many supper parties at Arthur Sullivan's that he had received an offer from (the name in this context is almost inevitable) Richard D'Oyly Carte. "Weedon," Carte had said, "seriously, if ever Art should fail, which I hope it won't, come to me and I will give you an engagement on the stage at once." Engaging *one* Grossmith had already paid him handsomely; what price, he may have thought, a G. & S. Grossmith duo?

And there can be no doubt that Weedon, if not immediately tempted, was flattered. At all events he thanked him and apparently said, somewhat ambiguously, that he had no intention of going on the stage, but that he would not forget the offer if he ever altered his mind. And now Art seemed indeed to be failing. The question of a switch of careers began to occupy his thoughts more and more. Should he attempt to make the change? Should he not? Eventually, though with considerable reluctance, he decided that he must.

[6] See page 31.

[7] It was "a splendid bit of pantomime," enthused the *Era*, when they performed the sketch at a benefit matinee in 1884.

Accordingly "in strict privacy" he secured an interview with Carte. But Carte, for once, had promised more than he could fulfil. He had nothing, he said, to offer him at that moment, but would write as soon as something suitable came up. The possibility of a G. & S. duo, if this is what had been in his mind, was not to materialise. Should he (Weedon) then stick to Art regardless? His "failure" there was, after all, very far from total. In May 1884, for example, another of his portraits was hung at the Academy. The subject this time was May Fortescue, an actress who had recently made news by instituting a breach of promise case against the son of an earl and claiming huge damages into the bargain. It was in consequence, declared the *Era*, a portrait certain to "attract the attention of the curious in matters relating to the stage, for in these days notoriety of any kind is dear to the gossip-loving public." His picture, however, was in excellent taste. "He has presented the likeness of Miss Fortescue in such a manner as to secure the admiration of the young lady's friends and admirers." And – the ultimate compliment – if other young ladies should leap into similar notoriety, they could not do better than "employ Mr Grossmith's skilful pencil to make them better known to the public through the medium of the Royal Academy or the Grosvenor Gallery."

But skilful though his pencil might be, the change "from studio to stage"[8] was nonetheless to come; and it came as the result of an apparently chance meeting in the summer of 1885 with Cecil Clay, husband of a then leading actress and producer, Rosina Vokes. There were rumours going around, remarked Clay, that he – Weedon – was thinking of going on the boards. Was this true?

"I confessed to him," Weedon recorded, that those rumours *did* have some foundation, that one manager had already offered him a small part,

"and I explained my situation. 'Dear old Weedon,' he said, 'I am delighted to hear it.' 'Why?' I said. 'Because,' he replied, 'I hope you will come with us to America.' 'What, to act?' I said. 'Yes,' he answered, 'to play some good parts in some good comedies, and I'll give you £15 a week.' 'When are you starting?' I asked. 'In two or three weeks,' he replied. 'Let me know tomorrow, dear Weedon.' 'Right you are,' I said, 'I will.' And I did. I accepted with joy, delighted to get away from my bad luck in London."

And less than two months later, on September 7th that year, he made his first stage appearance in a double bill at Liverpool, where the Clay-Vokes company played before sailing. "Dreadfully nervous," he gave what he considered a "wretched performance" in the evening's first piece. The house was flat; "no one seemed to care." It was only

---

[8] The title he was eventually – in 1913 – to give to his reminiscences.

157

fortunate that he was on stage no more than a few minutes; and only remarkable that he "bucked up considerably" in piece number two.

The American tour started unpromisingly (*he* thought) at Boston, and the company then proceeded on a wearying six weeks of one-night stands up and down the country from the heat of Virginia right over the border into the snows of Canada. But real success was close at hand; and it arrived – both for the company as a whole and for himself personally – with the production, as part of a triple bill, of *A Pantomime Rehearsal*, a one-act piece written by Clay himself some time previously but which up till then had never been performed professionally. In this he played Lord Arthur Pomeroy, "a rather good-natured, fatuous, conceited ass who had a colossal opinion of his own powers and ability in acting". His conception of and costume and make-up for this aristocratic "masher" were decidedly original. He created a near-sensation.

The following year he was back in America again, making a particular hit this time as the Hon. Vere Queckett, an ineffective little man "full of comic misery", in an Arthur Pinero farce, *The Schoolmistress*. He was "even funnier" in that than he had been in *A Pantomime Rehearsal*, pronounced the *Chicago Saturday Evening Herald*. "In his portrayal of unostentatious stupidity Mr Grossmith is irresistible." He had America where he wanted it. He could have stayed there a few years and made a fortune. But he pined for home and – no less to the point – he itched now for similar recognition in London. Accordingly he returned to England some time early in 1887.

But, once again, his hopes seemed doomed to disappointment. America and London were two separate worlds. Success in the one was no guarantee of even an engagement in the other; and it was not until October 8th that year that he made his London stage debut. The theatre was the Gaiety, the play an 1864 "comedy-farce" called *Woodcock's Little Game*. It could have been the opening he needed, for his own part was a crucial one, the title-role no less. But the style of it did not suit him, while the piece itself, as he realised, had dangerously dated, and in mid-December it was taken off. Its failure dragged his own reputation down with it; and in the wake of this disaster he found himself shunned by pretty well every London manager and unable to secure a fresh engagement of any sort.

Throughout this period – whether in America or back at home – he had continued to paint. And now, virtually giving up hope of the stage altogether, he decided to revert to Art once more and took a furnished studio in St John's Wood.[9] He turned out two or three more "pot

---

[9] For eighteen months after his return from America he lived – as an extended temporary measure – with George.

boilers". He secured a commission to paint the two young daughters of a solicitor. And it was in 1887 too that a portrait he had painted of George was hung at the Academy. It was a picture that showed his brother in a grey morning coat seated at a piano, one finger pressing down a key, head turned towards the spectator, pince-nez on nose and the lips "pursed up" in "the familiar smile". It had been, the *Era* suggested to its readers, "a labour of love". It was "a really admirable piece of work".

But *Woodcock*, damning to him though its outcome had seemed at the time, was in fact to prove his nadir. Part-way through 1888 the tide turned for him at last; and it did so in consequence of a telegram. That telegram emanated from no less a person than Henry Irving: would Weedon come to the Lyceum that afternoon? Eagerly Weedon complied; and Irving wasted no words. "Do you think you could play Jacques Strop," he asked him, "to my Robert Macaire?"

It was an unbelievable offer. For a moment it took his breath away. The play in question, *Robert Macaire*, was, in the phrase of the *Era*, a "curious farcical tragedy", French in origin, as were so many plays at that time. Macaire himself is a truculent, flamboyant, hardened criminal; Jacques Strop, his companion, on the run with him from prison, a pitiful, cowardly petty pilferer and the butt for all the stronger man's kicks and buffets, his insults and his irritation. Could he – Weedon – play that part? He was positive he could. He could play it, he told Irving as soon as breath returned, "better than anyone in London"; although then or a few days later he felt obliged to remind him of what had happened with *Woodcock*. Irving waved the reminder aside. But would not the stigma of that earlier failure tell against him too severely now? Weedon persisted. That, said Irving, was *his* risk, and one he was quite content to incur. But he may before long have begun questioning his own judgment, for at rehearsal Weedon seemed slow to grasp what was required of him. Irving struggled to make him understand, to explain: "Whenever I bluster as Macaire, *you* must echo me. See? Echo me – imitate me. That's simple enough, isn't it?"

Yet still Weedon was not fully on his wavelength, and he took the instruction too literally. He had imitated Irving – as Irving – many times as a party piece and he proceeded to imitate him in much the same way now. The other players on stage, about fifty of them, collapsed – some with laughter, others with fear; "never had such a thing been known within the sacred walls of the Lyceum." As for Irving himself, he glared at him for a moment and then gave him a push that all but propelled him off the stage. This in turn raised Weedon's own hackles and he only just saved himself from throwing up the part on the spot.

The moment passed. But Irving continued to feel unhappy about him. At those rehearsals, another member of the cast, John Martin-Harvey, recalled many years later, he worked "frantically" to get across to him the interpretation of Jacques Strop he wanted. Nor was Weedon's physical appearance calculated to inspire confidence. "He rehearsed in a silk hat and frock coat, carried an umbrella from which he never parted, and wore a moustache with side whiskers. However, none of Irving's efforts could change Weedon's method and he [Weedon] had a bad time of it."

So did the cast as a whole. But if the atmosphere remained tense and fraught throughout the period of rehearsal, all was forgotten on the first night. Sick with apprehension, Weedon waited in the wings for his cue, when suddenly there was Irving standing beside him and turning to give him a reassuring pat on the shoulder. "You're all right, my boy; don't be nervous." And he *was* all right. The audience took to him at once. And if his nervousness showed intermittently, the occasion turned out a triumph for him beyond all expectation. At the end of an intoxicating evening Irving after numerous curtain calls came forward, and in the course of a short speech said a few words generously predicting for this "brother of an old friend" a brilliant stage career.

II

Jacques Strop, as one later writer put it, was to prove for Weedon what John Wellington Wells had been for George.[10] It brought his name firmly before the London public; and his advance to stardom was now rapid. Before long "Wee-Gee"[11] had become as well known as "Gee-Gee" in the capital's theatrical and theatre-going circles.

Robert Macaire ran at the Lyceum for six weeks, soon after which Irving included it in the repertory of a three-month provincial tour. Following this, Weedon played Howard Algernon Briggs, a foppish "dude", in a comedy called *Prince Karl*, first – half a week – at Liverpool, then in London at the Globe. In February 1889 (still at the Globe) he played Sir Benjamin Backbite in *The School for Scandal*, and following that came his third major break when he was engaged by Beerbohm Tree to appear at the Haymarket in *Wealth*, a new play by a then top dramatist, Henry Arthur Jones, to open at the end of April. His part in

[10] Curiously enough, George was once – several years later – offered the chance to play Jacques Strop himself; at a charity matinee. But this was one offer he failed to take up. Doubtless he was doing something else at the time.

[11] The nickname was to be given to him about 1891 by an actress, Lady Monckton.

this was Percy Palfreyman, "a dreadful young loafing, betting city clerk"; and by now his particular talents had become fully recognised. A relaxed comedy character actor, he was at his best playing either harassed, misunderstood, unhappy little men (for, like George, he was physically small), *parvenu* vulgarians or absurdly conceited dudes. "I am almost invariably cast for cowards, cads and snobs," as he put it himself. He was, claimed Ellaline Terriss, an actress with whom he was to be associated for a period later, "the quaintest of low comedians", a "droll of drolls". "The more serious he got, on or off the stage, the funnier he became."

In July 1889 he played Juffin, an attorney, in a farce called *Aunt Jack* at the Court. In 1890 he talked Arthur Pinero into giving him the part of a money-lender, Joseph Lebanon, in his latest play, *The Cabinet Minister*, at the same theatre; the best part, he considered, that he ever played. Next came another farce, *The Volcano*; but this only ran seven weeks, there was no part for him in the piece that was to succeed it, and suddenly he was out of work. Brandon Thomas,[12] another member of the cast and one of his closest friends, was similarly placed, and at length in desperation the two of them turned joint actor-managers, taking over Terry's Theatre and putting on a triple bill. That bill included a revival of *A Pantomime Rehearsal*, in which Weedon resumed his old part, Lord Arthur Pomeroy, and a one-act play of his own, *A Commission*. *A Commission*, as its title – and its author's background – might suggest, owed its inspiration to Art. It was set in a studio, a simple if not especially original story of love, impersonation and mistaken identity (a lady sitter falling for the artist who is not the person she thinks he is). The cast of five included Weedon himself as Shaw, the artist's manservant, calm and unflappable, with Brandon Thomas magnificent (in Weedon's own estimation) as Gloucester, a model. "Weedon Grossmith treated his subject cleverly and made it pass the hour very pleasantly," was the verdict of the year's *Dramatic Notes*. In all the triple bill, using a repertory of items,[13] and despite moving on to three other theatres, played for more than four hundred nights.

There followed for him next a year or so of engagements with another manager, and then a further depressing two months out of work with no offers coming from anywhere. Thus temporarily in limbo, he was passing the time preparing another picture for submission to the

---

[12] Author – a few months later – of *Charley's Aunt* and a notable actor in his own right. He and Weedon had initially acted together in the Clay-Vokes company on that first tour of America.

[13] Among those pieces brought in later was *Rosencrantz and Guildenstern*, a Gilbert skit on *Hamlet*.

Academy when one day Arthur Law turned up at his house with his most recently written play. A single reading of this was sufficient to restore his spirits. He decided to try his luck at solo management by putting it on himself. That play was eventually called *The New Boy*.

"Mr Weedon Grossmith and Mr Arthur Law between them" (declared Clement Scott in the *Illustrated London News*) "deserve a public testimonial. They have given the playgoers one of the heartiest laughs they have enjoyed [for several years]. The fun of the farce or comedy – call it what you will – turns on the fact that a boyish-looking husband, married, as is so often the case with dapper little men, to an enormous, plump and good-natured woman, cheerfully consents to pass himself off as his wife's son in order to secure for her a valuable legacy. But this is not all. The miserable little married man is forced to go to school again, to be lectured and snubbed by an old dominie once his wife's admirer, to be whacked and bullied by a private-school lout in an Eton jacket, to be tossed in a blanket and hunted like a fox round a dormitory, to be compelled under threat to rob an orchard, to be hauled up before the magistrate and, as a last and crushing indignity, to be sentenced to six strokes with a birch rod. The sole consolations that the benedick receives are the proffered love, the rosy cheeks and the cherry lips of a charming schoolgirl who, true to human nature, makes the advance instead of the boy at this milk-and-water, bread-and-butter period of existence. To think of Mr Weedon Grossmith in this piteous predicament is to laugh. To see him is to roar."

It was, in other words, exactly the play for him. First at Terry's, then at the Vaudeville, it ran – he told an interviewer after seven months – to "phenomenal business", and had still more than broken even during a five week spell in August and September when he himself had been out of the cast taking a holiday. And nothing, he claimed, delighted him more about the play's success than the character of the audiences it had been attracting. "There are family parties – wives, children, sweethearts – all are brought to our feast of wholesome laughter, and now and then a clergyman unbends." It was a comment that was at once a reflection of the late Victorian middle-class attitude to the stage in general and of his own unquestioning acceptance of the values that attitude implied.

A man of varied interests away from his work, he had nonetheless two enthusiasms that overrode all others. The first was fishing, a passion that had consumed him from boyhood. Over the years he had fished in an untold number of rivers, ponds, lakes and reservoirs in and around London and the South of England. He would go anywhere, in the iciest weather, get up at any time in the morning, on the promise or even no more than chance of a good day's "sport". Fishing, for him, was not merely a pleasure in itself; it was also a means to health and a source of companionship. Though equally there were times when he found it just as enjoyable undertaken in solitude; when he might be "alone on the banks of a private pond or lake, perfectly quiet, sitting on a camp-stool, or hiding behind a bush watching the tip of a float, so shotted that it is only half an inch out of the water. How still it is! Then a twist, a slight movement, now it travels sideways, jibs, then suddenly disappears. The 'strike', the 'tang' of the gut line, you have hooked a good two-pounder, quietly, quietly, don't hurry, he shows his silver sides and red fins, get the net ready in [the] left hand, you keep your seat if possible, draw him along, you *have* him, and with a splash you put him in the 'keep net' pegged down to the bank. A little more paste on the hook, a little more ground-bait thrown in, you are ready again, and all so quiet and solitary . . ."

It either appeals or it doesn't.

Enthusiasm number two – one that had taken hold of him that much later[14] but which rapidly became scarcely less compulsive – was collecting old furniture, Chippendale, Hepplewhite and Sheraton pieces especially. At that time there were hundreds of such pieces cluttering up pawn-brokers, dealers and junk shops or stowed away privately, unwanted, potential firewood, and all going absurdly cheap, their value unrecognised. He snapped up as many as his then severely limited resources could afford, and over the years their value doubled; trebled; quadrupled – and more. At first he bought largely by instinct. Later he learned how to discriminate, and in due course he became an expert, widely recognised as such. And with this love of old furniture went a love of antiques and old things generally, including a particular weakness for tinsel portraits of actors.

A bachelor for so long and prizing, at least intermittently, his bachelor freedom, he at last got married in 1895. His wife, May Lever Palfrey, daughter (as with George's wife – an odd coincidence) of a doctor, was an actress with whom he had appeared on several occasions during the previous few years. "May," wrote Ellaline Terriss, "is a very lucky girl. But I wonder how she managed to keep a straight face when Weedon proposed." Their first home was The Old House at Canonbury, originally an Elizabethan structure and a secluded refuge within comfortable reach of central London, which Weedon had taken on lease for himself a few years previously. They had just one child, a daughter, Nancy, named after the character the new Mrs Grossmith had played in *The New Boy*.

From marriage to books. In 1896 Weedon published a novel. It was a novel with a typically Victorian title, *A Woman with a History*, a novel too that was semi-melodramatic, somewhat moralistic and typically Victorian in plot; though, remarkably for its author, it was a work that contained only incidental touches of humour. Perhaps because it was thus at variance with his public image, *A Woman with a History* had

[14] Apparently during his Fitzroy Street period (see pages 153–4).

only a short life – one edition full stop. But if this was the first and, as it would prove, only novel that Weedon would produce on his own, it was not the first or only novel to which his name had been attached. An examination of *The Diary of a Nobody* can be delayed no longer.

III

The number of nineteenth century novels that first saw print as serials published in magazines was legion. Most – indeed all but two – of those by Dickens, to take the name that comes most obviously to mind, began that way. It was thus quite in keeping with the practice of the times that *The Diary of a Nobody* too should come out initially in serial form. But it was probably unique – and, for a comic novel, thoroughly appropriate – that the magazine in which it appeared should have been the most widely read of all humorous magazines whether of that day or this; which is to say, *Punch*.

Francis (Frank) Burnand, editor of *Punch* since 1880, had been a friend of the two Grossmith brothers for some time. Over the years he had given George a generous number of *Punch* references, putting principal emphasis on his contribution to G. & S.,[15] as shown to most effect in that extensive paragraph about his performance and antics on the first night of *The Mikado*.[16] Nor was mention of his name confined to the magazine's text; he was featured too in a number of small cartoons. One of these portrayed him as "the aesthetic Bunthorne, the greenery gallery young man"; another, showing him as King Gama, sported the caption "The Performing 'Gee-Gee' "; another still, captioned "Carte and Gee-Gee", depicted a horse with Grossmith's head pulling a cart on which was riding Richard D'Oyly of that ilk.

But more even than feeling affection for him as a friend and boosting his name as a comedian, Burnand also admired "Gee-Gee's" capabilities as a writer. "First rate," he exclaimed in a letter on one occasion after hearing two of his most recent songs. "Better than W.S.G.[17] ever wrote, though if he *had* written 'em they'd have been lauded sky-high by the asinine critics"; and he had accepted from him a number of contributions for actual *Punch* publication. These had begun in 1883 and '84 with that sketch *The Society Dramatist* and that notable series of police court

---

[15] To some extent – and quite deliberately – at the expense of Gilbert. For Burnand was said to be intensely jealous of the latter's partnership with Sullivan whom he would have liked as a regular collaborator on his own account.

[16] See page 110.

[17] Gilbert – just in case there is any doubt!

skits, *Very Trying*, already referred to.[18] But *The Diary of a Nobody* was in a different class and on a different scale from anything he had done for any magazine before.

The first instalment, just over two half-columns in length, came out on May 26th, 1888. Thereafter the *Diary* was featured in twelve of the next sixteen issues (June–September), broke off for two months before surfacing once more in thirteen of the twenty-six issues published between November 17th and May 11th the following year. The payments ranged from fifteen shillings for the shortest episode (two-thirds of a column, August 25th) to two guineas on four other occasions, their sum in total being £38–10–6.

And with that things rested until three years later when, in the summer of 1892, there was the *Diary* being published as a book; and, moreover, with its text substantially longer than it had been in its magazine sequence. In particular, the last seven chapters were entirely new. But the earlier section had also been expanded here and there, and of the minor alterations the most noteworthy was an adjustment of some of the dating. In all the book had three hundred pages and sold at three and sixpence. The publisher was J. W. Arrowsmith of Bristol, the man who had previously brought out *A Society Clown*.

The *Diary* had begun in *Punch* with an editorial footnote:

"As everybody who is anybody is publishing reminiscences, diaries, notes, autobiographies and recollections, we are sincerely grateful to 'A Nobody' for permitting us to add to the historic collection"

and this idea was incorporated now into the book[19] as an "introduction" by the diarist himself:

"Why should I not publish my diary? I have often seen reminiscences of people I have never even heard of, and I fail to see – because I do not happen to be a 'Somebody' – why my diary should not be interesting. My only regret is that I did not commence it when I was a youth."

This is signed by – it is hardly necessary to add – "Charles Pooter, The Laurels, Brickfield Terrace, Holloway."

The *Diary* itself in its final, book form begins on April 3rd of an unspecified year and continues, with entries for one hundred and sixty-eight days in all, up to July 11th the year following; and in the course of it the reader is introduced to a magnificent cast of characters. There is first, and naturally dominating the whole, the figure of Pooter himself, a middle-aged clerk in an old-fashioned City firm, a man conscious and

---

[18] See pages 41–3.
[19] Following a dedication to Burnand.

proud of his particular niche in society, a bastion of petty snobbery, ever concerned with his rights, responsibilities and dignity. There is his "dear wife" Carrie; his brash, casual, irresponsible but irrepressible son Willie with his insistence on being called by his middle name, Lupin, his refusal either to settle into the routine-based, respectable way of life his father wants for him or to conform to the latter's prudish, old-fashioned mode of conduct; Sarah, their maid; Pooter senior's two great friends, Cummings and Gowing; Mrs James, of Sutton, ex-schoolfriend of Carrie; Lupin's on-and-off fiancée Daisy Mutlar and her brother Frank; Mr Perkupp, the "principal" at Pooter's office; Mr Burwin-Fosselton of the "Holloway Comedians"; Murray Posh of "Posh's Three-Shilling Hats"; Mr Hardfur Huttle, the loquacious American journalist; and half a dozen others and more.

It is without question an amusing book, a genuinely comic novel, its fun lying in the humour extracted – subtly, gently but with unfailing skill – from the ever-changing situations, the hopes and fears, the minor humiliations and disasters, the little triumphs and pleasures of everyday life. It can also be regarded as a historical and social document, a picture of life as lived in a lower middle-class household in a particular suburb of London at that particular time.

The book was illustrated by Weedon, with black and white line drawings, thirty-three of them in all (though most, for some reason, in the first half); and in their exact and careful detail they match and reinforce the text delightfully. Weedon, so an editor of one of the later editions considered, had the gift of "drawing the commonest objects – jugs, railings, lamp-posts, gas brackets – in such a way as to make them at once lifelike, significant and funny."[20] Those illustrations immediately became thought of as an integral part of the book, and formed in consequence Weedon's most recognisable contribution to the work. But in saying this, the question arises, how far did he share in the writing of the text? The fact that he did share in it is attested not only by the

[20] It should, however, be noted that one or two later editors and certain other people who have made reference to the *Diary* in print have not always been thorough in checking any necessary facts. Thus, for instance, Alan Pryce-Jones, in an introduction to the Collins edition published in 1955, failed even to get the date of it right. Again, the blurb of the current Penguin edition contains no fewer than three errors relating to George in one paragraph alone. But the prize in this respect must go to M. H. Spielmann, author of a history of *Punch* published in 1895. The *Diary*, he wrote, "dealt in an extremely earnest way with Mr Samuel Porter, who lived in a small villa in Holloway and had trouble with his drains" – which is to say, he not only slipped up on the name of the leading character, but the reader will search in vain for a single reference to drains in the whole of the book. Nor, come to that – and reverting to the quotation in the narrative above – will he find railings; or lamp-posts; or gas brackets in any of Weedon's *Diary* illustrations. Oh dear!

title-page of the book itself, but by all other existing evidence, both written and oral alike. Yet balancing this – and suggesting that his share may have been less than is sometimes assumed – must be placed two other factors, hitherto ignored. First, when the *Diary* was going through its *Punch* sequence, its only illustrations were certain incidental, effectively anonymous and very small cartoon-type figures, best described as "matchstick" in style and totally different from the substantial, flesh-and-blood creations he put into the book. And second – even more significant – all the *Punch* payments were made to George alone, indicating that, whatever part Weedon played thereafter, none of the text *initially* was his.

Nevertheless, if a question mark must be put against Weedon's share of the actual writing, this is far from claiming that he had no influence on or made no contribution to the book's content. And this leads conveniently to a more general point, and a point of particular relevance to a biography. All fiction – or, at least, all fiction having any basis of realism – has some foundation in the writer's own experience; and to this rule *The Diary of a Nobody* was no exception. Rather, the number of allusions and episodes in the book that can be linked directly with facets of and episodes in the two brothers' own lives is considerable. The items in the following list cover only the most obvious:

1. The location, the most obvious of all: Holloway, North London, an area both of them had known since childhood. For Holloway is no distance from Hampstead, and Hampstead was the district in which they grew up.[21]

2. The innumerable theatrical allusions right through the book; the use by Lupin, for instance, of theatrical "slang" in the entry for November 18th; a mention too, among various actual theatres, of the Savoy (April 21st). Or again, more specific still, it has been asserted that Weedon, when making his drawings of Burwin-Fosselton, took as his sitter Tom Heslewood, a close friend and contemporary costume designer.[22]

3. Similarly there is a reference (June 4th) to that popular contemporary ballad parodied by George, *The Garden of Sleep*.[23] There is a character, a Mr Stillbrook, who sings comic songs. While on November 2nd Lupin is described as "positively dancing in his room and shouting out *See me Dance the Polka* or some such nonsense" – an engaging dig by George at himself.

[21] See pages 26–7.
[22] Though this was a somewhat back-handed compliment to him if so, for the actual character is portrayed as bumptious and insensitive, if not downright impossible.
[23] See page 132.

Fig. 12a. Weedon Grossmith. Drawn by "Spy".

Fig. 12b. The Laurels, as drawn by Weedon.

168

4. Another such dig occurs on November 14th. "Everybody so far has accepted for our quite grand little party for tomorrow. Mr Perkupp [the principal] in a nice letter which I shall keep ..."

> Compare *A Society Clown*: "... I must plead guilty to pasting in a book, or keeping in my desk, every letter addressed to me personally that has a good name attached."

5. And a third on December 18th: "... I am sure [my diary] would prove quite as interesting as some of the ridiculous reminiscences that have been published lately." *A Society Clown* was published less than five months before this remark first appeared; and the same idea is of course implied in both that first editorial footnote and Pooter's later "introduction".[24]

6. "April 30th. Perfectly astounded at receiving an invitation for Carrie and myself from the Lord and Lady Mayoress to the Mansion House to 'meet the representatives of trades and commerce'." In June 1887, just eleven months or so, that is, before the first *Punch* episode of the *Diary* appeared, "Grossmith, G." had been at a lunch at the Mansion House as one of a company composed largely of "well-known representatives of the theatrical profession". While the previous January he had also been there to a juvenile ball.

7. And still on that Mansion House affair: the (fictitious) *Blackfriars Bi-weekly News*, in printing the names of the guests present on that occasion, referred to the Pooters (after initially leaving them out) as, first (May 12th) "Mr and Mrs C. Porter" and then (May 16th) "Mr and Mrs Charles Pewter". And who besides Pooter knew all about having his name wrongly spelt?

> "People never get the name of Grossmith right. About August 12th it'll be Grousesmith; September 29th, Goosesmith; Christmas, Ghostsmith; and the last day of the old year, Grogsmith."
>
> (George Grossmith – *The Trials of an Entertainer*)

8. On two occasions (April 24th, November 14th) there are passing allusions to "Bezique". Weedon in his reminiscences has a reference to his (and George's) own parents playing this card game.

9. May 30th of the second year: Mrs James initiates the first table-turning session at The Laurels. The manifestations or otherwise of spiritualism were something of a Victorian preoccupation. Weedon, for instance, mentions being persuaded to hold a seance at The Old House. But the main spur to the inclusion of a spiritualist sequence in the *Diary* derived almost certainly from George's long acquaintance with his

---

[24] See page 165.

169

erstwhile *Entre Nous* partner, Florence Marryat, an ardent seeker after spiritualist truth. There is virtual admission of this. Mrs James sends Carrie a book to read: *There is no Birth*, by Florence (excruciating pun) Singleyet; in 1891 she (Florence Marryat) had published a book called *There is no Death*. Even more to the point she had once – back in 1876 – persuaded George to take part in a seance with herself. It was an experience which, as his own account makes apparent, he found difficult to take seriously. But spiritualism was just the sort of thing to cause differences of opinion in the Pooter household.

10. July 2nd of the second year: a reference in a paragraph quoted from the *Bicycle News* to a "Mr Westropp" – curiously, the one name in the book to have a real-life Grossmithian counterpart, that of George's second secretary.[25] And, more curious still, the use of the name here can hardly have been chance or coincidence. For this passage was part of the section not written till the *Diary* went into book form, by which time the real Westropp had been with him a considerable period. Most likely, therefore, the reference had to do with some private joke.

11. November 22nd, 23rd, 24th: Burwin-Fosselton comes to The Laurels to give his "Irving imitations". "Mr Henry Irving and his Leetle Dog" was to feature frequently as an imitation in George's entertainments (including the one he gave before Queen Victoria) in his early post-G. & S. days; Weedon, as previously mentioned, had also been in the habit of doing – for private amusement – his own Irving imitation.

12. "April 15th, Sunday: At three o'clock Cummings and Gowing called for a good long walk over Hampstead and Finchley"; a walk Weedon had done on several occasions while at Simpson's School, and on one of which he and his fellows had been caught smoking by a prowling Mr Simpson himself. It was a memory that remained sharp with him ever after.

13. "November 6th ... In the evening we went round to the Cummings', to have a few fireworks." Both the brothers had a weakness for fireworks; Weedon especially being prone to seize the slightest excuse for setting some off.

14. April 28th of the second year: at Mr Paul Finsworth's. "There were a great many water-colours hanging on the walls ... Mr Finsworth said they were painted by 'Simpz', and added that he was no judge of pictures himself but had been informed on good authority that they were worth some hundreds of pounds, although he had only paid a few shillings apiece for them, frames included, at a sale in the neighbourhood." Though George was not unknowledgeable in this respect, there

[25] See page 138.

170

is no doubt which of the brothers had been the more often on the receiving end of similarly optimistic and wild statements about pictures and Art in the course of his career.

15. December 21st, a typical Pooter humiliation: ". . . I left the room with silent dignity, but caught my foot in the mat."

An incident in Weedon's youth:

> " 'Father, are you under the impression that I have been drinking?'
> "He simply said, 'I am no judge,' and went on with his game.
> "I made no further answer. I kissed my mother and wished her good night; I bowed to my father with stilted politeness. But as I approached the door I most unfortunately caught my foot in the rug and absolutely rolled on the floor . . ."

16. And finally, Willie Pooter's insistence, earlier mentioned, that he be addressed as "Lupin". Lupin, in his father's phrase, is "a purely family name"; the maiden name, it seems implied, of Carrie. And who else throughout his life was called by a similar "family name"? Why, Walter "Weedon" Grossmith, no less. Clearly, however little of the *Diary*'s text he may have written word for word, Weedon's contribution to and influence on the details of that text was no slight one.

For an apparent trifle, written however skilfully, the success and continuing popularity of *The Diary of a Nobody* has been remarkable. It became one of Arrowsmith's most famous books; and it is doubtful whether there has ever been a time when it has not been in print in one edition or another. It has been dramatised at least three times (by Basil Dean and Richard Blake in 1954; by Ian Taylor as a one-man show in Bristol in 1975; and for television more recently still by Basil Boothroyd); it has been read as a serial on BBC radio (January 1977). It has been a favourite book of several public figures; from a historian and humorist (Hilaire Belloc) to a one-time cabinet minister (Augustine Birrell); from a Lord Chief Justice (Lord Hewart) to a poet laureate (Sir John Betjeman). While in 1910, when preparing his fifth edition, Arrowsmith wrote apparently requesting a foreword or appreciation from no less a figure than Lord Rosebery, prime minister for a spell during the 1890s; and Rosebery's reply may serve to sum up the affection for the work felt down the years not only by celebrities like himself but by countless other people, men and women, old and young, both "nobodies and somebodies":[26]

---

[26] A phrase used by the third "G.G.", acknowledging that it was a book into which he too dipped frequently.

"My dear Sir,

You are quite right in thinking that I am devoted to that small classic, *The Diary of a Nobody*, and I have, I suspect, purchased and given away more copies than any living man.

To write an appreciation of a book I esteem so highly is, I am afraid, beyond my power; for it is now so familiar to me that the keen edge of my discrimination has worn off. But I regard any bedroom I occupy as unfurnished without a copy of it. And that is an appreciation more sincere than any that I could write."

And yet its influence has been greater even than that. Thus Harry and Laurence Irving, the actor's sons, were "apt to judge new acquaintances by their reaction to the Pooters"; and it has made and cemented friendships. It also on one occasion – in the early 1930s – had a notably humanising effect on legal proceedings. A Mr Bawl had just been found guilty of blackmail and violent assault: had he anything to say before sentence was passed? He had; and the exchange that followed could have been taken, if not quite from *The Diary of a Nobody* itself, then certainly, and even more suitably, from one of George Grossmith's *Very Trying* sketches:

Accused: My Lord, I have nothing to say, except that I wish I had hit him harder and more constantly, and sent him more insulting postcards. I most enjoyed pulling his beard till the tears came into his eyes, as the cabman did to Mr Pooter after the East Acton Volunteer Ball.

The Judge: (*starting eagerly*). Mr Pooter slipped and banged his head on the floor on that occasion, I believe?

Accused: No, my Lord. That was at the Mansion House Ball.

The Judge: (*with strong emotion*). So it was – so it was. The charge is dismissed with a caution. Mr Bawl, I shall be happy if you will dine with me tonight.

And, when the time came, off they went to the Judge's house "arm-in-arm".

For the two brothers themselves, though, in the context of their lives as a whole, the *Diary* was very much an incidental. Apart from a passing allusion by George in an 1893 interview to the effect that Weedon had been part-author with himself of "several sketches which have appeared in *Punch*", and an acknowledgment in *Piano and I* that he had been "concerned in two [previous] books", neither seems to have given it publicly so much as a mention. Yet both, wrote the editor of the Penguin edition in 1945, "are more likely to live because of [it] than of anything else they did". More so even than, in George's case, the role he played in moulding the Gilbert and Sullivan operas? Perhaps. For however great his influence in that respect, the immediacy of his impact, as with that of any performer, was bound to fade with time; whereas the *Diary* lives on in print to be read anew by generation after generation exactly as it was written. But the judgment is clearly one that, could they have known about it, would have caused both of them the utmost astonishment, wrapped up as they were in all the hard work and demands of their respective careers as entertainer and actor in the 1890s and early 1900s.

CHAPTER NINE

Family Life and Final Years

For George Grossmith indeed the second half of the 1890s and the first few years of the twentieth century were, career-wise, essentially a continuation of the five and a half years that had elapsed since his departure from the Savoy. During that time his fame and popularity as an entertainer remained at its height. More, there seemed no reason why that popularity should not continue indefinitely.

Most years – as before – he began a new tour around the end of August, progressing with an all but unceasing flow of engagements or other work right through to the end of the following April. He also made three more trips across the Atlantic.[1] While back at home, his presence was still in demand for private functions and charity appeals:

> "A lady wrote to me not far from Lincolnshire to ask if I could give a recital without fee to enable her to raise sufficient funds to start her invention of a new chutney and sauce. She added, 'If you will kindly do this, I will supply you with chutney and sauce free for the remainder of your life.' As I am forbidden to touch either chutney or pickles, I was reluctantly compelled to refuse the lady's kind offer."

---

[1] Following a recital in St James's Hall before the second of these (1902) *The Times* gave him one of his rare unfavourable notices, complaining about what it called "a considerable amount of rather a cheap form of wit at the expense of the British aristocracy" in a new sketch entitled *Somebodies and Nobodies*; and going on to add: "If there is not the same amount of spontaneous sparkle in Mr Grossmith's jokes as there was a few years ago, if sometimes they seemed forced and unnatural, Mr Grossmith, perhaps, is hardly to blame; for even a highly successful entertainer must feel the enormous difficulty of joking perennially."

He also received his share of requests for autographs. Equally he came in, both as actor and entertainer, for the inevitable anonymous letters. He had even on occasion received love letters – though only on occasion;[2] he lacked the requisite looks or build to set lonely female hearts throbbing in that type of way. Again, he was forever being asked to help find openings or engagements by and for budding – but all too often unsuitable – aspirants to stage or platform. Once it had been:

> "I took your letter of introduction to Mr D'Oyly Carte, Mr Grossmith, and I sang to him. He said I didn't sing well enough for the chorus, so I thought of going in for your sort of parts."

Now it was:

> "A young man called upon me to ask for my advice. He was short, pale, thin, wore pince-nez, and he was dreadfully plain. He said that his friends had advised him to go in for musical entertainments, as he was so much like me"

– which, if anything, was even less flattering than the other.

Throughout his post-Savoy period too he continued to produce new material. Every year he needed new songs, new sketches. These he would work on for the most part during the summer, in between his various tours, though the ideas which sparked them off might have come to him at any time during the previous months and at all sorts of odd and inconvenient moments – particularly out of doors.[3] There was, for example, a parody of a then theatrical "craze", *The Ibsenite Drama*:

> She: Don't keep secrets from me. Are you still ill?
> Dollghost: I am more than ill – I am dying.
> She: You never told me that – you know that *I* am dying. Don't keep secrets from me. Why are *you* dying?
> Dollghost: I am dying because – because – it is hereditary.

There was a sketch entitled *Do we Enjoy our Holidays?* And there were a couple of songs concerning babies. One of these, part of his *How I Discovered America* sketch, was a parody of an American type of quartet singing in four-part harmony, set to music of a mock revivalist hymn style. It was called *The Baby on the Shore*.

---

[2] In an interview he gave in March 1888, he claimed, it seems, to have had "several". But by the time of *A Society Clown* a few months later, that "several" had been whittled down to a solitary "one".

[3] This, of course, had always been the case. The tune for *See me Dance the Polka*, for instance, had apparently come to him while walking along Bond Street, and he had not relaxed till he had got the crucial notes scribbled on his shirt cuffs. In the case of the *Careful Man* (see page 93) the lyric was written on a train going down through Kent and the music composed on the backs of envelopes on the return journey later. "As a matter of fact," he once remarked, "I can compose best away from my piano."

> "The sun was shining brightly,
> Yes, shining as it never shone before.
> We were thinking of the old folks at home,
> And we left the baby on the shore."

But it was not a case of leaving it there quite, so to speak, as they had found it; for the last verse ran thus:

> "The moon was slowly rising,
> Yes, rising as it never rose before;
> We were feeling weary, very weary,
> And we sat upon the baby on the shore!
> Yes, we sat upon the baby on the shore,
> A thing which we'd never done before;
> If you see the mother, tell her gently,
> That we sat upon her baby on the shore."

The other song with a baby theme, by contrast, had the infant mercilessly active in its own right – *Keep the Baby Warm, Mother*:

> "I often give up hope, dear,
> Because it loudly cries
> Whene'er the yellow soap, dear,
> Gets in its little eyes.
> And when it's in the mood, dear,
> It gives me awful knocks,
> And will not take its food, dear,
> But tries to eat its socks"

while – still on the same subject – in a sketch which he called *Awful Bores* he came out with the following:

> "The baby is brought down to be introduced to me. It is always in a perpetual state of hiccups. I wonder what fond mothers would think of a grown man in a perpetual state of hiccups?"

But babies to him were not offputting merely because they hiccuped. Babies had on occasion, especially in his early days, been a very real problem to him at recitals. "The moment a baby makes its presence known to an audience, it is all up with the entertainer. Competition is useless and he may as well retire from the platform." Off the platform too babies had sometimes been known to take a dislike to him. Singing and being rude about them was, he may have felt, one way of getting his own back.

These, too, were the days when he was at the height of his fame and popularity socially. Each year the number of his friends seemed to grow still greater. Children, if not babies, adored him; adults likewise revelled in his company. But of all his friends the one that perhaps meant more to him than any other was Corney Grain. Over the years Grain's career had proceeded along lines both similar and dissimilar to his own. Primarily he remained as he had begun, a piano entertainer like himself. But from his first appearance at the Gallery of Illustration in 1870,[4] his fortunes had been linked indissolubly – as solo performer, actor, writer and eventually co-partner – with the German Reeds; and *un*like Grossmith he never went over to the regular stage. As entertainers, though, whether in public or at private functions, their talents – and material – were very much of a kind; a fact that, on one occasion, led to what Grain described in his own reminiscences as an "awkward incident". The unfortunate perpetrator was an unnamed male.

> "Mr Grain" (urged the latter) "do give us your sketch of *The Drinking Fountain*. I think it's quite your best."
> "I said I would with pleasure" (recorded Grain) "but for the fact that I didn't know it, as it was Mr Grossmith's sketch.
> "Then ensued an embarrassing silence, and the company in desperation rushed at the weather as a conversational relief."

Normally, though, any confusion of this sort would have been a matter for relish rather than embarrassment. For the two men were widely seen to be – and vastly enjoyed being – platform rivals, each delighting in seizing any opportunity to make jokes at the other's expense. In particular, the difference in their respective physiques was an obvious source of amusement, not only to themselves but to others; and back in 1888 this difference had been delectably hit off by the cartoonist Leslie Ward – "Spy". One evening Ward had watched the two of them "chaffing" each other at the Beefsteak. After they had gone he had sat down at the writing table to sketch them while the picture of them was fresh in his mind. And the result showed the huge, tall, paunchy Grain on the right "waving aside with a fat and expansive hand" the minute and impish Grossmith on the left. In due course Ward had several copies of this drawing reproduced. It became one of the most famous of all his character studies.

The friendship of the two men, then, as Ward so well realised, was based – and deeply based – on fun. "I daresay Mr Grossmith and myself may both be considered old enough to know better," Grain once wrote, "but there is a great charm in playing the fool in private life." An evening they each looked back on with special pleasure was a party at Burnand's when Grossmith, at the latter's suggestion, organised a "bogus band". In this he had Weedon and himself down to play violins, Rutland Barrington to play the piccolo, Grain to conduct. And in apparent

[4] See page 58.

deadpan earnest this comedy quartet, together with three other participants, proceeded to wave, scrape and blow at half-speed through a
well-known overture, watching with delight the expressions of surprise
their antics produced among their audience. The appeal to Grossmith
of such a hoax was irresistible for, as will have been recognised, he loved
nothing better than a straight-faced practical joke. Unless it was a quip
or verbal leg pull. There was, for instance, an occasion in America when
he and another companion fooled any number of people by pretending,
though they were no more than a few minutes walk away, to be unable
to find the Niagara Falls. Similarly, while out among the London crowds
celebrating the Queen's Diamond Jubilee, he had his family creased
with suppressed laughter by his insistence on studiously asking each
policeman he met "what all the flags were flying for?"

Then there was the time in Baker Street when he was accosted by a
religious fanatic. "Have you seen Jesus?" the latter demanded, fierce
and wild-eyed. Grossmith nodded, completely unabashed. "Yes," he
said, pointing, "he went down there, turned first right, second left and
right again." He was also liable to accost complete strangers on his own
account with some preposterous or disconcerting remark. "Why, my
dear old friend Mrs Lean, how are you?" he once gushed to a very stout
– and surprised – elderly lady down at Broadstairs. ("I think you are
mistaken," she told him. "I'm Mrs Fluber, of Liverpool.") And he could
be just as devastating in writing as in the flesh. There had been a
performance of *Mother Goose* at Drury Lane when one of the wires
holding the airship broke and the two actors in it, Dan Leno and Herbert
Campbell, crashed down on to the stage, one on top of the other. The
incident made the next morning's papers; and for the matinee that
afternoon Grossmith secured a box and, to the resultant displeasure of
Campbell at least, sent Leno and himself a telegram: "Dear Dan and
Herbert. Do please fall out of the balloon again today. I want a good
laugh." "Having nothing better to do the other day," he once began a
letter to the critic Clement Scott, "I visited a penny waxwork show. I
was not even represented in the Chamber of Horrors." But his best quip
of all was one put over at second hand. The venue was a Lord Mayor's
Banquet. Amused (or, query, irritated) by the fact that everyone present
except his wife and himself seemed to have a title, he gave false names
for the two of them to the major-domo announcing on the door. And
the man duly boomed out those names to the assembled throng without
batting an eyelid: "Sir Walter and Lady Closet!"

Away, however briefly, from the platform and the public eye, the
social function and the party, Grossmith was never short of activities to
fill available moments of leisure. Racing – as a spectator; lawn tennis;

skating – principally in Canada; taking photographs – a hobby sustained from boyhood; all these deserve a mention. So, even more, does fishing, a pastime sufficiently absorbing (even if he never took it to quite the same lengths as Weedon) for him to list as a recreation along, at one time, with the tennis, in *Who's Who*. All these were orthodox enough, but on top of them he had another interest – again listed in *Who's Who* – that was more eccentric: "shipbuilding and locomotive yards". The atmosphere of such places had a magnetic appeal. Thus whenever he was in Edinburgh he would visit the museum to look at Watt's "old-fashioned beam engine"; in Belfast he was allowed to wander at will around the shipbuilding yards of Harland and Wolff; while in New York he spent many an hour happily investigating the docks.

As the earlier years of the 1890s had been punctuated for him theatrically by *Haste to the Wedding* and, more particularly, *His Excellency*, so the years that followed were punctuated by his appearance in three other stage shows. The first of these was produced on February 20th, 1897 and marked – as *His Excellency* had not – a return to the Savoy; though to a Savoy opera with which, for once, neither Gilbert nor Sullivan was associated. The piece in question had, instead, libretto and lyrics by Burnand and R. C. Lehmann and music by Sir Alexander Mackenzie; its title was *His Majesty*. But *His Majesty* ran into rough waters almost from the start. D'Oyly Carte, who should have been in charge, was for much of the time unwell and left most of the arrangements to his wife, Helen; and she, with worries about him never far from her mind, had been somewhat gloomy about it all along. During the six months or so of its preparation she made Grossmith something of a confidant,[5] pouring out to him the problems and difficulties the piece seemed constantly to be causing in a series of voluble letters – including one on the very day of its opening:

> "The one great thing I want to impress on everybody tonight is that we must above everything try and get through in decent time. If we take as long as we did yesterday and allowing for perhaps three or four encores it would, as I said, be a quarter to twelve before we were over. Sir Alexander does not understand the seriousness of this, but *you* do . . ."

No doubt. But if *His Majesty* was having problems as a whole, he meanwhile was having enough problems coping with his *own* part to have time to concern himself with what people around him were doing. Dressed in a medieval style costume that included canary-coloured tights and a beard, he was cast for the title-role, Ferdinand the Fifth, King of

---

[5] There was even talk at the beginning of his "sharing some of the risk" (that is, financial) involved in putting it on.

Vingolia, a ruler with certain idiosyncrasies (a bicycle and a bullet-proof umbrella being among his properties). Despite all this, however, it was in essence a dull part; and if his return to the stage for *His Excellency* had hardly been an unqualified success, his reappearance for *His Majesty* was, as near as made no difference, disastrous. The first night found him at his nervous worst. His old whimsicality, his former stage dominance, his rapport with the audience – all were lacking. It was a "painful thing", wrote the *Referee*, "to find an old favourite in such straits". He experienced particular difficulty with his songs (not that he was the only member of the cast to have problems in this respect; the music, especially that for the patter numbers, being condemned by many critics as too serious and elaborate for the words it sought to fit);[6] and apart from a lengthy – and somewhat marginally relevant – imitation of Beerbohm Tree, he made virtually nothing of the character at all. "Under the circumstances," the *Referee* concluded, "we cannot help thinking that he was not unwise in refraining from appearing before the curtain at the end of the performance."

Failure – or refusal – to take a curtain call; and, of all theatres, at the Savoy; there could hardly have been a sadder come-down for the man who had been star of every piece in which he had previously appeared. And the question has to be asked now, much as it was asked then: to what was his lack of impact due? He himself had no doubts – and there seems no reason to challenge his diagnosis. The whole work, he claimed in an interview the following week, had been entirely remodelled during rehearsals and *his* part had suffered particularly from the alterations; it had become that of a juvenile lead rather than a comic, and that was – for obvious reasons – no good to him at all. But, even so, he might have coped had he been in full health – and this, it had become all too evident, he was not. He had been off colour and obliged to rest the previous September. More specifically, the run-up to the production had told on him heavily. And now, on or immediately following the first night itself, he found his voice going almost completely. On Wednesday, February 24th, after just three performances,[7] he decided to withdraw, at any rate temporarily, from the cast. The news, from the point of view of Helen Carte, could hardly have come at a worse moment; but her letter of reply showed motherly concern. "What I think you ought to do – and *must* do – is to take a good long rest. . . . It isn't your fault that you should be ill. But it *would* be your fault if you risked your own health and the success of the piece by trying to play when not strong enough."

---

[6] "Insufferable balderdash" – no less – the *Saturday Review* called it.
[7] The total has also been put, inaccurately, at four and six.

It was a point he now accepted himself. "I trifled with my illness far too long," he later admitted. Accordingly, he went down to Folkestone to recuperate.[8] By early April he had fully recovered. But by then it had also become clear that *His Majesty* was doomed. Neither cuts nor other changes, neither the effective playing of his erstwhile *Ruddigore* understudy, Henry Lytton, who had taken over his part, nor – even more ironically – that of Walter Passmore, a comedian on whom his mantle in G. & S. had been the first fully to fall,[9] could save it from an early demise.

Then in 1898 he joined Weedon (the only time the stage careers of the two of them merged professionally) in a brief essay at production and management, with a farcical comedy by Harold Ellis and Paul Rubens called *Young Mr Yarde*. This play, yet another adapted from a French original, had a story involving deliberately switched identities. In it Weedon played the hero, George his valet who impersonates him. It was, in its way, a neat piece of self-casting; for the two brothers had sufficient natural similarity of voice, figure and mannerisms that, taken in conjunction with George's ability at mimicry, helped to make this well-worn theatrical device rather more convincing than usual. But, that apart, *Young Mr Yarde* had little to commend it. It did well enough during a short tour of the provinces where they began. But when they brought it to London, it ran there – at the Royalty Theatre – little more than a fortnight.

His final stage appearance of all was at the Globe late in 1900, in a comic opera called *The Gay Pretenders*, the pretenders – or impostors – concerned being the two bogus claimants to the throne during the reign of Henry VII. Grossmith himself, looking "very odd" in velvet and ermine, played one of these, Lambert Simnel; John Coates, soon to become known as a serious tenor, played the other, Perkin Warbeck. But it was an unlikely subject for a comic opera; and, in consequence, *The Gay Pretenders* in no way made theatrical history. If the first act had its merits, the second – as Grossmith saw it – was "little more than a variety entertainment". It lasted in all just seven weeks; and it only endured that long because Grossmith and another backer came forward to sustain it financially.

---

[8] His doctors, it appears, had recommended the South of France.

[9] Passmore's G. & S. career had begun in 1893 with a small part in *Utopia Limited*, and between then and 1902 he was to play six of Grossmith's old roles in various Savoy revivals. Nor should another coincidence respecting *His Majesty*'s casting go unnoticed: Charles Herbert Workman, who would in turn follow in Passmore's shoes, was Grossmith's original understudy as Ferdinand.

The reason he himself had given it financial backing, however, was not solely to prolong its run for any gratification of his own. More significant perhaps was the fact that, as with *Young Mr Yarde*, it was a piece in which a second Grossmith had an interest. And in this case that second Grossmith was not Weedon, but rather – as actor, co-producer, co-manager of the theatre and, in addition, author of the libretto – George III, his son, the new Gee-Gee junior, by then a leading stage figure in his own right. It was also the one time father and son acted in public together; and, that said, it seems now an appropriate moment to turn to George Grossmith in the context of his family and to consider briefly his relationships with his wife and children.

II

George Grossmith made a happy marriage. Of that there is no doubt. His wife was one of those rare people who inspire love and affection from everybody they meet. Gentle, kindly, dignified, serious-minded, though far from lacking her own sense of humour, outgoing, but with no public ambitions for herself, she gave her husband devoted backing throughout their span together, and was present in the audience on most, if not all, of his theatrical first nights. Equally important, she was someone with whom he could at all times discuss his problems (he had dedicated *A Society Clown* to her as his "truest friend" and "best adviser");[10] and she would share many of his leisure moments too. If she had no interest in "shipbuilding and locomotive yards" (when they were in New York, for instance, she had more than once gone off round the shops while he went off to the docks) she had certainly been known to go with him on the occasional fishing excursion.

The house in Blandford Square in which they had begun their married life proved eventually too small for their needs, and about 1885 they moved to a much larger home, 28, Dorset Square, behind Baker Street. There they remained for seventeen years, and 28, Dorset Square became the house always to be most closely associated with their name.[11] As the years went by, it grew more and more crowded with souvenirs, mementoes, gifts and other acquisitions. An interviewer, shown round

[10] He also dedicated to her a couple of his songs: *Ben Tom Jim Jones* (1882) and *How I Became an Actor* (1883).

[11] Since October 1963 Grossmith's residence there has been commemorated by a blue enamel "London County Council" plaque on the front outside wall. A similar plaque, unveiled at the same time, commemorates the later residence of George junior at 3, Spanish Place off Manchester Square.

in 1897, noted photographs and pictures galore – portraits, cartoons, water-colours and tinsels – along with no fewer than three pianos. Of these latter the prize item was a Zumpe dated 1770, about five foot long, square in shape and still with a fair tone, that Grossmith during his travels had rescued from a children's playroom. Three years previously, in 1894, he had lent it for display in a musical exhibition at the Royal Westminster Aquarium.

At Dorset Square the two of them entertained extensively, and would assuredly have done even more in this line had Grossmith himself not been away so much. There were luncheon parties, there were dinner parties. There were parties on occasion when the guests were exclusively or predominantly friends of *his* – lawyers perhaps; many of his closest friends were at the Bar. There were others when the gathering might be one of scientists, theologians and theosophists, particular friends of *hers*. But visitors to the house were by no means always invited in advance. On Sundays especially the drawing-room became a mecca for casual callers, almost invariably welcome. Gilbert, Sullivan, Irving, Tree, Oscar Wilde, Whistler, Toole, Florence Marryat, Marie Corelli the novelist – these were just a sprinkling of the famous people recorded as having turned up at Dorset Square, whether as invited guests or casual callers, at one time or another.

But the reason they had needed a larger house was not solely to accommodate increased possessions or for the extra space essential for coping comfortably with large parties. It had far more to do with an expansion of the household itself, in the arrival over the previous years of the next generation. In all the two of them had four children, born in steady progression. First (May 11th, 1874) came George; then (1875) a daughter, Sylvia; a second son, Lawrence (March 29th, 1877); and finally (1880), balancing the numbers with admirable tidiness, a second daughter, Cordelia.

"It was his own desire, as well as his nature, to be one of us, and I often think many fathers would find it to their advantage if they followed his example." So wrote Grossmith of his own father, and the latter's relationship with Weedon and himself as boys, in *A Society Clown*. But it was one thing to say this in respect of somebody else; it was not always so easy to follow that example himself. There were times indeed when he was very much "one of them", the George Grossmith whose love of mischief and joking made him for them all a delightfully amusing and – perhaps especially for the two girls – lovable and affectionate companion. On holiday with their nurses at Broadstairs (or, once or twice thereafter, Folkestone) during their early years while he was still at the Savoy, they would look forward eagerly to Sundays when he and their mother were free to come down and join them. Then, relaxed and bounding with energy, he would lead the way in climbing the cliffs, jumping around the rocks and splashing into the sea, finally taking them back to their rooms – to the inevitably less enthusiastic reaction of Mrs Gee and the nurses – all gloriously scruffy and dishevelled.

In later years, instead of going to the sea, they went alternately to Switzerland and to Goring-on-Thames in Oxfordshire where they would rent the old-world vicarage for several weeks.[12] There they roamed the vicarage garden, stripping bare the gooseberry bushes, playing tennis and waiting for their father to emerge from the vicar's study, where he would be polishing his latest songs and sketches, to organise a firework display, a trip on the river or some other activity.

Back at home too he took the lead in countless escapades: sliding down the banisters right from the top of the house, bumping down the stairs on teatrays – though always when their mother was out; and in organising their parties and entertainments. 28, Dorset Square had a ballroom, and this was requisitioned as the centre of activities for all these occasions. They gave what they called an Annual Juvenile Dance which, like most of their parties, found the adults outnumbering and enjoying themselves quite as much as the juveniles. These parties nearly always included a short play written for them either by Grossmith himself or by Weedon; for all four of them – unremarkable to relate – grew up with a love of acting and performing.

Climbing cliffs, sliding down banisters, writing plays for them to perform – that was one side of Grossmith as a father. But there was another. This, it must never be forgotten, was the Victorian era. And, very much a creature of his age, he tried at first to be the archetype Victorian papa, a martinet, the unchallenged head of his household, stern authority; and this came out in certain unattractive ways. For example, though he took all the daily papers, he refused to let anybody else in the house look at even one of them till he had read them all himself; and, if necessary, would actually sit on them to make sure of not being thwarted in this. All his love of fun and mischief admitted, he was on the whole (to quote Cordelia) "pretty strict with us; and when it came to conventions of manners and morals generally, nothing Bohemian would suit him at all." Not even in such "rigid" days as those, George junior was similarly to claim, would anyone have imagined an actor's house to be like it. "Practically silence at meals. 'Wipe your feet on the mat.' 'Go back and close the door quietly.' 'Walk properly and

---

[12] This was in addition to the cottage rented each autumn at Datchet (see page 106) to which the children, it seems, did not normally go.

185

don't strut.' 'Rinse your hands thoroughly before using the towels.' 'Eat properly.' 'Speak properly.' 'Behave properly.' 'Complete silence in the afternoon while I am having my nap.' "

Which could – obviously – be trying. And relations between Grossmith and his elder son were frequently somewhat edgy. There was no question, it seemed at first, of the latter making his own life the stage. "My inborn love of the theatre," he recorded, "was frankly not encouraged; my amateur performances, especially those at school, were frowned upon." It was suggested he choose an alternative career. He plumped for the Army; he actually qualified for entrance into Sandhurst. And then at the age of eighteen he received, out of the blue, that offer of a part in *Haste to the Wedding*.[13] The hereditary instinct was not to be denied. It would have been too much to expect him to turn the offer down. His father, though, had misgivings about the whole thing, which found forcible expression when the question of salary came up. A weekly figure of £2–10–0 had been suggested.

"Ridiculous!" he snorted. "The boy has had no experience whatever, and from what I can judge of him will probably be no good. Give him a pound."

Shades of Grossmith himself and the reaction of George the First to his own stage debut fifteen years earlier in *The Sorcerer*. But the probable reason why he in turn adopted this attitude was that, consciously or unconsciously, he was jealous; the not uncommon jealousy of a father, past youth himself, of the youth of his son; a resentment too at having to share the family limelight that until then had been his (and Weedon's) alone. "Do you know," he told the actor Squire Bancroft a couple of years later, "things are really very sad. The first time I came back from America I found myself spoken of as 'Weedon Grossmith's brother', and now after my second visit I am only 'George Grossmith's father'." According to Bancroft this was all said somewhat plaintively. But according to Grossmith family belief the remark was in essence one of petulance. And no doubt some of this petulance stemmed from a realisation that his efforts to be a martinet at home were, overall, patently unsuccessful; so unsuccessful, indeed, that in the end he gave up trying. The younger generation simply took after *him*. They had too much bounce and high spirits of their own to be kept down for long.

And with those high spirits, any jealousy on his part notwithstanding, they grew up keenly conscious of themselves and their achievements both as individuals and as a family. They were each a "Grossmith"; and they revelled in the identity. "I am having a lovely time," Sylvia wrote

[13] See page 146.

to him on one occasion from Switzerland. "The hotel is full of Americans. Lots of nice American girls, so you would be very happy; and some of them are very sweet to us. But they don't know our name or they would be even nicer." This sense of identity comes across at its most diverting in a series of thick-covered exercise books kept on a table at Dorset Square, each of which bore as a title the two words *Retired Tired*.[14] These books, *Retired Tired*, formed in effect a running family dialogue, a daily (or, rather, nightly) commentary on Grossmith life. Their tone was one of sustained teasing and banter, few holds being barred. Two entries must suffice to give their flavour. Example number one, the first entry in the first book, also makes clear their primary purpose:

> December 9th, 1894. "Someone must write in this book every night, in case anyone is locked out – unless we all go to bed together. *Mother.*"
> "Which would be most improper. *Gee-Gee.*"

The second example brings in one of their favourite and most regular themes – inebriation and (or) protested innocence of same:

> January 21st, 1895: "Eleven fifteen. Though I go to bed early and sober, my 'signature is never distinct'; this I am told. Let me try once more to write, *Mother.*"
> "Twelve ten. Signature quite distinct! But who left the electric light burning in the sitting-room? *Father.*"
> "Two thirty. Signature absolutely distinct. Great carelessness has been displayed with regard to the electric light! But who has sat in the butter dish??? *Offspring.*"

And meanwhile the offspring in question, George junior, had been growing up fast. Following *Haste to the Wedding* he played in a couple of brief running pieces at other theatres, and then in April 1893, after a frustrating period in which no engagements at all were forthcoming, he secured a part in a musical comedy, *Morocco Bound*, at the Shaftesbury. The part was that of Lord Percy Pimpleton, "a prize idiot with three lines to speak". It was his breakthrough. For from those three lines that part developed through his determined interpolations into the biggest in the piece. Musical comedy, a new, expansive, flamboyant genre, was clearly to be his forte, and in the autumn of 1894 he was snapped up by the impresario George Edwardes for its liveliest and most colourful venue, the Gaiety. Tall (close on six foot) and thin, suave and debonair, his parts here and elsewhere were those either of rich,

---

[14] The phrase itself had its origin in *The Diary of a Nobody*.
"October 31st . . . I wish Carrie had not given Lupin a latchkey; we never seem to see anything of him. I sat up till past one for him, and then retired tired.
"November 1st. My entry yesterday about 'retired tired', which I did not notice at the time, is rather funny." (!)

inane young men with, as he put it himself, brainless sounding names like Bertie, Algy or Archie, or jaunty, virile Lotharios. "Where was there," demanded Seymour Hicks, a fellow Gaiety actor for a time, "a quainter looking object than clever George Grossmith junior, with a face hardly less extraordinary than his curious legs, and a humour as unctuous as his father's at his best?"

In him, as a later commentator was to write, the male side of musical comedy reached its zenith; and during the first decade of the new century he was to epitomise the hedonism and vivacity that was the sunny side of Edwardian England. Comedian, dancer, singer, producer, librettist, writer of lyrics – Yip-i-addy-i-ay, written for one of the most sparkling musicals in which he starred, Our Miss Gibbs, was to prove his answer to See me Dance the Polka – he was also the man chiefly responsible for introducing revue into this country. And to the whole world, both on and off the stage, he presented an ever-smiling image. He set fashions, and was nicknamed "the schoolgirl's dream" and "the Hope Brothers' Beau". What he wore one day, all fashionable and half suburban London would be wearing the next. In 1895 he had got married – to an actress, Gertrude Rudge; and in due course they had three children of their own: two daughters, Ena and Rosa, and a son, George, the present "Gee-Gee".

Lawrence Grossmith too – "Lawrie" to most of his friends and family – had been growing up likewise. Beginning his adult career as an engineer with a firm in Bath, he soon decided that neither engineering nor Bath greatly suited him, and by 1896 he too was on the professional stage; and he too was to marry an actress, Coralie Blythe. As for the girls, they also had both got married, Sylvia to a barrister, Stuart Bevan, Cordelia to an architect and author, George Frederic Turner; while in or about 1904, and on a quite different note, they brought out a George Grossmith Birthday Book with a quotation in prose or verse selected from the full range[15] of Grossmith's works to that date for every day of the year. The dedication was to Grossmith himself:

"Dear Father,
    The compiling of this little book has been a great pleasure to us. It has not only reminded us of your later sketches, but it has recalled the songs you composed and sang to us when we were children."

And how, through all these years, had things been going for Weedon? After The New Boy he – Wee-Gee – had at first experienced, theatrically,

---

[15] Well, almost the full range. For at some stage Grossmith, largely for his own amusement, wrote an unpublished murder story; and only the males of the family were allowed to see it. Whatever its qualities as a whole, it had a splendidly macabre opening: "Drip! Drip! Drip! And the blood came through the ceiling."

Fig. 13a. Grossmith in a scene from *His Majesty*.

Fig. 13b. George Grossmith III in *The Toreador*
(Gaiety, 1901).

Fig. 13c. Lawrence Grossmith.

a long period of mixed fortunes. It was not in fact until 1901 that he struck real gold again, and this came when he put on another play of his own, a farcical comedy, *The Night of the Party*, at the Avenue Theatre. *The Night of the Party* was his first full-length piece. It had as its hero, the fate of *Young Mr Yarde* notwithstanding, a valet who impersonates and changes places with his employer. But there seems little doubt that he handled this theme with greater originality and comic skill. *The Night of the Party* ran more than six months in London and proved no less successful in the provinces and abroad. It was, proclaimed the *Tatler*, "a capital bit of fooling".

In this Weedon, quite apart from being the author and producer, not only played the principal role but designed the scenery and painted the poster as well. And still under fifty at the turn of the century, he pursued his acting and playwriting career in unflagging style right through the prewar period. Highlights for him during these years included a one-act play, *The Van Dyck*, with Beerbohm Tree in 1907, a sublime piece of nonsense in which the two of them played, respectively, a bragging little art collector and a burglar who pretends to be a lunatic. He was "wildly funny" in a 1909 farce, *Mr Preedy and the Countess*, similarly devastating in another such laughter maker, *Baby Mine*, in 1911. And in 1913 he published his own volume of reminiscences, *From Studio to Stage*.

But what, during this prewar decade, of George himself? For him, alas, those years had not been the happy and successful years they had been for his brother and for all his children. For him, by contrast, life during this period had lost much of its savour. For back in 1905 – on February 28th that year – his wife had died.

III

It was not a sudden event; she had been painfully ill for fourteen months previously. But this made the loss no less, his grief no easier to bear. It was a blow indeed from which he never truly recovered. More, the whole long drawn out tragedy could not have come at a worse time. For around the period her own illness began he had begun to break up physically himself.

The reason for this it needed no magic power to ascertain. To put it simply, he had worn himself out. He had now been touring in effect for more than fifteen years. The strain of this had started to tell on his health, as already indicated, as early as 1894. He had of late given up entertaining in private houses. On medical advice he had long since given up suppers, hitherto his favourite meal. Throughout this period too he had suffered from insomnia. Now that insomnia was worse than ever. He was still, in 1905, no more than fifty-seven. Yet he

190

was fast becoming, as Cordelia was to put it, "an old man before his time".

During his wife's illness he had sacrificed all his long-distance engagements in order to be constantly within reach of her – which had meant paying forfeitures to the places he had let down. He had done this willingly. And now drained, dispirited, lonely, miserably restless, he wanted simply to give up; to retire. But his family, his friends, his doctors all urged him to carry on, to keep active, to prevent his mind dwelling on his loss. He gave way. A new tour was arranged, though a tour with a poignant billing, a tour of "farewell" recitals. This was to be the last occasion, each place involved was informed, that he would give his entertainment entirely by himself. The tour was to begin on August 23rd with a matinee at the Spa Theatre, Scarborough. Scarborough was a place where, in the past, he had always done well. But this time the advanced booking was dreadfully slow. Was he – on top of everything else – losing his appeal? He was close on despair; and, tearfully, he admitted as much to Sir Henry Irving, who happened to be in the Yorkshire resort, as part of a holiday, for a few days that week. And Irving in response came up with an immediate suggestion: he would himself attend Grossmith's matinee and have this intention publicised; that, surely, would bring the people in.

It did. And when the great actor, now an invalid, was led down the aisle of the auditorium to take a front row seat in the stalls, they gave him a standing ovation. But thereupon the curtain rose, and attention switched to Grossmith on the platform. Quick to appreciate the likely effect upon Irving of a reception so fervent, he made no special acknowledgment of or comment on the latter's presence. Yet he was obviously not quite himself, for a short while later, when singing *The Happy Fatherland*,[16] he suddenly and hopelessly dried up.

And then, in a brief flash, inspiration came. With a comic expression he looked down at Irving and said: "You're making me nervous, sir. I shall have to ask you to leave." The remark was greeted by the audience with a delighted roar; and that laughter perhaps released some of the tension that had built up inside himself.

Chatting once more with Irving when the recital was over, Grossmith asked him a pointed question. Which would he choose: to live ten years if he rested or two if he continued to act? Irving answered without hesitation: he would act.[17] Which answer can hardly have come as a

---

[16] Increasingly over the years Grossmith filled out his programmes with previously used material.

[17] He had his wish – in the sense of not having to give up – though the span left to him was to be measured in terms rather of days than of years. He died in fact a mere six weeks later, while on tour at Bradford.

surprise for, as Grossmith knew, the actor was a person to whom work meant everything. But in asking that question, he (Grossmith) may have been thinking less of Irving than of his own future. And, unlike Irving, his thoughts were running more and more along the lines of rest.

It was not that the tour went badly as a whole. "Never in our experience has he been in better form," the *Brighton Gazette* (for example) enthused in October. "Never has he displayed a prettier wit or launched his satiric arrows with truer aim." Rather was it that as the weeks passed the fact of success – or otherwise – seemed to become meaningless. For he found he was losing interest in what he was doing; and this was "a calamity". At the end of that tour in April he again expressed a resolve to retire. Again, though, he was persuaded against it. But as his billing over those latter months had presaged, he was no longer to give his entertainments entirely by himself. Instead he engaged a couple of young and unknown female performers – one a singer, the other a reciter – to tour with him, in the hope their support would make life easier and relieve him of some of the strain.

But their recruitment, it soon became clear, had solved nothing. On the contrary, their presence only added to his anxieties. For the public, or so it seemed to him, resented their intrusion, and his audiences in some cases fell away badly. That winter (1906) he was ill again, and forced to cancel yet more engagements. The following season he increased his female supporting cast to three – the reciter, a pianist and, ultimately, a different singer – only to find this equally disastrous; and after a post-Christmas series of matinees at Steinway Hall on which again he lost heavily, he paid off his assistants and reverted to solo work. Immediately his audiences – in most instances – began once more to increase. Yet this made little difference to his underlying longing to give up.

For there was frankly, as he saw it, no need to go on. With all his family married he had no one now to work for except himself; and it was not as though he needed the money. Financially the promise of that first provincial tour back in 1889–90 had been more than fulfilled. And suddenly, towards the end of 1908, he came to his decision. He told his current secretary to cancel all his few remaining engagements except one, a Saturday matinee at Brighton. That Saturday matinee (November 7th) would be his last recital of all. It passed off as a run-of-the-mill event. The *Brighton Gazette* reporter, it is clear, had no idea the occasion had any special significance. "The versatility and unbounded humour of Mr George Grossmith," he wrote, "seem inexhaustible, and the ravages of time apparently have no effect whatever on his genius for

Fig. 14. Grossmith in the 1900s – "an old man before his time".

making people laugh. . . . His sense of humour was undiminished, and he sustained a varied programme with all his accustomed skill and originality." It could hardly have been less like a valediction.

"I shall simply slip out unobserved and leave people to say in future years, 'Oh, what has become of that curious little man with the pince-nez who used to sit down at the piano and give funny songs?' " So Grossmith told reporters when, before long, the news of his retirement leaked.[18] And as he had slipped out in a professional sense, so, shortly afterwards, he did the same in a private sense too. Some time in 1909 he retired to the coast, to Folkestone, breezy and bracing, and a small semi-detached house there in Manor Road which, if nothing special in itself, was – he was delighted to find – "on the estate of a real live earl". It had been a wrench – a great wrench – leaving London, his home, after all, from birth.[19] But if life now became less strenuous, he was for a time very far from inactive. He was put up for a local club, the Radnor. He took an interest in the Folkestone Art Club; played a part in supporting local charities; was in demand as an opener of bazaars; and, more perhaps than anything else, welcomed with eagerness the occasional visits of old friends. Thus when Rutland Barrington, on a provincial acting tour, showed up one day, he (Grossmith) readily agreed to compose the music for a song his ex-colleague had written. And meanwhile he had himself been busy on the writing front putting together his second volume of reminiscences, *Piano and I*.

Piano and I was published by Arrowsmith in 1910 as, in effect, a sequel to *A Society Clown*, covering as it did the general outline of his career since his leaving the Savoy. But unlike that earlier work, it is a book that disappoints. For whereas *A Society Clown* had bubbled with liveliness and personality, *Piano and I* comes across as dull and featureless, as though the writing of it had been hard going, a real physical effort. The narrative is a ramble, much of it a self-confessed jumble, the style at times gauche, twee and even faintly embarrassing. There is, too, an exhaustion of vocabulary, certain all too common adjectives, for example, being dragged in over and over again. There are of course a few good stories scattered among its pages here and there, but one or two others are grumpy, self-righteous even, and would have been better left out. The book was dedicated to his four children, "in grateful remembrance of the constant affection which they have always displayed

[18] They were particularly – and in a way understandably – surprised he had not given a farewell recital in London.
[19] Home of late had been 55, Russell Square. He (and his wife) had moved to this new address about 1902, driven to the change by the incessant noise from Marylebone Station, opened a few years earlier, and situated only a matter of yards behind their former house in Dorset Square.

to their ever devoted father";[20] and unlike *A Society Clown* – the one way in which it scores – it was illustrated, notably by a series of caricatures of him drawn by an American, Wallace Goldsmith. "Mr Grossmith drapes himself gracefully over the corner of the piano and proceeds to tell you all about it," read the caption to one of these. "The versatile Mr Grossmith with the piano well in hand brings odd characters to view," ran another.

In July 1911 Grossmith was one of five celebrities to contribute to a magazine called the *Bookman* his *Recollections of Sir W. S. Gilbert*, who had died that May.[21] After *His Excellency* the hostility between the two of them had taken some time to thaw. But thaw it did in the end. "I am really glad," Gilbert had written in December 1898, "that all is smoothed over between us. I hate quarrelling with an old friend"; and thereafter amity – on both sides – reigned unchallenged. In December 1906 Grossmith was called upon, with Jessie Bond, to reply to the toast "The Savoyards" at a celebrated dinner given by the Old Playgoers' Club at which the librettist was guest of honour; and his *Bookman* piece was more than generous to the man who, whatever the tension between them at times, had done so much to further his career. "Goodbye, 'Bab', you have gone; but your last act of charity was to leave behind your brilliant work to endear you in our lasting memory."

Gilbert had died suddenly, of heart failure, in the act of rescuing a girl caught in difficulties swimming in his lake at Grim's Dyke. And for Grossmith too the end was not far off. It was early the next year, 1912. On Wednesday, February 28th, he was seen out and about, being wheeled in his bath chair along the Leas close to Folkestone's front, and looking, it was thought, in slightly better health than he had been for the previous three or four months. He was known, too, to be anxious for a special word from London. George junior had been put up for the Beefsteak; would his proposal be accepted? It was – late in the evening of the Thursday. The news was telegraphed to him at midnight by Weedon. But that telegram arrived just a few hours too late. For at two o'clock that morning, Friday, March 1st, he had died. It was a quiet, peaceful death. As with Gilbert, the cause had been heart failure. As with his retirement from the platform, he had surely gone the way he wanted to go.

Many people mourned. The newspapers and magazines spread themselves with obituary notices, and not only those in the British Isles but

[20] He had also, many years earlier, dedicated a song to them: *The French Verbs.*

[21] Not that this was the first time he had been called upon to write an appreciation of a recently deceased public figure. Back in 1895, for instance, he had contributed a similar piece to the *Pall Mall Gazette* on Corney Grain.

some American and Continental ones as well. The new King and Queen (George V and Mary) sent a letter of sympathy to the new George Grossmith, who now in his turn would drop the "junior" from his name.[22] The former queen, Alexandra, sent a wreath. While an Irish entertainer, Percy French, wrote a not unmoving doggerel lament:

> "Lay down the pipe and the tabor,
> Set the bell tolling instead,
> He is resting at last from his labour –
> George Grossmith is dead!"

His funeral took place on March 5th at Kensal Green Cemetery, the ground where his parents and (seven years to within a day) his wife had likewise been buried. Among those present were Weedon and his wife; George (junior) and *his* wife; Lawrence;[23] Sylvia, Cordelia and their husbands; Beerbohm Tree; Squire Bancroft; Rutland Barrington – as a solitary link with his old G. & S. days; and – as a similar link with his more recent days as an entertainer – Montagu Leveaux, a later secretary.

> "And who is there now of us mummers,
> To take up the mantle you threw?
> Ten minutes we give the new comers –
> We spent the whole evening with you."

The sense of loss might be heavy, the feeling of sadness linger. But as it was for laughter that George Grossmith is remembered, so it is only fitting that his biography should end with a smile – and a smile, indeed, provided by himself:

> "You receive congratulations from a most distinguished peer,
> Who says, 'We like to have you to amuse the people here.
> But it struck me you were not as funny as you were last year.'
> Oh! the trials of an entertainer."

---

[22] Though this in no way affected his popular image. He was still being referred to as "Young George" even in the 1920s.

[23] Weedon died in 1919; George junior in 1935; Lawrence in 1944.

A NOTE ON SOURCES

A Note on Sources

"A man will turn over half a library to make one book." So said Dr Johnson, and good old Sam's maxim has certainly applied in the present case. Among the most important works I made use of were, first, those written by the Grossmiths themselves: George's own volumes of reminiscences, *A Society Clown* (Bristol, 1888) and *Piano and I* (Bristol, 1910); *The Diary of a Nobody* (Bristol, 1892); *The George Grossmith Birthday Book* (Bristol, 1904?) and his various published songs and other writings; the reminiscences of Weedon, *From Studio to Stage* (London, 1913) and George III, "*G.G.*" (London, 1933); an unpublished typescript, *The Grossmiths at Work and Play*, written about 1936 by Cordelia; and, going right back, *Amputations and Artificial Limbs*, by William Robert (London, 1857).

Second come a number of books and articles *about* one or more of them: *Bouncing Boys*, by Andrew Halliday (?), in *All the Year Round*, August 5th, 1865; *A Family which has Lived on its Legs*, by J. M. Bulloch, in the *Cripples' Journal*, July 1925; *Gaiety and George Grossmith*, by Stanley Naylor (London, 1913); the chapter on Grossmith in *Players of the Period*, by Arthur Goddard (London, 1891); *George Grossmith and the Humour of him*, by Raymond Blathwayt, in the *Idler*, 1893; *George Grossmith Interviewed*, in the *Era*, March 31st, 1888; *George Grossmith to an Audience of One*, by John Hyde, in the *Windsor Magazine*, August 1897; *George Grossmith's Family*, by J. M. Bulloch, in the *Gilbert & Sullivan Journal*, October 1925; *How the Dying Irving Helped Grossmith*, by B. C. Hilliam, in *The Times*, October 12th, 1962; and the anonymous *Life and Theatrical Excursions of William Robert Grossmith, the Juvenile Actor* (fourth edition, Reading, 1829).

199

Third must be mentioned the whole extensive literature on Gilbert and Sullivan; in particular *The D'Oyly Carte Opera Company in Gilbert and Sullivan Operas*, by Cyril Rollins and R. John Witts (London, 1962); *The First Night Gilbert and Sullivan*, by Reginald Allen (New York, 1958; London, 1976); *Gilbert and Sullivan*, by Hesketh Pearson (London, 1935); *Gilbert, Sullivan and D'Oyly Carte*, by François Cellier and Cunningham Bridgeman (London, 1914); *The Savoy Opera and the Savoyards*, by Percy Fitzgerald (London, 1894); and *Souvenir of Sir Arthur Sullivan*, by Walter J. Wells (London, 1901).

Fourth come the still more numerous biographies, autobiographies and memoirs of other contemporary figures, ranging from those such as *The Life and Reminiscences of Jessie Bond* (London, 1930) and *Rutland Barrington, by himself* (London, 1908) in which references to Grossmith crop up in some quantity, to those where he gets no more than a single passing mention.

Miscellaneous sources include those manuscript items referred to in my "Acknowledgments", plus *Chronicles of Bow Street Police-Office*, by Percy Fitzgerald (London, 1888); *The Lost Theatres of London*, by Raymond Mander and Joe Mitchenson (London, 1968); and the introductory material written by the editors of various later editions of *The Diary of a Nobody*.

Finally, as fascinating as they are invaluable, come the files of contemporary newspapers (both national and local) and periodicals. Where this book would have been without, say, the *Daily Telegraph*, the *Illustrated London News*, *Punch*, the *Reading Mercury*, *The Times* and, above all, the *Era*, is a question I do not intend to ask.

INDEX

Index

203

208

211